D0732405

Behind the Mask

BEHIND THE MASK

Destruction and Creativity in
Women's Aggression

DANA CROWLEY JACK

HARVARD UNIVERSITY PRESS
Cambridge, Massachusetts
London, England
1999

Library of Congress Cataloging-in-Publication Data
Jack, Dana Crowley.
Behind the mask : destruction and creativity in women's
aggression / Dana Crowley Jack.
p. cm.
Includes bibliographical references and index.
ISBN 0-674-06485-2 (alk. paper)
1. Women—Psychology.   2. Aggressiveness (Psychology).   I. Title.
HQ1206.J26   1999
155.6'33—dc21
99-22221

To Rand, Darby, and Kelsey
and to my mother, Dorothy

Contents

Behind the Mask

HEARKENING TO
WOMEN'S VOICES

In this book, sixty women share their lived experiences of their own aggression. Exploring the territory of aggression with these women, I found a land inhabited by our worst fears but also by possibilities for powerful action and change. Thinking about aggression is always weighted with wariness about its link with hurt and death. As I heard of pain caused by aggression, both received and given, I wondered if I could remain open to listening. How could I sustain an attitude of hearkening, "the most intense wakefulness of wanting to hear . . . the condition of the possibility of hearing"?[1] Listening to a woman's voice and all that surrounded it—feelings, context, history, reaction to me, my own responses—required both a sharpened, focused attentiveness to the meanings she was trying to convey and, at the same time, the kind of unfocused, gathering-of-sounds listening I do on spring nights when the frogs begin their chorus. In that open hearkening, I hear the wind in the trees, the owls, far-off dogs barking, a distant truck—a widening ring of sound that conveys many different realities that surround the frogs' pond.

I found it difficult to maintain this unfocused, gathering kind of hearing. Sustaining a listening openness to aggression led to places that felt terrifying, hopeless, filled with the deepest questions, the deepest dread. Listening, I heard not only the woman but the voices in her thoughts that came from her family, her culture, her history. Then I heard past her and into her context. Was she in poverty? In a privileged situation? Was she in violent relationships, or did she face less obvious types of power and aggression? I heard past her specific context into wider spheres of aggressive acts. I heard into society, where violence is a daily fact in people's lives. I heard into nature, where we ruthlessly invade the earth, annihilate species, rip apart delicate webs of life that took millennia to evolve.

At the college where I teach, a student mounted stereo speakers in the tall cedars that surround our building. Through these speakers came, first, the sounds of a rain forest in Brazil—birds, insects, monkey calls, other animals. Several days later the recording changed: this song of the earth was interrupted by noises of a survey crew, of bulldozers, followed by days and days of chainsaws, the crack of falling trees, the roar of large trucks.

During this time I was interviewing women. The juxtaposition of their stories with the sounds of human assault on nature brought home to me two things. First, history has been brutal to women. Under male domination, the feminine has been repressed and devalued. The earth, long associated in Western thought with the feminine, has also been devalued and brutalized. Second, I learned how painful it is to listen, to hear the sounds of aggression in a sustained way. As we listen, sounds enter through the labyrinth of the ear into the body, into our felt existence. More often, we turn away to block them out. It is difficult to encounter—to come into relationship with—aggression in this intimate, bodily way.

As I walked to my office each day, I wanted to stop the sounds of clearcutting. I wanted to avoid the panorama of awareness opened by the noises, take the back stairs, block the sound. At times I wanted to stop listening to the pain women conveyed about the hurt they experienced and dealt out to others. But, unbidden, my listening grew larger still. I heard past each woman, past her context, past our violent society, past our aggressive relationship to nature, and into the age-old questions about violence and suffering. Why do fear, hostility, and the urge to dominate, which underlie aggressiveness, appear as such human predispositions? How have we become so alienated that we support the destruction of that which gives us life—women, the earth? How do we become so blinded as to destroy others? Why do appalling, seemingly unbearable events happen to some people while others appear to live charmed lives?

Women's lives, including mine, are witness both to the destructive effects of aggression, given and received, and to the transformation of that aggression into positive action. How do some women overcome aggression directed against them and transform it into new life possibilities? Why do others become submerged in hatred and anger, propelled by these feelings to retaliate destructively against the violations of body and spirit they have endured? I realized that the women could tell us; knowledge comes from their stories.

Most students of aggression have not asked such questions. They focus more narrowly, using the scientific method to isolate aspects of behavior or mind associated with the individual and aggression. The bigger questions that evolved from my listening to women are not the questions of psychology alone. They are human questions which we all confront at some point or another. But I have no answers, only the questions and the women's stories.

We know that men are more physically aggressive and authoritarian than women, that men commit more violent acts and are more approving of aggression than women across a range of realms as diverse as international relations and war, social control and law enforcement, interpersonal relations, and the portrayal of violence on television (Eagly and Steffen, 1986). Acceptance of the "fact" of human aggression forms a cornerstone of our images of the future, even though women's attitudes and behaviors differ from men's. Bringing women's perspectives on their own aggression into larger dialogues about this subject is critical for society.

Almost all of what psychologists have thought and felt about aggression has been shaped by a male perspective. This means that we understand aggression from the point of view of those who have been dominant. It also ensures that men's fears of women's aggression, as well as men's projections and desires, have been built into our concepts and conclusions. Since women's aggression develops within a different social reality than men's, women's accounts may offer a new perspective on this human problem.

Over the centuries, women evolved the shapes, patterns, and strategies of their aggressive behavior in direct relation to male dominance and male violence. Women's social reality has differed from men's, not only because of inequality, but also because men's aggression against them has been culturally reinforced and approved throughout most of history. Today, the threat of male violence crosses all races, classes, and nations to affect all women, though the actual risk of being attacked varies with women's ethnicity and social class.[2] The 1997 UNICEF "Progress of Nations Report: Women Commentary" declared violence against women and girls the most pervasive abuse of human rights in the world today.

Despite these realities, the greatest silence around women's aggression has been about the two factors that have most affected its forms, its display, and its consequences for women: the threat of male violence and social inequality. Although I call attention to women as recipients of violence, I attempt to explore aggression beyond the dualistic model of oppressor/oppressed, in which women are powerless victims. Rather, I look at the creative, subversive, and resisting nature of women's practices concerning aggression.

Throughout history, women have been punished for obvious displays of aggression; they have been forced to camouflage their intent to hurt others, their opposition, and even their positive forcefulness, to deliver their aggression in culturally sanctioned but more hidden ways. The lack of available models by which to understand women's aggression has shaped my purpose: to represent the forms and meanings of women's aggression from women's perspectives.

On spring nights, the owls sound different from our front yard than from the path that winds up the forested hill behind the house. Where I stand affects what I hear. I knew that the way I heard these women was influenced by my own childhood pain and adult transgressions. Though my privileges make my life radically different from the lives of many of the women, I have tried to take these differences into account by attending to all the aspects that enter into the space between listener and speaker, such as economics, power, and ethnicity.[3]

In this work I follow the voice-centered method first articulated by Carol Gilligan (1982) and now used by many others (see

Belenky, Bond, and Weinstock, 1997; Belenky et al., 1986/1997; Brown, 1998). Interview narratives are seen as dialogues generated within a relationship of interviewer and subject; the investigator attempts to listen to the point of view of the subject. Doing so requires taking a reflexive stance in order to notice how we help shape the very texts we study (Fine, 1992; Goldberger, 1996). It requires listening intensely to the unknown of self and other without expecting to hear something determinate. In this model, self-awareness and the ability to hear others from their own standpoints are interconnected.

I entered into the complex territory of women's aggression using six ways of listening to their narratives: open listening (the body's responses and other nonverbal signals are taken into account as part of reflexivity), focused awareness (meanings are not taken for granted; the speaker is asked to explain key words or phrases), and attending to moral language, to inner dialogues, to the logic of the narrative, and to meta-statements, those places in interviews where people spontaneously reflect on something they just said (Jack, 1999b). Used to analyze the interviews systematically, these ways of listening make it possible to examine the unique subjectivity of each woman, the site of her resistance, conformity, and change. They focus on uncovering the speaker's point of view and meanings, a critical first step toward detailing the diversity of women's experiences. As women grapple with contradictory social norms governing their behavior, it is possible to see how changes in women's roles affect their aggression.

Listening systematically to moral language, for example, provides a way to examine what standards a woman uses to guide her aggressive behavior and to judge herself. Such standards can be traced to their cultural and familial origins. Moral language also provides a way to think about the relationship of the general to the particular. It is possible to honor each woman's individuality, in its full richness of personal history, by observing what values she has accepted and strives to attain. The "general," then, is the human tendency to evaluate the self; the "particular" is the specific content of the moral self-evaluation, what gender ideologies or cultural values a woman uses to inhibit or judge her aggression. Analyzing

moral language across all the interviews gave me a deeper understanding of how culture manifests itself in individual lives and at
various locations. Each of the other five ways of listening also allows such a close examination of the interaction of person and
social context.

In the interviews, women defined aggression themselves in response to open-ended questions such as "When you think of your
own aggression, what comes to mind?" I asked them to describe
their aggressive acts, what led up to their behavior, and their feelings before and after their actions. I listened for their intent, for
their expectations of consequences, and for the actual outcomes of
their aggressive acts, as well as for changes in their self-experience
related to those acts. Though I followed a set outline of questions,
I also followed each woman's lead to inquire more deeply into the
meanings she attached to her actions and into the context in which
they occurred.

I am most interested in how a woman brings her anger, will,
and desire into relationships with other adults, and what her
thoughts about doing so reveal about power, gender ideologies, and
personal and social change. I asked no questions about aggression
toward children other than "What do you teach your children
about how to be aggressive?" Probing into a woman's relationship
with her children raises a host of difficulties, including the requirement to report child abuse to authorities if it is suspected. Fur-
thermore, a vast literature already exists on child abuse and its
relation to social and psychological factors (see, e.g., Cicchetti and
Carlson, 1989; Egami et al., 1996; Milner and Chilamkurti, 1991;
and Rodriguez and Green, 1997).

My goal is to delve into a largely unexplored area: the psychology of aggression in women. The kind of exploratory study I
have conducted is necessary because we have no reports of women's
subjective experience of their own aggression (Björkqvist and Niemelä, 1992). Further, many contemporary researchers regard aggression as a particular category of goal-driven behavior. According
to the generally accepted definition, an aggressive act is "done with
the intention to harm another person, oneself, or an object"
(Björkqvist and Niemelä, 1992, 4). It is the actor's intent that defines

an act as aggressive, yet rarely do researchers inquire into intent by asking the actor. The interpretation of an actor's intent often serves as a screen for a researcher's projections about aggressiveness based on stereotypes of gender, ethnicity, and class. At the same time, an actor's description of intent may be self-serving or blinded by denial. Thus intent, the very heart of our psychological definitions of aggression, carries a large measure of ambiguity.

Why, then, should we trust what these women say about a subject that often brings social judgment and shame? Psychology has a long history of bias against self-report and interview data, assuming that people will try to present themselves in a good light in order to conform to social expectations. But since the social expectations or norms affecting aggression are themselves a focus of my interest, they are not unwanted variables. Because my task is to understand women's aggression from their perspectives, interviews, with all their inexactness and saturation by social norms, provide the information I seek. Searching for "objective truth" in narratives is not the goal. Rather, I am interested in mapping the psychology of women's aggression, particularly its relationship to social norms, social contexts, and the experience of self.

Exploring women's lived experiences of aggression sheds light on long-standing problems in women's psychology. For example, many women incorporate the cultural myth that women are not aggressive while their own experience contradicts it. I wanted to understand the psychological dynamic of internalizing this myth while struggling with a lived experience that belies it. Most women say they want their daughters and younger women to be more assertive, even aggressive, in pursuing their dreams and protecting themselves, but don't want to add to the violence and harm in the world. Women want the freedom to be authentic, to move out into the world without fear, but do not want to destroy others in active self-expression. In resisting social authority and convention to become one's own self, how do some women take the path into destruction, either of self or of those they love? How do others use this aggressive force for positive purposes, to push at the outer and inner constraints of their lives?

To look at the interaction of self and society, I chose to interview women from a range of social contexts that endorse differing forms of aggressive behavior. Within these contexts, I sought women whose aggression appeared usual, not extraordinary.

The women whose voices fill this book include rich, middle-income, and poor; old, middle-aged, and young. They include a range of ethnicities within the concentric circles of social power from margin to center. They are police officers, attorneys, a correction officer, a former military servicewoman, the head of security at a major business, athletes (a mountain climber, a marathon runner, the captain of a university rowing team, and a wrestler), a Holocaust survivor, a politician in a state legislature, an administrator in higher education, an international photojournalist, architects, social workers, lesbians in a battered women's group, college students, a legal secretary, elementary school teachers, a Buddhist teacher, and an instructor of tai chi. In addition, I interviewed six women enrolled in the Seattle Birth to Three Project, which works with high-risk, substance-abusing mothers.[4]

Some of the sixty women were clinically depressed, some addicted or in recovery from addiction. Thirty-six had been abused as children, as adults, or both. The forty-one white women and nineteen women of color ranged in age from 17 to 75. Eight women were lesbian.[5]

By talking to police officers and attorneys, I planned to examine conflicts resulting when socialization for femininity collides with a profession's demands for stereotypic male behaviors. I also chose police officers to clarify how women authorized by society to use force against others think about their own aggression. Whereas certain kinds of aggression are condoned for women in the professions, socially marginalized and lower-class women are punished, even caricatured, for their more overt, often antisocial aggression. In their narratives these women give voice to those who are most often "shut up and shut out" of psychological research (Reid, 1993; Bing and Reid, 1996). While lawyers and police officers reveal how women think about integrating socially sanctioned power into their aggression, women at the margins have fewer options for exerting their aggression through socially acceptable channels. With abused women, who came from all social locations, I sought to explore how having been subjected to violence or abuse affected their perspectives on their own aggression.

Though I selected women from various social contexts, I found that they often do not experience their power in ways tagged by social markers. Some attorneys, though they have social power, feel marginalized because of gender, ethnicity, and/or personal history. Some women at the margins feel a greater sense of personal power and freedom to use creative aggression than those who wield social authority. In real lives, outer formal structures are only part of what affects how a woman uses her aggression; we must consider her subjective experience as well.

In their aggressive acts and in the meanings they attach to them, no two women reconcile social expectations and personal experience identically. No single woman is representative of her ethnicity, her profession, her class. A particular woman's voice and view should not be considered as speaking for her occupation or her ethnic/racial group, but simply *from* that social, economic, historical context with all its complexities of position and power. Throughout the book, I identify age, ethnicity, and occupation as a reminder that context and subculture affect a woman's view of her aggression, but the narratives also remind us that these are only part of the picture.

Interviews lasted an average of two hours; many women were interviewed twice, some three times over two years. To analyze the interviews I used Ethnograph software.[6] The process of analysis was like viewing pointillistic paintings. Up close, one sees only little dots, or segments of thought; when one steps back, the dots form a picture. I present some women's stories in depth, using them to convey the patterns I discerned across all the interviews. Another way of describing the process is to return to the metaphor of hearkening. Analysis by Ethnograph allows a different kind of listening—a hearkening to the many voices versus the one. Then, when I return to the one voice, my hearing has been deepened by systematic attention to the many.

During my research, my family traveled the length of Chile, hiking in remote areas of the Andes. In Santiago I interviewed four Chilean women. I wanted to listen for cultural differences in the perceived costs of aggression and in types of aggressive behavior. The women with whom I talked were all professionals who spoke fluent English, and thus are representative only of a very small minority of Chilean women. Their interviews are similar in themes, perceived costs, and strategies of aggression to those of U.S. women in comparable social positions. They are part of the sample of sixty women.

Two years later my family spent six weeks in Madagascar as Earthwatch volunteers. We helped collect data for Patricia Wright, who is studying patterns of female dominance in lemurs. Watching primates interact heightened my skepticism regarding the innateness of aggression and brought home how easily people have projected human purposes onto other species. Wright (1993) has found that when female primates lead, levels of violence and aggressive interchanges are lower than when males dominate. Strong bonds among females appear to keep males in place not through aggressive dominance but through displays of female solidarity and quick reprimand (de Waal, 1996; Wrangham and Peterson, 1996). Watching the lemurs reinforced my interest in aggression's origins and its relationship to power and human culture.

I was drawn to study aggression by listening to women's experience of their depression (Jack, 1991, 1999a). I learned that silencing the self leads to depression, and that many women attempt to silence their anger and aggression, aspects of self they fear will disrupt relationships. In order to learn more about depression, I decided to approach it through aggression, which felt like a seldom-used back door, much more forbidden for women to move in and out of than depression. Entering there, I found a complexity of which I have examined only a small portion. I attempt to present women's perspectives in ways that allow an appreciation of the links between their aggression and their depression.

When talking about their aggression, women often speak of "crossing the line." In this book I document social and psychological factors that contribute to the line each woman draws between acceptable and unacceptable aggression, and the costs to self and society both when she crosses the line and when she stays within a line too closely drawn.[7]

1

THE PUZZLE OF AGGRESSION

Lyn (age 39, white, student) ended her seventeen-year marriage to a physician a year ago. She lives with her two teenage daughters in a city in the Pacific Northwest, and she has recently returned to college to complete her B.A. Like many women in our culture, Lyn was raised to be nice, to stifle expression of anger, aggression, and sexual desire. As an adult she finds herself in a dilemma: how to be herself without destroying others:

> Well, aggression in my life was just, you just don't do it as a girl. That's just not something that is appropriate. It's not. I really believe in nonviolence and I really am trying to work that out in my own lifestyle. It's very hard to take my cultural upbringing and just want to do nonviolence by not confronting anybody rather than an active nonviolence, which is saying more when I need to protect myself, I need to protect myself. That kind of aggression is not the kind I am hearing people talk about—wars or, you know—it's a being yourself, being myself and not destroying other people with that.

Lyn's thinking creates a bind: self-protection, which she calls active nonviolence, leads to a fear of hurting others. But if she is nonviolent, which to her means "not confronting anybody," she has no way to protect herself. As she listens to cultural dialogues about aggression, she hears about war with its implications of physical violence, power, and death. She finds little in such a discourse that reflects her struggle between nurturing others and standing up for herself:

> There is an aggressive stand-up-for-me part, and if I take that too far, it does not become socially helpful. And so I don't want my whole self to be turning on doing everything I want to do and damn everybody else, kind of thing. Because there is a place for interaction and I do not know where that balance is yet. I don't know where the balance is between nurturing other people and standing up for myself, so I am playing with that gentleness-aggression, you know. It is real fluid right now.

Maria (age 32) has practiced law for eight years in a large city, litigating on behalf of minority clients and Indian rights. She is married to a white attorney; they have two preschool-age girls. Maria was raised by her Native-American mother on a reservation; her Latino father never lived with the family. Her attitudes about aggression differ from Lyn's:

> Aggressive means strong to me. I don't see it in a negative sense, I see it as a positive attribute that I want my daughters to have. To me it's a positive thing, it's good if you're aggressive. I don't think we should dress it up and call it assertiveness or whatever, I think we should call it what it is . . . I think it's something that you definitely can cultivate and I think as a woman you almost have to . . . because in a lot of ways it still is a man's world, and that's probably your strongest suit sometimes.

Responding to the question "What did you learn about aggression from your mother growing up?" Maria says: "I learned that it's feminine, that it's a very sexy thing, that it's not anything that you should be ashamed of or hide." Unlike Lyn, she was not raised to be "nice" or "good": "To strive to be that only invited ridicule where I came from. You can go ahead and be who you are and not be a 'nice girl' and you're still okay."

Maria does not fear her own destructiveness; rather, as a minority woman in a racist society, she fears what might happen to her if she does not fight for herself:

> With all the attorneys I work with there's still this attitude that it's nice that Maria's a lawyer. "Gee, isn't it nice that she's Indian, but by the way, the big cases and the big briefs will be done by Kaylan and Jerry, or Chris and Tim." I mean, I still have to fight, even at this age, to say not only am I valued, . . . if you don't give it to me, I'm going to take it from you, and I will scream racism and I will scream sexism. I have had to. And nobody enjoys being a watchdog . . . I do not enjoy being this minority liaison, I don't like it. I still think I have those biases and stereotypes working against me, and I have to deal with them day to day.

Maria battles injustice even though she does not relish the fight, using her anger to oppose racism and sexism on behalf of herself and her clients. She has "a lot" of conflict about how aggressive she should be in certain situations: "I'm still not comfortable with my own aggressiveness but I'm learning more about how to reel it in and when to let it out." Between her troubled acceptance of the status quo ("trying to find [my] place within this professional world") and her resistance to it ("I have to fight"), Maria constructs her understanding of her aggression and how she should express it.

If a woman stands outside the myth of the unaggressive woman, a myth historically applied to white upper- and middle-class women, what meanings does she attach to her aggression? How does positive aggression, including this ability to oppose others, relate to women's self-development?

While her 18-month-old daughter plays on her lap, Chrystal (age 25, unemployed) says growing up was "hard. Very, very hard." Chrystal, an African-American woman raised in poverty, has been affected by a social context of racial discrimination, devaluation, and socially structured violence. Talking about her struggle, she focuses only on the family context within which she had to form her identity and find her way. The central theme of her life is a feeling of disconnection from others:

> My mom had to give me up when I was six months to my grandmother because she couldn't take care of me. Both my parents

are heroin addicts. So when you go to live with another family, even though it is your blood family, there's a lot of sisters and brothers and then when one is brought in, you know, you're raised like brothers and sisters, but it's always that little gap in between? . . . You can't find your place, you know, if you can't be with your mom or your dad, and you're in this place where it seems like you're always being treated different.

Trying to find her way into her family, the group that first teaches the power of belonging and the searing pain of exclusion, Chrystal felt "always that little gap in between" herself and others. Her feeling of being different, of not finding her place within her own family, led to sadness, isolation, and wordless rage: "Everybody in the family got spankings when they acted up. But I got more . . . whuppings than anybody else and then after a while, you know, a kid, you spank them and they'll cry, and then you stop. But I wouldn't cry. So as I got older it went from a switch to extension cord, and then to brooms, and to even being punched, and I would not cry, and that would . . . just piss [my grandmother] off."

In Chrystal's family words were not used to convey vulnerable feelings or to share concerns, nor to seek solace or achieve closeness. Her grandmother, raising eight children alone in poverty, was not able to help Chrystal learn to cope with her feelings constructively. "My grandmother . . . she's not the type person that you can go and talk to. And when I was growing up and I'd say, 'Mom, can I talk to you?' [she'd respond] 'Get away from me! I'm tired! I'm doing this!' It's yelling. She doesn't talk, she yells. So you know, it wasn't like I had anybody to talk to." Chrystal learned to use angry words and fists to bridge the gap between herself and others, a way of protecting her vulnerability while fighting for some form of connection.

Violence, drugs, and despair were at the center of Chrystal's life from the time she ran away at 15 until she stopped using drugs at 24 and began to examine her feelings. At 18 she got involved with a man who started beating her after their first child was born: "I guess he was kind of a control freak and I was, I just wanted somebody to at least half-ass seem like they cared about me." After five years and three children, she escaped him and lived on the run. Pregnant with her fourth child, concerned about her increasing patterns of violence and continued drug use, she entered a treatment program and began working with an advocate from the Seattle Birth to Three Project. When our three interviews took place she had been off drugs, with only occasional lapses, for a year.

For Chrystal, aggression has an emotional outcome:

> After I beat somebody up, I feel better. Every time I do something like that I feel a release, you know, like I just let go of something that was tightening my—it feels like something in your chest, like you can't breathe and you don't have no control. It's just like release, like all the weight is gone, there's no more tightness . . . It's like if you don't do something you're gonna explode, you're like walking on tiptoes, you don't know what to do.

Chrystal's body speaks what her voice cannot. Because she is convinced that others will not listen to her words, her body takes over. Powerful, seemingly uncontrollable feelings take her breath away. She uses a language of the body to express her pain, both as she tells me about the pain and, more directly, as she communicates her anger and isolation by beating someone up.

Chrystal was once referred to a psychiatrist because of her uncontrollable anger. She says, "I kind of went off on him because he was asking me so many questions and the way he was asking really, you know, I guess pissed me off." The psychiatrist prescribed "anger management" to help her learn to control herself. He did not invite her to explore the origins of her anger in the devaluing experiences of abuse, poverty, and racism, nor suggest that she consider how she might use her anger more positively to resist such devaluation. Instead, as often happens, he individualized the results of social injustice: she must contain herself. Chrystal had been told that the source of her aggressiveness was in herself, evidenced by her lack of control—of drug use, of aggression, of her unruly self.

When aggression is seen as a way to release pent-up anger, the logical antidote is anger control or anger management. But there is a broader explanation, one that can include Chrystal's social/relational context. What can we learn, for example, by examining physical aggression as a type of relational connection? What material and social conditions underlie women's physical aggression? How much does the ideology of femininity, the myth that women are not aggressive, intersect with ethnic and class stereotypes to permeate social judgments about women's aggressiveness?

Anna (age 40, white) is an artist whose works have been exhibited internationally. She is now in law school, committed to using law for social justice, particularly for protecting the rights of lesbian and gay people. A lesbian herself, from a working-class background, Anna knows first-hand some of the difficulties of being an outsider in mainstream society. She is also well acquainted with being the target of aggression, having been sexually and physically abused as a child by two different stepfathers. She attended a Catholic grade school where the idealized goodness stressed by the nuns sharply contrasted with the cruel reality of her family life, strengthening her conviction that she could "never tell" about the abuse. At age 11 the threat of her stepfather's abuse filled her mind daily: "I'd pray every day that the abuse wouldn't happen and I had this fantasy that he would die in this car wreck. I prayed for a car crash. It was a lot like I'd made a deal with God. I said, 'I will be good forever, I will be very good, I will be excellent forever if we could make this deal and you make him die.' And I really thought I was making a serious contract with God."

In return for this promise of angelic goodness, God was supposed to free her mother and her sisters, and they were supposed to have a better life. But after what she had prayed for came to pass—"He actually died in a car wreck, a truck went off a bridge and he died, which was too close, you know?"—Anna's mother was shattered and became an alcoholic.

> Then I was really pissed when it happened, because it was like there was this fine print about, well, my mom was supposed to be happy about it, my sisters were supposed to be rescued, we were all supposed to be rescued by this. And they're not happy,

this is awful. So I felt like God sort of cheated me on the deal. So then I didn't feel like I was necessarily obligated to be good forever because there had been this fine print.

Anna was left with her guilt—about the abuse, the death, and her mother's reaction: "My mother was just destroyed, which made me feel very bad. I felt *very* guilty about being so selfish. I wouldn't take it [his death] back, for nothing would I have taken it back. It still remains to me the best solution that was possible from many perspectives, but I felt tremendous guilt."

Now, at 40, Anna has integrated these difficult experiences as well as her anger about the abuse. The moral contradictions she lived as a child—the saintly goodness presented by the nuns next to the hidden evil she was forced to endure; her promise to be good forever in return for the death of her abuser—left her deeply suspicious of "goodness" and its ability to mask aggressive destruction.

Anna talks about her own development from such a difficult childhood to her creative adulthood:

There's a line from a Dylan Thomas poem, it's about a flower, something about the force that drives its greenness.[1] I mean, think about how a tree, in the course of a day, moves a tremendous amount of water. You never see it, but it does, it's constantly doing that. But I think that anger is just—it's like, what kind of tree would I be without it? Anger is where I expand. You know, mystics can spend a lot of time and energy trying to be only all things good and beautiful, but another option is just to take that anger and let it be the force that does drive the green. And I think it's that anger that helps me send off another feeler, another branch over here . . . So in a sense, anger is perhaps the healthiest emotion we have to ensure our growth, you know? Because if I hadn't found it, I wouldn't have grown . . . And so I think anyone who's aggressive is fueled by, "I'll be angry if I don't accomplish this, it will anger me to lose the opportunity, it will anger me not to be as big as I should be."

How can anger become a force that drives the green of growth rather than a force that feeds aggressive destruction? Each of these four women's pattern of dealing with what she terms her aggression profoundly affects her sense of self and her life course. What do Lyn, Maria, Chrystal, and Anna, located so differently in society because of their ethnicity, class, socialization, and opportunities, have in common in the experience of their aggression? What accounts for their variations in attitude? How can Chrystal feel better after she hits someone while Lyn fears she will destroy someone simply by being herself? How has Anna learned to use her anger constructively? We will look for answers to such questions as we listen to the women's voices.

As the women tell their stories, the clarity of a single concept of aggression fractures into dissonant, contradictory perspectives. Because there is no such thing as *a* woman's perspective, we should expect this, particularly when women speak from differing contexts, ethnicities, classes, and ages. But if we listen more deeply we can hear some underlying similarities as women talk about aggression within the context that concerns them most: relationships. To recapture a unifying thematic yet allow differences in plot, we must let women recount their own experiences.

The Mythology of Aggression

Several powerful cultural messages affect the meanings women attach to their aggression. The most pervasive of these is the myth that, while men are naturally aggressive, women are naturally unaggressive.[2] Others are that women are less competitive; express aggression in indirect, "sneaky" ways; suppress their anger because of passivity or training; tend toward irrational and overreactive outbursts; need psychological treatment if they are "overaggressive"; use aggression only in defense of their children; and are commonly motivated to aggression by jealousy (see Macaulay, 1985; White and Kowalski, 1994). The popular idea that women are more empathic than men also suggests that they will be less destructively aggressive.

The belief that aggression is characteristic of men but not of women is reinforced by what we see in society. Men are more physically aggressive and commit more crimes of assault and murder than women do. According to the FBI's Uniform Crime Reports, obtained from over 16,000 police departments, females (juvenile and adult) commit only about 13 percent of all violent crimes and 8 percent of all homicides.[3] This social fact of male aggressiveness is often attributed to biological differences between the sexes, particularly to the male hormone testosterone. But the claim that testosterone is the "hormone of aggression" that drives men to mayhem and war is open to serious question.[4]

The "naturalness" of male dominance was popularized during the 1960s by descriptions of gender hierarchies and male aggression among nonhuman primates, our closest cousins. Robert Ardrey (1966) and Konrad Lorenz (1966), who described a strict dominance hierarchy between males and females, portrayed male aggression as part of the plan of nature. We now know that such portrayals were based on projection and on observations of only a few species. The claim that male's greater aggressiveness has ensured their dominance in all species of primates, including the human species, has been contradicted by more contemporary researchers. Patricia Wright (1993), who studies lemurs in Madagascar and monkeys in South America, observes:

> Reviewing the data that primatologists have obtained from recent in-depth field observations, we realize how naive and biased the earlier images were. There are approximately 200 species of primates, and in about 40 percent of them females are dominant or equal to males in status. At the family level, six out of ten families have females equal in rank or dominant over males and one of these families (Cebidae) has genera with females either equal, subordinate or dominant. Only in the great apes (Pongidae), the Old World monkeys (Cercopithecidae), and the bushbabies and lorises (Lorisidae) are females below males in the gender hierarchy. Long-term studies have shown that in one species of great ape, the female has the option of transferring out of her social group into a new one if circumstances, including the male's behavior, do not suit her. (127–128)

Whatever the role of biology, social determinants play a dominant role in fostering and shaping aggression in humans.[5] Racism, poverty, fear, powerlessness, and cultural beliefs mold aggression; socialization and power shape its expression. Beliefs about aggression, particularly that it is a product of biology, serve political purposes, justifying both wars and men's violence against women. Male power, reinforced by the threat of male violence, has taken on the aura of "naturalness" in our world.

In Western cultures overt displays of aggression by women have often been met with death or physical punishment. Thus, women have developed "women's ways" of enacting aggression, often less physical than men's ways, some not easily recognized as aggression. As a matter of survival, women have learned to *appear* unaggressive. In addition to disguising aggression outwardly, they have learned to undertake an inner activity against themselves, to stop anger or aggression from being overtly expressed, so as to appear passive and nonthreatening. Much of women's nonaggression and deference to male authority is part of a strategy of "compliant relatedness" that women use to ensure safety and attain intimacy within inequality (Jack, 1991).

Alternatively, women living in dangerous social contexts have learned to appear aggressive and hostile as a means of deterring attack. Aggression becomes an interpersonal style, an attitude that warns, "Better not mess with me." Or, in work situations that call for a certain amount of aggressiveness, women readily demonstrate the expected behavior. Whether their style is behind your back or in your face, women enact their aggressiveness within a society that believes men are and should be more aggressive than women. They learn early the moral prohibition against harming others, the physical threat of retaliation for aggression, and the social rule that aggressive women are ostracized.

Women are not always compliant and nonthreatening, nor is their aggression always a performance or an attitude. They join men on the battlefield, in the courtroom, and in sports arenas. In personal relationships, they fight back against their aggressors, both physically and emotionally. They resist domination, combat inequality, and push for social change. And women hurt others. They abuse, kill, inflict harm on the human spirit, and dominate others through pain and intimidation. Not only men batter women; violence occurs in lesbian relationships at about the same rate as in heterosexual relationships (Obejas, 1994; Renzetti, 1992). Women also abuse children. According to a Justice Department study released in 1994, 55 percent of murders by parents of their own children are committed by mothers.[6] Violence is not limited to men.

When women stand up to inner or outer authorities, when they hurt someone purposely, when they positively fight for justice— these are critical points of change. In these moments of giving in or aggressively defending, of resisting or succumbing, the sense of self is being transformed. So is the structure of relationship. To understand the various motives and meanings of women's aggression we must move beyond arguments about who is the most aggressive to examine the specifics of women's aggression and the social contexts that shape it.

Despite convincing evidence that gender differences in aggressive behaviors are socially created, the common belief remains: aggression in women is an anomaly. Each woman must come to terms with this cultural message. Even women who, as girls, were taught to fight with their fists, to attack rather than be attacked, must deal with the social judgment that their aggression is more deviant than a man's. As women check themselves against the myth that their gender is not aggressive, they often silence themselves or resist the myth in ways that jeopardize themselves or others.

Social expectations and the fear of being judged by others affect what parts of their experience women are willing to reveal and what parts they hide. Deborah (age 41, white), a police officer for fourteen years, talks about an incident during her previous job as a security officer, when she and a woman colleague physically subdued and apprehended two female shoplifters:

> I felt pretty good that we caught them, that we held our own actually, and it kind of sounds weird to be saying that . . . I held my own even though they were, she was a big woman and obviously, experienced and that kind of thing. *[Why would you say that it sounds weird to say that?]* Oh, I was thinking that probably

society would not like to hear that it felt good . . . it's gender-related too. The guys, if they win, they're like, "yeah, yeah, yeah!" You know, "That's great!" The testosterone is just raging and flowing and they're feeling really good about themselves . . . So to feel good about winning and aggression, I would never have told anybody. *[How did you think other people would respond at the time?]* Well, I remember the police officers at the time were saying "Hey, good job, good job," you know, and I was just "Thanks, thanks." I just didn't want to appear exuberant about it or anything . . . to feel good about winning and aggression, I would suppress that.

Fear of straying into testosterone territory, of infringing on male identity by enjoying her aggression, leads Deborah to hide her real feelings. By doing so she inadvertently perpetuates the stereotype that women do not like winning a fight or subduing another person. Femininity, in this instance, clearly is a social performance that excludes enjoying physical aggression, even in a job that demands such aggression.

Deborah's vigilance over her feelings arises from her knowledge that women who appear too "manly" are considered deviant. Women in traditionally male jobs told me they were called "lesbian" or "dyke" for their choice of work. Our culture's homophobia inhibits women's willingness to risk being seen as aggressive and thus incurring these labels.

Social rules also dictate that women use very different behavioral styles from men as they oppose, argue, get their way, and intimidate and hurt others. Like the other women I interviewed, Arliss (age 27, white, student), who spent four years in the air force, is well aware of these social rules:

I feel, for women, that they do it [aggression] so subtly. But for the men that I know, they can do it more . . . they can get away with it and everything. I mean if you blow up at somebody and use aggression to get them out of your way or whatever, then everything's going to be okay afterwards. But as a woman, if you use that same tactic, you're not going to be friends afterwards more than likely. But that's been a real hard thing for me because

I am a woman, but then I've been immersed in a male field. So I know both ways and sometimes it's hard to decide which one to use. Should I use the male style or the female style? I kind of flow back and forth between the two.

In the air force, Arliss says, "I learned that being subtle and the female ways of doing things usually didn't work except in positions where the figure happened to be a very high figure—authoritative figure. But with people who were just a little bit higher than myself or my co-workers, or people who were below me, I could use that male style of aggression and get away with it." In her current part-time job as a waitress, Arliss uses nonverbal communication to convey her hostile messages to rude customers: "Probably my more female aggression comes out then because I get very selective about my word choice and my facial expression is not very animated but just that kind of eyebrow raising, staring them down kind of thing."

Types of aggression follow social rules that depend on power, gender, and context. While people usually tailor their aggressive responses to these three factors, subordinates may monitor them more carefully and use subtler, less visible aggressive styles, as Arliss so clearly describes. She recognizes that a woman cannot simply reverse the terms, "blow up at somebody" like a man, and get away with it. She thinks that doing so will affect relationships negatively, a view shared by other women who perceive that angry displays directed at co-workers have greater relationship cost and personal cost for themselves than for men (Davis, LaRosa, and Foshee, 1992).

The myth that women are not aggressive is reinforced by stories that children learn early in life. The tale of Beauty and the Beast lays out the Western mythology of gender, aggression, and sexuality. Man is a beast; woman is an unaggressive beauty. In relation to man, woman possesses "magic" powers either to call forth his aggressive nature, as did the witch who turned the prince into a beast, or to transform him from a beast into a prince, as does Belle.

Aggression is usually understood as "the beast within," an aspect of "man" waiting to erupt when provoked. This archetypal tale brings man's aggressive, bestial nature to the surface, and teaches how a woman should relate to this male trait to remain safe. Safety lies in a woman's ability to love in spite of a man's aggressive, brutish nature. In fact, her love will *transform* his aggression, though she may always recall his dangerous potential. Thus, to achieve love and happiness in a world where male rulers—princes, husbands, authorities—hold this negative power, a woman must direct her force in certain ways. The more she enacts the characteristics of "good" femininity—beauty, forbearance, compliance, submissiveness, gentleness—the more successful she will be in eliciting a prince, not a beast. Either way, the woman is responsible: she is a witch (rhymes with what?) if her man is a beast; beautiful (Belle) and feminine if he is not.

Fear and sexuality figure in this story, as they do in the world. They run through Belle's capture and defenselessness. The story presents men as danger or as protection; they attempt to rescue women from other men's aggression, though they are not always successful. Belle's own destructive or self-protective aggressiveness never appears; its absence implies its nonexistence. Also absent is any mention of the consequences if Belle should choose to fight the beast. But this omission does not diminish the threat of retaliation for any resistance she might offer. The menace of the beast's potential violence hovers, implicitly, from the outset. It makes Belle's unaggressive response comprehensible. She uses her own force to transform the threatening male's potential sexual and physical aggression into love; she transforms her fear and anger into goodness and compliance in order to find happiness with the beast.

Society's Double Messages

Another, more recent cultural voice contradicts the myth that women are not aggressive. This voice, which arose with the women's movement and with the entry of large numbers of white, middle-class women into the labor force during the 1970s, contradicts the claim that women are "not aggressive enough to make it."

Controversy about women's aggressiveness fills the media, usually in the form of arguments about whether they are as aggressive as men. "Just as fierce" says Katherine Dunn (1994): "With the possibility of genuine equality visible in the distance, it is self-destructive lunacy to deny the existence of women's enormous fighting heart. We don't just deserve power, we have it. It includes the ability to inflict damage." "Deadlier than the male" says Alix Kirsta (1994) in her book on women's violence and aggression. "Shoot the women first," says Eileen MacDonald (1991), quoting advice given to antiterrorist squads because women terrorists are thought to be more deadly and ferocious than their male comrades. Further, the popular media call attention to increasing aggression among adolescent girls. An article in *USA Today* (August 11, 1993, 5D) entitled "Girls Are Muscling in on the Bully Act" cites experts agreeing: "We're seeing much more expressed aggression on the part of females, and I think we'll see it even more." In zines and music lyrics, women are claiming their aggression as part of pushing for equality.

Society gives women conflicting messages about how aggressive they "should" be. On the one hand, they must be aggressive enough to make it in the marketplace, particularly in formerly male professions: they must be ambitious. On the other hand, if they are "too ambitious" they are seen as aggressive and criticized or punished. While gaining equal opportunities, women still have to maintain behaviors that are more traditionally feminine. As Theresa (age 40, Latina, attorney) says: "I think about how aggressive I 'should' be every day. Women won't be liked unless they are 'nice and polite,' but they won't be respected—it's easy to be walked all over if you aren't aggressive enough." Another attorney, Robin (age 48, white), the first woman to make partner in a large international law firm, recognizes that women and men are judged by different standards:

> There was a woman who entered [the firm], in fact we started work the same day, who was viewed by the male partners as being too aggressive and unfairly criticized for it. Now I never saw anything different about her than I saw about myself, but for some reason, some behavior that she engaged in, whatever it was, had irritated someone who had said something, you know, to someone. That same kind of behavior in a young male lawyer I can think of, who's very much kind of a "I have to have my own way" kind of person, it was not viewed as a negative.

Knowing that the label "too aggressive" may affect their careers, yet not sure which behaviors will be so labeled, women monitor their own behavior, looking for the elusive middle ground of appropriate self-assertion.

Brooke (age 35, white), an attorney in private practice, makes the same point:

> This client was talking about this woman who was "overly aggressive." But what he meant is that she was overly ambitious, in his mind. She was seeking a job that she was not qualified to do, and so it was inappropriate ambition. It's aggressive if you are inappropriately ambitious, but it's just a matter of degree always. There's a much higher threshold for a man to be overly ambitious to the point of being overly aggressive. It's a much, much lower threshold for women.

In thousands of daily interactions, women learn what behavior is considered appropriate. Stories like Brooke's, passed from one woman to another, serve as modern cautionary tales warning women to suppress, mute, and disguise what others may perceive as overly aggressive behavior. Yet, at the same time, the workplace values male over female characteristics and requires women to show "enough" aggression (see Case, 1995).

This double bind stood out in a Supreme Court decision regarding a consulting firm's refusal to promote Ann Hopkins to partner because "she was sometimes overly aggressive, unduly harsh, difficult to work with and impatient with the staff." Ruling in favor of Hopkins, Justice Brennan wrote: "An employer who objects to aggressiveness in women but whose positions require this trait places women in an intolerable and impermissible Catch-22: out of a job if they behave aggressively and out of a job if they do not."[7] Many of these issues in the workplace have less to do with aggression as such than with cultural policing to keep women and men within recognizable lines of gender.

The fine line between being not aggressive enough and being too aggressive is policed by women as well as by men. Elizabeth Jones (age 43, white), an obstetric/gynecological surgeon who practices in a large city, recounts a tense scene in the delivery room:

The woman was in labor and the baby's heart rate showed great stress. I planned on moving the mother to the C-section room, but wanted to try a vaginal delivery first. The nurses were flustered because they couldn't find the packs for delivery. One nurse especially was floundering around, fumbling to find things, couldn't locate the stirrups, etcetera. Meanwhile, I was quickly preparing for delivery and gave orders for them to prepare her. The nurse said behind me, "I hate it when you're like this." They were responding to my tone of voice! I was simply giving orders. As a woman, you can't give orders but have to soften it to make it sound like a request.

Dr. Jones, who has been criticized by hospital officials for refusing to stop performing abortions, was singled out for censure by the hospital for "long-standing improper behavior." According to confidential reports she showed me, certain staff members had complained that she was "hostile" and "rude," used "offensive language and tone," and had "verbal outbursts." Basically, the behavior consisted of showing any signs of anger, either in her tone of voice or by criticizing hospital personnel. The director of the hospital wrote to her: "You are hereby warned and advised that *any* future instance of apparent long-standing improper behavior . . . including, without limitation, displays of anger and hostility toward other physicians, staff, and patients . . . may result in restriction, suspension, termination, or nonrenewal of medical staff membership or practice privileges."[8] Many people rushed to Dr. Jones's support when they learned of this letter, including patients, other physicians, and members of the hospital staff.

Dr. Jones voluntarily consulted a physician center for an outside assessment concerning the allegations of her "disruptive" behavior. According to the letter sent to the hospital director from the center, she "does not fit the typical 'disruptive' physician stereotype . . . she is thoughtful, articulate, fiercely loyal to her style of Ob-Gyn patient care and aware of how [pro-life] movements can see and use her as an icon . . . She was also extremely receptive, insightful and emotionally sensitive to our probes. She reiterated a desire for formal conciliation."[9]

When the hospital administrators wanted to find grounds to dismiss Dr. Jones, they did not point to incompetence or any behavior that could be measured by specific outcomes. Rather, they seized upon behaviors that could be *interpreted* by others. The smallest departures by women from submissive, deferential behavior—including tone of voice—may be labeled angry or hostile because they deviate from traditional norms of femininity. Given her indisputable competence, this was the one area in which Dr. Jones could be attacked.

This "Catch-22," as Justice Brennan called it—the demand that women be unaggressive but that they be aggressive enough to succeed at work—clearly causes dilemmas for women as they try to thread their way through its contradictions. Mary (age 43, white), a psychotherapist who works in a large organization, describes the bind caused by a collision of expectations about required interpersonal behavior:

> I define aggression as something that's necessary to get anywhere in this world of patriarchy. For women to be aggressive especially, I think of it in terms of being able to speak your voice, to stand up in situations, to go for what you want, to be able to succeed. I wish it weren't necessary because I don't agree with the system we have to work in. In the patriarchal thinking, the hierarchal structure, we have to get to the top. I think in negative ways, you know, oftentimes it steps on people's faces, and . . . that's not good. I mean, it's impossible to stand on the line, to not hurt anybody and be aggressive. Or at least that's a goal I have personally, to be able to do that, to be aggressive enough to get myself where I want to go and not hurt anybody in the meantime.

The dilemma Mary describes—how to be self-assertive without hurting others—is created by society's contradictory messages about how women should behave. No clear line can be drawn between assertion and aggression because observers have the power to label behavior. Attempting to be "assertive" but never "aggressive" is a bit like flying a plane and straying across enemy lines into a no-fly zone: there are no markers or signposts indicating that you have moved into forbidden territory.

The Connotations of Aggression

When we use the word "aggression," we assert a set of relations based on force and power. We also assert a set of social beliefs in labeling an act or a person as aggressive. As our society defines it, aggression designates male; the term derives its meaning in relation to female "absence" of aggression. In all measures of masculinity, "aggressive" forms the core of masculine qualities.[10] A man's aggressive behavior, even when it is negative or destructive, enhances his masculinity. A woman's destructive or dominating aggressive behavior detracts from her femininity. Consider this statement by eminent researchers on aggression: "The preponderance of evidence indicates that males, as a group, are always more aggressive than females, as a group, regardless of how the aggression is expressed or measured" (Eron and Huesmann, 1989, 55).[11] They go on to assert: "What it means to be a man or masculine in our society must be re-examined, since the preponderance of violence in our society is perpetrated by males or by females who are acting like males" (65). Women's aggression, for these researchers, takes its meaning in relation to men's behaviors: violent women are just imitating men; "real" women are not violent. How our culture socializes boys for aggressiveness certainly must be reexamined, but so must such fundamental issues as how our beliefs about aggression have guided researchers' perceptions and interpretations.

Aggression by women connotes destructiveness and a challenge to male authority. One of the surest ways to neutralize the force of an intelligent, sexually assertive, independent woman is to depict it as destroying others, particularly children or men. Strong women are imagined to rob their men of potency. As castrating "virility vampires" (Dijkstra, 1996, 141), they drain the male life-force through their own "masculinism" or "abnormal dominance"—by actions as innocuous as speaking in a harsh tone of voice. Powerful, dominating mothers are believed to steal their children's initiative and mold "sissy" boys and unnatural girls.

The idea that a woman's sexual and emotional self-assertion destroys others is inherited from late-nineteenth- and early-twentieth-century intellectuals such as Darwin and Freud. Darwin's idea that the most primitive living organisms had been "bisexual," containing within themselves both male and female generative functions, was used by Freud and others to argue that sexual *difference* provided the cornerstone for cultural evolution: "The greatest achievement of human evolution had been to widen the differences between men and women in an exponential fashion" (Dijkstra, 1996, 133). Thus the regressive pull of bisexuality was seen as the greatest threat to civilization, and bisexuality's definition was broadened to include not only biological generativity (sex) but also social characteristics (gender). "Masculinism" in women was seen as the mark of the primitive beast, and so was any sign of "effeminacy" in men. The biological, psychoanalytical, and philosophical schemes devised to extirpate such primitive remnants from humanity have shaped our present ideas about the social function of gender.

At the end of the twentieth century, with gender spilling over its former lines of demarcation, such arguments are again being mobilized, though without their explicit ties to Darwinian theory. Aggression is still the bedrock upon which gender dualisms are erected: active/passive, warlike/peaceful, competitive/cooperative, separate/connected, and more. The thought of women's aggression arouses inchoate fears of an unnatural blurring of gender lines that have been drawn by evolution. If women are overtly aggressive, then gender, as our society has defined it, will no longer exist.

Underlying these long-standing issues around gender and aggression is a fear woven deeply into the human psyche. What the culture fears, wants to control, and denies is women's *intent to do harm*. Women give life to the human race. Their intent to do harm is incompatible with their biological function as mothers and their social role as nurturers of the young; they must curb aggression so as not to hurt children. In addition, women must stay out of dangerous, confrontational situations in order to stay alive to fulfill their biological role of raising their offspring (see Coghlan, 1996). This is part of why women's aggression is particularly taboo.

The fear of women's destructive potential is learned early. Children intimately know their mother's absolute power over their well-being. In the memory of a young child, dread of the mother's negation may generalize to fear of the destructive potential of all women. Many cultures integrate aspects of this early image of mother as destroyer into their myths of the feminine. Before patriarchy, the triple goddess included maiden, mother, and crone. The crone was the destroyer. This crone aspect of the feminine both personified human fears of death and destruction and gave hope of transformation into new life or new patterns. The Indian goddess Kali, dancing with her necklace of skulls; Ereshkigal, the queen of the underworld in the ancient Sumerian *Hymn of Inanna;* the goddess Hecate; and numerous others all fall into what Jung calls parts of a Dark Mother archetype: "the place of magic, transformation and rebirth, together with the underworld and its inhabitants . . . presided over by the mother. On the negative side, the mother archetype may connote anything secret, hidden, dark; the abyss, the world of the dead, anything that devours, seduces, and poisons, that is terrifying and inescapable like fate" (Jung, 1970, 16).

Kali symbolizes women's power to give life and thus to deny life. She also represents the power and the need to destroy what is no longer necessary. Western patriarchal society wants to forget about the destructive, aggressive side of femininity and to celebrate only the virginal maiden and the nurturer. This renders women innocent and unhurtful and thus contained and controllable.

Relations of power underlie the social meanings of aggression. Whenever interests conflict, aggressive acts or threats can be used to enforce one person's will over another's. But threats are coercive only insofar as they create fear. Then fear can serve as aggression's stand-in to enforce dominance. When couples engage in violent, physical arguments, women fear men's anger and aggression; men do not fear women's (Jacobson et al., 1994). In couples with a male batterer,

> fear is the major gender difference between male and female violence. Without fear, there is no control. For us [researchers], fear became a barometer of control. The women consistently

> manifested it in the laboratory during the arguments, whereas
> the men did not. The women consistently reported fear when
> describing arguments at home, whereas the men did not. (Ja-
> cobson and Gottman, 1998, 82–83)

Particularly in intimate relationships, male dominance is main-
tained through fear, backed by the threat of physical aggression.

In the wider culture, the long history of men's control over
women is believed to stem from men's greater brute strength and
inherent aggressiveness. These characteristics allowed men greater
social power, manifested in laws, economic sanctions, and other
coercions, always backed by the threat of force. Fear of aggression
underlies the social contract wherein individuals trade certain limitations on personal freedom for protection from higher authorities. Because women are perceived as carrying less aggressive threat
and less social power, they have been left out of the "tit for tat"
social contract that is based on the view of human nature as inher-
ently aggressive. They have been extended a contract based on inequality: chivalry, a quid pro quo, protects women of a certain color
and class against men's aggression in return for their deferential
behaviors.

The terms of this unequal contract were made explicit in the
rhetoric around manliness and civilization during the early 1900s.
In the words of Sir Almroth Wright, an eminent scientist: "When
a man makes this compact with a woman, 'I will do you reverence,
and protect you, and yield you service; and you, for your part, will
hold fast to an ideal of gentleness, of personal refinement, of mod-
esty, of joyous maternity, and who shall say what other graces and
virtues that endear woman to man,' that is *chivalry*." The historian
Gail Bederman observes: "If either sex broke this compact, all bets
were off. When a woman became violent, unrefined, ungrateful, or
'when she places a quite extravagantly high estimate upon her in-
tellectual powers,' the contract was broken. Woman must then bear
the brunt of unfettered masculine violence" (1995, 159). The gender
quid pro quo requires traditional "feminine," that is, submissive,
behavior, including caretaking and nurturance, in return for the
promise of male forbearance.

Woman's role in the social contract between the genders also includes an expectation that she neutralize or de-escalate male aggression. Through her neutralizing acts, she plays the role of a "civilizing" force in society. Women's role as nurturers of children includes soothing; they calm an infant or a child with voice tone, gentle touch, reassurances, distraction—by the general deescalation of negative arousal. Through being ministered to by their caretakers, who are usually female, children internalize an expectation that a woman's function is to soothe or neutralize frustration and aggression. Women attempt to neutralize their own aggression to remove its threat from their caretaking abilities.[12]

This image of the feminine "soothing self" that neutralizes aggression shapes the perception of how women should behave. This may be one reason why battered women so often are asked, "What did you do to make him angry?" The social contract based on inequality and the notion that men will refrain from aggression so long as women fulfill their part of the bargain—deferential, submissive behavior—lead society to fault a woman whose man hasn't protected her. The question really means, "Why didn't you defuse his anger?"[13] Women's force and power are supposed to function for neutralizing and caretaking, not for opposition that may lead to conflict.

Further, female caretaking and nonaggression have been seen as morally superior to male aggressive self-interest and violence. If women become angry or aggressive, they lose the one claim to moral superiority that male culture is willing to give them (Hayles, 1986). Falling from their superior moral position makes them "one of the boys," and thus negates the social contract of chivalry that promises protection for specific types of women. Women of color, as well as poor and working-class white women, were exempt from this patriarchal contract.

While gender appears to be the major system of power that affects women's aggression, intersections of race and class also position social power and influence women's behavior. Of most interest here is how a woman experiences these intersections herself and how, or if, she articulates the meanings of her aggression in relation to them.

Carrie (age 30, African American, social worker), the mother of two school-age children, describes confronting the principal of a largely white school. She had received a letter that her kindergarten-age son had "been a problem on the bus lately" and had behaved poorly at other times.

> I have to go and face the principal. First of all, I'm an African-American woman. I'm a single parent. I've got two kids by two different fathers. Okay, label me, label me? Now I found this area that I think is beautiful. It's got a golf course . . . But you know what? We're talking about rich people living out here. Now I'm living in an apartment complex, okay? . . . I just go in and I speak from the heart. I've been there, like I told you, I've been there. You know, it's like it's been throughout my whole life and it's time for me now to go and speak for my kids. I'm speaking from experience. Speaking from the heart means being honest and putting your all into it. You know, everybody has a righteousness, a goodness, and when you just let go and in everything you do, you don't have a hidden motive. You're not out to get anybody. You're not out to degrade anybody or put anybody down but what you're out to do is just be open and honest. You're not sitting out there with any vengeance, "Well I'm going to stick this to you because I . . ." You're saying, "Look, you know, let's really be real about this. Let's work together on this. This is what I see and this is how I'm feeling and this is what's going on here and this is what's been happening with me or whatever. This is what's going on."

To Carrie, race and class are entwined with gender in terms of the power relations that affect her aggression. She sees that others might label her on the basis of these social markers and interpret her aggression negatively. Even though she uses these markers to describe the context of her actions, she attempts to make them less controlling by "speaking from the heart." Her goal is to cross the distance created by such social positionings to engage positively with the principal and to prevent future injustices to her child. Her social position affects her; it does not determine her.

Few women I interviewed frame their aggression as explicitly in terms of race and class as does Carrie, but social location influences the forms of their aggression. Numerous factors, all induced by social inequalities, such as racism, poverty, physical and emotional abuse, incest, and other sexual abuse, create disconnections that can lead to destructive aggression. Or, at times, women transcend these social inequalities and their resulting traumas to courageously love, overcome, and heal through positive aggression. What distinguished the stories of the women of color from those of the white women was the greater detailing of demeaning treatment by society and of the barriers to their equal social participation. Like many white women, many women of color had faced abuse; but poverty and racism often added layers of anger and difficulty. Because of the small number of subjects, I cannot generalize about women's aggression by race and class. These categories are dynamic and changing; all women are constantly re-forming them as they resist and revise the meanings of their aggression.

In ordinary usage, aggression is a slippery and elusive concept, at one time designating an act, at another an aspect of personality or a way of interacting. Aggression can be external, manifested through behavior, or internal, manifested through feelings, fantasies, anger, and hostility. It can be used constructively, to fight injustice, set things right, move societies toward equality, break harmful silences, pursue goals. Destructively, we use it to tear things apart, dominate and control others, harm, kill, and maim. Some aggression, such as that on the athletic field, in the courtroom, in the military, or in the boardroom, is socially sanctioned and governed by rules. Other aggression is forbidden and punished.

In this book I focus on aggression's meaning for women's interpersonal relationships and its role in their psychology. As an aspect of interpersonal relations, aggression always carries the social connotations it has accumulated over the centuries, yet it feels intensely personal. As women describe it, aggression defies logic; it sits in paradoxical relationship to love. Love would seem to exclude aggression, the wish to hurt; aggression "should" not be present where love and its substrate, empathy, mediate the gap between two people. Yet anger opens fissures, love cracks, and aggression strikes through the gaps in angry words, blows, cruel acts. It happens in what seems like a second: a morning of lovemaking, close-ness, a later irritation over critical words, angry self-defense, es-calation into aggressive hurt. Women sketched this scenario often. Love seems a changeling, transforming before one's eyes from har-monious connection to betrayal, rage, and hatred. Aggression is also a changeling, assuming many guises because direct acts lead to pun-ishment: it erupts here as boiling sugar to pour on an abusive part-ner, there as yelling at children, elsewhere as honey-coated talk with the intent to harm. Though these interactions often feel unchosen and unplanned, they are patterned by generations of gender in-equality, fears, and cultural conventions regarding women's ag-gression.

Freud's Legacy

Psychologists understand aggression primarily in terms of its mo-tivation, as "an act done with the intention to harm another person, oneself, or an object" (Björkqvist and Niemelä, 1992, 4); or in terms of its goal orientation, as "an act whose goal-response is injury to an organism" (Dollard et al., 1939, 11); or as a trait, "an aggressive personality" (Dodge and Coie, 1987); or as a socialized set of be-haviors that is stable over a lifetime (Eron and Huesmann, 1989). A common assumption underlies all such definitions: that aggres-sion is an attribute carried within the individual. In this widely accepted view, aggression in the individual is "pushed out" or "compelled" by inner forces, such as aggressive energy, instincts, hormones, brain centers, anger, or frustration (Felson and Tedes-chi, 1993).

Freud's ideas shape our models of aggression. In his view, sex and aggression are basic drives. The individual pursues self-interest and pleasure, using aggression to achieve desires, and "man's" nat-ural state is one of anarchy. People must renounce a certain amount of gratification of sexual and aggressive drives in order to avoid social chaos; civilization is a thin veneer that cracks whenever ordered social relations break down to reveal the basically self-interested, aggressive nature of man. Incessant wars seem to pro-vide evidence of Freud's thesis: at the heart of civilization lurks the threat of its violent undoing through aggression, with its presumed maleness and innateness.

Women occupy a place in this story as the "civilizing influence," the ones whose love tames the sexually aggressive men and fosters peaceful communal life. Freud argued that in women aggressive drives are repressed and redirected inward, resulting in female masochism. Women who behave aggressively have been, and still are, considered "masculine." Thus aggression presents proof of maleness, while in women it is seen as unnatural, since the essence of femininity, according to Freud, is passivity. Further, a woman's aggression signals insubordination, a breaking of the implicit social contract upon which patriarchal civilization rests.

Those who study aggression today must contend with two enduring ideas inherited from Freud: a model of the self as a self-contained, self-interested individual (based on a male prototype) who is innately aggressive, and the myth that women, by nature, are passive, not aggressive. These ideas have discouraged researchers from even thinking of women's aggression as worthy of study (White and Kowalski, 1994). Only recently has women's aggression been studied as a phenomenon in and of itself (Björkqvist and Niemelä, 1992).

The assumptions that underlie investigations of aggression matter because of the conclusions that flow from them. The assumption that aggression is a quality, a trait, or a drive within the person supports and justifies a competitive, capitalistic society that pits individuals against one another—my gain is your loss, you have to play hard in order to win, and those who lose are at fault. The supposition that aggression is innate in man but not in woman explains (and therefore partially "justifies") men's violence against women and accounts for economic disparities between genders (women are not aggressive enough to "make it"). As part of a racialized discourse, such assumptions bolster stereotypes and fears while masking societal violence against people of color. These ways of thinking about aggression obscure its interpersonal, cultural roots. The notion that aggression is an innate quality transforms social relations into personality traits and places aggression's cause in "human nature" rather than in power, shame, or separation.

Thus critical social issues—such as poverty, racism, and violence against women—can be ignored while attention focuses on characteristics assumed to lie within the individual.

Relational Perspectives

Relational theorists view aggression from a radically different perspective. They assume that one of our basic, biosocial motivations is to make secure, intimate connection with others; they see even aggression as a channel through which we relate to others.

John Bowlby's attachment theory (1969, 1973, 1980) takes into account our animal nature and the types of environments within which humans evolved. Arguing that animals of all species are most vulnerable to predators when alone, Bowlby proposes that attachment behaviors, which create and maintain physical and emotional closeness to others, ensure safety, security, and comfort. In humans, the desire for companionship is especially pronounced when a person is distressed, ill, or afraid. Under ordinary conditions, the threat of loss of a valued relationship arouses anxiety and anger; open conflict often causes psychological discomfort similar to that caused by physical separation. It is easy to imagine, from this theoretical perspective, that people may avoid aggression because it drives others away. Because women's aggression is less accepted by society than men's, women may have particularly strong reasons to fear that if they instigate conflict they will be left isolated and alone.

Children learn patterns of relating from their primary family and internalize these as fundamental ways of connecting with others (Mitchell, 1988). If a child's entry into human relationships occurs through aggressive interactions, such behavior becomes the familiar way to reach others. Since any contact is better than no contact at all, the child (and later the adult) relies on aggression as a form of relatedness. From this perspective, aggression is not a drive internal to the individual; rather, it is a particular way of being connected to others. Whether or not destructive aggression becomes a central form of connection for a certain person depends on the person's culture and family contexts and the person's responses to those contexts.

From the relational viewpoint, aggression can be either defensive (benign, functional) or destructive (malignant, dysfunctional), depending on its effect on the bonds of relationship. Functional aggression "serves life" (Fromm, 1973, 218) and may help an individual overcome obstacles to reunion and may discourage the loved person from going away again (Bowlby, 1973). Dysfunctional aggression tends to destroy the bonds of intimacy rather than restore them. Anger can become dysfunctional aggression when separation is prolonged, repeated, or constantly threatened. Thus inquiry should be focused on what features of relationship discourage functional anger and aggression and elicit the destructive forms.

Aspects of Women's Aggression

Women are socialized to be nurturant and to focus their energies on creating and sustaining relationships. A long line of research confirms that women's sense of self is more interdependent, more based in relationships than men's.[14] Compared to men, women are considered to be more empathic in critical aspects of human activity such as moral reasoning, parenting, interpersonal relationships, work, and knowledge (methods of scientific inquiry). Also, women are taught to see themselves as more responsible for the emotional tone of relationships than their male partners, and often experience an unwanted ending of relationship as a moral failing (Gilligan, 1982).

All theories of development agree that growth requires conflict, that is, the ability to assert oneself, encounter opposition, and negotiate differences. Though we may dream of it, and experience it at times, there is no such thing as "conflict-free perfection—a state of complete happiness and integration," presumably made possible by a "properly relational, nurturing environment" (Schapiro, 1994, 13). In fact, the ideal for relatedness is not the absence of conflict but the ability to engage in conflict without paralyzing fear or destructive harm. In the closest of relationships conflict is inevitable, and the ability to engage in it positively is fundamental to the survival of an equal, mutually satisfying relationship. Without conflict, one person in the relationship is likely to experience a loss of self, a disappearance of self into the outlines of the other.

The development of a distinct self occurs not through detachment from relationships but through experience of the "self-opposed-to-other" within relationships. If conflict is necessary for growth, if one needs not only empathy and attunement but the ability to oppose others and express one's will, then healthy aggression is mandatory to the development of self and to positive connection.

This is precisely why many puzzles of aggression occur for women. First, a woman's interdependent sense of self may be threatened by her own angry aggression that arouses her fear of isolation, separateness, and retaliation. Second, women have few models for using aggression positively, for expressing anger creatively, for being themselves without being domineering. Yet anger and aggression are necessary for self-development. We cannot stand up for ourselves without opposing others. Third, women's aggression often occurs within unequal relationships, both in intimate relationships and in broader social ones. Women's ways of expressing aggression have evolved through the centuries as they have lived intimately with others who had power over them, and, at the same time, have borne and raised children. Traditionally, women have not been allowed to directly oppose men. At this time of major changes in women's social roles, images of how to be aggressive swing between stereotypes of masculine dominance and feminine indirection. Each woman must invent her own forms of aggression by balancing a complexity of personal intentions, fears, and social messages. As we will see, women are doing so in a variety of creative, positive ways as well as in a range of destructive, despairing ways.

While a great deal is known about how girls and women silence themselves, we know less about how to change this behavior. Cultural prohibitions against women's aggression, paired with inequality in male-female relationships, often keep women from engaging in positive, creative conflict. Instead, they often turn it into self-reproach, depression, or hostile destructiveness to others. Women must be able to call on their aggression to right imbalances in relationship, to stand up for themselves, and to protect themselves. They must bear the threat of separateness if they are not to lose themselves in relationship.

There is not just one version of femininity, or of female aggression. What a girl learns about dealing with conflict and opposing others varies with her location in society. Urban, poor, and working-class girls appear more willing to engage in open conflict and to exhibit aggressive behavior (Brown, 1998; Fordham, 1993; Phelps et al., 1991; Taylor, Gilligan, and Sullivan, 1995; Way, 1995); many white, middle-class women are socialized to suppress their anger and learn to rely on indirect forms of aggression (Jack, 1991; Miller, 1991). Signithia Fordham (1993) sees the "loudness" of African-American girls as a metaphor for their subversive resistance to an image of their "nothingness" promoted by dominating images of white femininity. African-American mothers may socialize their daughters for survival more than for "goodness," knowing the adversity and devaluing stereotypes they will face in the culture. Listen to Carrie: "My mother taught us to 'sleep with one eye open.' That was the saying. 'You always have to do, try that much harder. You have to do that much better. You have to, in order to get ahead, you have to—it's going to be hard.' So I guess I was basically raised to survive what I'm about to face." Mothers like Carrie's model an assertive, self-directed woman who carries authority: "She shouted. She let it roar. And it came out! And when she came home, we had certain things that were expected of us and if they weren't done, then you heard about it."

Despite these differences in socialization for aggression, girls and women of all ethnicities find it more difficult to oppose males with whom they are intimate (Taylor, Gilligan, and Sullivan, 1995; Way, 1995). In the sphere of intimate relationships, conflict and positive aggression become even more complicated for women than in the social world with all its contradictory messages.

The meanings a woman attaches to her aggression as well as the forms it takes must be understood in the context of her social world. Most research has focused on white, middle-class children; given the variety of lifestyles, ethnic and religious backgrounds, and social statuses, these findings cannot be generalized to all children.

At this stage of our knowledge, it may be more useful to speak of local systems of socialization and relationships that inform a woman's understanding of her aggression. These may differ substantially. Yet all women face two common issues because of their gender: the threat of male retaliation for their aggression, and socially structured male dominance.

The relational perspective leads to an obvious question: Where does aggression fit into women's psychology? At every stage of development, a girl's desire for relationships can come into conflict with her positive aggression, compromising both. Relational psychologists have done much to revalue disparaged characteristics traditionally considered to be feminine, but in the process they have overlooked the characteristics that are most dreaded and disowned. If women seek to resolve conflicts by following an ethic of care with the injunction not to hurt others (Gilligan, 1982), then we must reexamine the issue of hurt as we seek to understand women's aggression.

Relational Aggression

In answering questions about their own aggression, women invariably talk about relationships. Laura (age 50, Japanese American, attorney), makes this perspective explicit:

> It's not as though the aggression was in me, but the aggression was kind of like in the ebb and flow of my relationship. So it's not as though in a certain period in my life I was an aggressive person. But in certain circumstances within every long-term relationship, you have these times of working things out and that involves maybe some more aggressive acts than others. I guess, for the most part, I don't think aggression is self-generated. And as a result, I can't look back on my life and say, "Oh, this was a time I was most aggressive." Unless we're talking about a certain relationship within that time.

Laura and the other women I talked with see aggression as fundamentally interpersonal: it arises within relationship, its expression takes different forms depending on one's family background, social location, and social expectations that are part of one's ethnicity. They portray aggression as arising in certain situations in relationship that are accompanied by fear, anger, or the need to defend oneself. These situations—injustice, inequality, disconnection, and violation—are part of the ebb and flow of relatedness: rather than standing apart as a one-time event, aggression appears as a series of interactions ranging from subtle to violent as relationships cycle through times of transgression, distance, and pain.

Issues of power also weave through women's talk about their aggression. Laura continues:

> I think that aggression is responsive in a relationship. I think when one in a relationship feels either overpowered or recognizes efforts to be dominated, then one's got to develop aggression in return. I know myself, I've been aggressive when in a relationship, in my bad relationship, I would come out being aggressive when something was very important to me that I knew I needed to power on in order to be heard, for instance. Or, in order to even have a level playing field. I would have to be more aggressive coming out of the gate in order to end up even.

For Laura, who spent her early childhood in a relocation camp for Japanese Americans during World War II, the playing field has not been level. Relations of power, both intimate and social, affect her understanding of her aggression. But all women, regardless of their social location, see some type of aggression as necessary to preserve self in relationship, especially when the playing field is tilted to their disadvantage.

A common element crosses all the women's interviews: *Aggression is a type of relatedness, a particular form of interaction, a way of connecting.* It is an interactive event, it occurs in the relational space between people, it arises from the inevitable clashes of people's wishes, desires, and wills. For the present, let us define aggression as *forcefully bringing one's will, desires, and voice into rela-*

*tionship to oppose or displace those of another, for either constructive
or destructive purposes.*

Rather than a powerful, dangerous eruption of the "beast
within," aggression is an integral part of the struggle between the
need to establish, maintain, and protect intimate bonds with others
and the need to escape the devastation and shame that accompany
the loss of such bonds. As an interpersonal event, aggression arises
out of specific forms of relationship; our focus must shift away
from inherent qualities within the individual to look at qualities of
relationship, and at the self in its social context of relationships.
Power is part of all social interactions. We cannot know the meaning or intent of an aggressive act without knowing both its relational setting and its meaning within that setting. Aggression's expression is shaped by the structure of a relationship, including
power, gender, and economics, and by the quality of the relationship—its feeling tone, its violations, its intimacies.

Aggression requires a target. The severity of aggression is usually judged by its impact on the other, not by its impact on the self
(see Storr, 1991). In fact, aggression carries consequences for both
the self and the other as the interaction alters the relational space
between them. After a woman behaves aggressively, she sees the
effect on the other and judges what she has done. This judgment
profoundly affects her sense of self.

Wendy (age 45, white, artist) presents this relational perspective on aggression:

> You aggress against other people. You aren't just aggressive in a
> vacuum or something. You'll aggress against something or some-
> body; it could be against the environment or against your
> mother. Expressing anger can be something that can explode out
> of you wherever you are. You could be all by yourself in the
> basement and throw a hammer or something, and that would
> be anger. But aggression seems to me to be something you do to
> someone else.

Anger is an emotion, often a response to being violated or perceiving injustice; aggression is an act, a movement through voice or
behavior, that affects relationship. As women tell it, anger and self-

protection are the factors that most often initiate the move into a type of relatedness they call aggression.

Women call a broad range of thoughts and actions aggressive: simply being themselves; standing up for themselves; opposing others; being honest, ambitious, or loud; initiating sex or sexually pursuing another; developing their own interests. They think about their aggressive acts "every day," deciding whether to inhibit them, use them strategically, camouflage them, enlarge them, use them to fight for change. Sometimes women consider aggressive interactions negative and hurtful; at other times they celebrate their ability to engage in such acts, believing their aggression preserves them from obliteration in a world full of inequality. The actions women call aggressive include ways of being in relationship that depart from the traditionally prescribed yielding, compliant behavior.

While I have defined aggression itself as a type of relatedness, I use the term *relational aggression* to indicate that, most commonly, women's aggressive behavior is directed at affecting a relationship. Women's relational aggression takes many forms. Women talk about using aggressive force to affect relational space both positively, by removing barriers to relationship, and negatively, by displacing another's will, power, or feelings. While women and girls do manipulate and damage relationships by means of withdrawal, exclusion, and the spreading of rumors (Crick and Grotpeter, 1995),[15] their aggressive repertoires are by no means limited to these forms. For both girls and women, the goal of aggressive activity is to restructure the relationship and thereby affect the persons within it.

To enlarge our possibilities for listening for the forms of women's relational aggression, it may be useful to recall the original meaning of the word "aggression." Its positive and negative possibilities can be seen in the Latin *aggredi*, which means "to go forward, to approach." Its root is *gradi*, which means "to step, to walk, go." Shipley (1967, 198) notes that "the basic root (through Sanskrit *griddhra*, greedy), is Aryan *gardh*, to desire, hence, to step toward." Thus aggression, in origin, includes *desire* and *movement toward an object of desire*. Further, the movement delineated by the word is itself neutral, not necessarily harmful.

When a woman intends to affect a relationship in a way that will hurt another, her destructive activity signals rage, disappointment, or frustration about the *quality of her relationship*. Her harmful acts indicate her despair over what could have been or should have been, including what the relationship symbolizes that she cannot have or lacks herself. The relationship can be of any type—intimate, professional, or with society at large. A woman wants to correct an imbalance of power or of pain by causing pain, to reconfigure the space between herself and other(s) by forceful action. She wants to affect or disrupt the existing structure of relationship. Some women enter the gap between self and other like the furies, churning with rage from previous relational injuries such as abuse and abandonment. Others enter a space of cold distance to attempt to fill it with hot emotion, or bring their own icy silence to increase the distance. Whatever the form, a woman often resorts to destructive aggression when she feels she cannot communicate her feelings directly and have them heard.

Aggression can also be positive. A woman engages in positive aggression when she forcefully removes obstacles in order to restore mutuality in relationship. Sometimes an aggressive attempt to remove obstacles leads to authentic relatedness, sometimes to retaliation, sometimes to loss. Or, if a woman feels under attack, perceives injustice, needs to protect herself, she may enter forcefully into the space between self and other to preserve life or foster positive relationships with others and with the social world. New forms of self and relatedness are achieved by such aggressive acts. As Lyn says: "Aggression for me is standing up for myself. And . . . that is how I have made any changes in my life."

Let us listen to one woman's narrative about an aggressive interaction, remembering that other patterns from different social contexts will be described in later chapters. Julia (age 39, white, teacher), the mother of three children, talks about fears of harming her husband:

> Harming him verbally, and I've hit him a couple of times and it just scares me. You know, what have I been reduced to. He never has hit me. It's just feeling that whole association of aggressive-

ness with violence and that being such an unacceptable thing
. . . And it all has to do with feeling disrespected and sort of on
some deep level—it's hard. The situation I was remembering is
I hit him accidentally. I was trying to hit the mattress. *[And then
you hit him?]* But he was there! (laughs) And by hitting the mattress I was really hitting him psychologically, I think . . . We were
in bed and the lights were out and we were talking about something and I was just feeling so backed in a corner because he was
so logical and didn't leave any room for another way of looking
at things. And he was also actively shaming me for my loud voice
and the way I was expressing myself that I just hit as like a way
to get his attention. To just shake him out of his—it was a smugness. It was sort of a smugness of rationality and logic.

Julia hit her husband (accidentally) in response to an interchange that left her feeling "backed into a corner because he . . .
didn't leave any room for another way of looking at things." Her
use of spatial metaphors calls attention to aggression as a way to
affect relational space. She feels cornered and crowded out of mutuality; even her loud voice that seeks to make him listen gets
shamed. Though Julia does not remember the exact content of this
argument, she does remember the feeling of being unable to defend
herself against her husband's "smugness of logic," a type of rational
aggression that carries the culture's approval.[16] When he uses cold
logic, Julia says, she feels "attacked so tangibly, even though it's
verbal, that I feel like blocking that, stopping that. Impressing upon
him how violent it feels even to be talked to with a calm voice but
without any heart." Her husband's rational style, seemingly devoid
of emotion, feels choked with control and power.

Julia says her goal was to "shake him out of the deadness. Almost like piercing a hardness or a separateness. I don't think it's
putting him in the same position I've been placed in. And it's not
hurting for its own sake. It's more to rattle." Yet she also says: "It
was definitely that feeling of 'I've got to change this. You've got to
listen to me.' "

Julia articulates a theme that permeates the women's narratives: aggression arises out of disconnection, those gaps and failures
of attunement. It signals the "fracture of connection" (Gilligan,

1982, 43) and stands as a red flag marking the failure of dialogue. Its goal is to pierce the separateness to create some change, to rattle the container (the relationship) to rearrange how people are positioned within it. Julia also illustrates that aggression stems from anger over perceived violations of the self and over value judgments that assign blame, rightly or wrongly, for the feelings of anger.[17]

Julia's husband, she says, "dismisses what I'm saying, and that brings out a lot of aggressive feelings in me." An unresponsive, demeaning partner creates not only an experience of separation where closeness is desired, but also an experience of inequality that arouses anger.[18] The demand/withdraw pattern that Julia describes is common to unhappy couples. The demander, usually the woman, pressures the partner to change through emotional requests, complaints, and criticism. The withdrawer, usually the man, retreats through "stonewalling," passive inaction, or defensiveness (Gottman and Krokoff, 1989). Those who demand change, intimacy, or engagement are in a less powerful position than those who want to maintain the status quo: "By withholding resources that women want (i.e., involvement, closeness, or new behaviors), men maintain power over women" (Babcock et al., 1993). While Julia's example is from an intimate heterosexual relationship, similar scenarios can be played out in any kind of relationship.

Aggression often springs from a lack of language, a lack of understanding, and a feeling that one has been objectified—cast into a fixed, immovable role that does not reflect one's real self. With her husband's actions as a catalyst, Julia realizes that she must move; at least some of women's aggression is a movement from object to subject, from feeling acted upon to becoming an agent. But, as Julia says, it is more than this. Suddenly, in a moment of angry clarity, a woman recognizes an injustice that is bigger and more profound than the catalyst, her partner's behavior. Her anger insists there is a person within her, a *self that must be heard*. In that moment, the partner's word, tone, or dismissal reverberates through layers of past relationships and events—father, mother, abusers, playmates, employers, silences, institutional barriers, teasings, cruelties. The woman recognizes that she has betrayed herself and has been betrayed, kept from something she could have done, been, or created in her life. She feels a sense of terrible injustice—and she strikes. She perceives her partner as the source of anger, but in fact the anger stems from the rage of disconnection, fostered by the inequality in the relationship.

Often women's aggressive actions come from parts of the self that are unknown, unpracticed, and disavowed by the culture as unfeminine. When not recognized as our own, negative feelings—anger, fear, hatred, jealousy, hurt—can be denied as if we had no power over them; we can remain "innocent" or victims, or we can attack the wrong targets. Julia retaliated for her husband's refusal to hear her with a vehement strike against his dominance, which only separated them further.

The issues between Julia and her husband are power and intimacy: who has control over the level of intimacy, over the prerogatives of relationship? That Julia's use of physical aggression is unintentional makes it no less an actual blow. But her action does not carry the same meaning as if it were (accidentally) done by her husband toward her. Although women and men report giving out equivalent levels of physical and verbal aggression in intimate relationships, women are more likely to be seriously injured or killed by their male partners' aggression.[19]

It is possible that Julia's aggressive act may be the beginning of movement from blind anger over inequality and disconnection toward conscious choice. She may be able to name her emotional reality; they may assess the relationship, acknowledge dead ends, leave differences behind or leave each other, make decisions together about their future. Her aggression may be part of a process of bringing choice back into relationship.

But in fact Julia's attempt to change the structure of the relationship fails. Following well-trodden feminine paths, she switches the object of attack, turning against herself with shame and blame: "I felt like I was a mess. Like what's wrong with me?" "Why can't I be logical and articulate?" "Why can't I win on his terms?" She withdraws, shrinks, ambushes herself. Her act, though it was unintended and did not hurt her husband, "made me feel like I was uncivilized or that I really didn't have any power because I was pushed to behaving irrationally." She feels as if her action reinforced her position as the "disrespected," subordinate one in the relationship. Julia quickly backpedals, frightened of the implications of her aggression: she has violated the patriarchal structure of civilization, a structure that equates masculinity with aggressiveness and labels female aggression as especially uncivilized. She has also violated her own desire to achieve more equality and closeness in relationship by, instead, increasing separation. And she has resorted to a stereotypic, male form of force which she condemns.

Julia quickly abandons her feelings to realign with her husband, uniting her voice with his and the culture's to condemn herself. This is the most familiar, most expected female response to anger in relationship: conciliation through self-blame. It will deflect her husband's retaliation and preserve the bond with its familiar spatial arrangements: his wishes, style, and preferences take up almost all the room.

Julia's example illustrates one of the puzzles of women's aggression. Men's dominance in intimate relationships carries the culture's backing. Economic structures, history, and the threat of violence stand behind each man, though any individual man may not utilize any of them. Within these cultural expectations of who carries more power, women must work out ways to handle conflicts, push their own agendas, and create egalitarian relationships in both the public and the private realm. Women do resort to physical force, but usually only when hitting back self-defensively against male aggression (Jacobson et al., 1994; Jones, 1994). They often demand changes and then "lose it," as Julia did, with an explosion that simply lets off pressure and then continues the status quo of power in the relationship. Women's puzzle is how to use their force positively in order to alter the structure of relationships when, from the outset, they are not presumed to carry as much power as men do.

Julia's relational impasses and attempts at aggressive breakthrough are linked to her severe clinical depression. She traces both anger and depression to her inability to express herself because she fears hurting someone else. Yet, she observes: "The hurt that I trace back as being one of the sources of not speaking or not acting is imaginary. I mean, in many ways, it's not substantial." Silencing the self is associated with women's depression. Since many women interpret their own words as aggressive, particularly when those words seem to oppose other people, how much does the general prohibition of female aggression affect women's vulnerability to depression? The easy answer, that depression equals anger turned inward, deserves closer scrutiny. As we will see, aggression and depression have a common origin: disconnection. Aggression's relationship to depression may lie not only in whether anger is turned outward or inward but also in the ways in which women stop their "aggressive" speech or acts.

As women talk about their aggression, they contradict, interrupt, and challenge each others' perspectives and judgments. They quickly dispel the simplistic myth that women are not aggressive, inviting a look at the differing patterns of women's aggression and the underlying factors that create these patterns. My struggle throughout this book is to stay close to the complexity of lived experiences of aggression and to represent the meanings women make of their actions.

2

Ways of Occupying Space

As women tell stories of their aggression, they use metaphors that differ from popular images of battle, conquest, and pride. For many women, even standing up for themselves is a daunting, aggressive act. To "take up space," to "know how far you're going to go with your anger and aggression," or to "get out there and push it" are issues women mull over as they talk about how aggressive they can be.

> I never claimed my space. I was forever giving up my space. It was fear of conflict, fear of confrontation. (Alice, age 46, white, secretary)

> I kicked her door open and I went in there and got in her face. And she jumped out of bed and I backed up out of her room but only backed up so far, and she came right up in my face, and it was like this, I'm not gonna back down from you . . . And she kept getting in my face. (Mary, age 43, white, psychotherapist)

> I was uncomfortable [after hitting my husband] but it immediately came to me that I'm a better person than this. I don't have to expand who I am by becoming a person who lashes out all the time . . . When you lash out the first time you get this horrendous fear that now I've stepped over the threshold, so now I could continue doing it. And that I either had to jump back on the other side right then, or it could become a real—somewhere in my head, in who I am, in my soul, whatever, that I have a

point that, you know, that's the barrier. And I had crossed that line. (Camille, age 69, white, retired biologist)

What makes me really aggressive is for my husband to take his anger out on my son. So that was the limit. So I said, "If you are angry talk to your people"—meaning his sister—"and don't take it out on my son." You know, but I said it like in a really angry voice. And then I thought, "Was that me? Did I say that?" (Consuelo, age 24, Mexican American, student)

Women use metaphors that portray aggression as a way of occupying the emotional and physical space between people. The metaphors reveal moments of feeling trapped in relational space ("pushed against the wall"). They reflect how women respond to others' force with head-on collisions ("I'm not gonna back down"), by deflecting or yielding ("giving up my space"), or by feeling pushed to "the limits." Images of containment and expansion, of pushing and being pushed, of crossing over lines or barriers all imply using force or being moved by forces within relational spaces.[1]

Societal norms supply a kind of map people use to navigate the interpersonal world, a map outlining the boundaries of acceptable behavior. Norms create differing maps for women and men, and locate safe havens for people who share cultural practices and identities. Where a woman perceives herself on the social map determines whether she feels central or marginalized, where forbidden territory starts, and how much space she is entitled to in her relationships. These mental maps tell a woman how to engage in conflict—how to struggle with others about whose emotions, will, or "self" will prevail. The maps are dynamic and changing; individuals continually redraw the lines that are supposed to restrain their force and that designate the limits others may not cross. A woman's use of spatial metaphors identifies where she locates the shifting social and personal lines that lead her to judge an act as aggressive.

Consider the word "pushy." As Alice says, "If a woman is claiming her space, she's aggressive and pushy. If a man does exactly the same thing, he's doing something that's not considered negative." "Pushy" combines notions of force and space; of pressing with force against a spatial limit or boundary. It reveals a host of underlying assumptions about how women "should" behave. On a physical, sexual level, women are supposed to soften, receive, and take in; not to harden, erect, and penetrate. They are called sexually aggressive when they show desire or actively pursue. Within relationships, women are not supposed to occupy as much physical or emotional space as men; they are to step aside when needs collide. Women are called pushy if where they are expected to give in, they stand firm or move toward; if where they are expected to defuse, they instigate; if where they are expected to defer, they control. Women's aggression challenges deeply held conceptions of how one gender but not the other may use force and occupy space.

Each woman knows her culture's norms about how much social space she is allowed and in what contexts. From personal experience, she also carries a sense of her own force, of when and how she can be forceful, and of what barriers she should not push past to avoid being labeled an "aggressive bitch" either by herself or by others. This sense of how to use her force in relational space is based in her particular physical and social experience.

Speaking the Body

When a woman says she "has no backbone" or "stands up for herself," her metaphors weave her physical experience into her emotional and interpersonal experience. Her images convey how much force she exerts in a relationship through a language that references the body. Women know that their bodies powerfully affect social interactions. Their metaphors expose the relation between their feelings of vulnerability and strength and the forms their aggression takes ("back down," "got in her face"). They reveal how women's bodies are in women's minds.

We live an embodied existence. Physical experience affects how we understand our social worlds; conversely, our social worlds interpret and shape physical experience. A number of theorists have argued that infants' preverbal, physical encounters with the world provide a basis for thinking through metaphors (a type of cognitive schema) that organize the way we make meaning (Johnson, 1987; Merleau-Ponty, 1962; Piaget and Inhelder, 1971/1997; Stern, 1985). Mark Johnson gives an example of "force" as an *embodied schema* or specific metaphorical structure that provides a bridge between the personal body and the "body" of the world.[2]

> We begin to grasp the meaning of physical force from the day we are born (or even before). We have bodies that are acted upon by "external" and "internal" forces such as gravity, light, heat, wind, bodily processes, and the obtrusion of other physical objects. Such interactions constitute our first encounters with forces, and they reveal patterned recurring relations between ourselves and our environment. Such patterns develop as meaning structures through which our world begins to exhibit a measure of coherence, regularity, and intelligibility. (Johnson, 1987, 13)

All infants sense external forces that impinge on their bodies—the texture of surfaces, the soft mattress, the hard floor. And all experience internal forces—hunger, the need to defecate, to urinate, to move. These universal physical sensations become reference points to which the developing mind relates more complex perceptions, creating embodied metaphors that link bodily experience, mind, and external world. Equally important in structuring embodied schemas is culture, which interprets, socializes, and assigns meaning and value to the uses of force and space.[3]

Gendered Force and Space

Around the world, cultures use gender as a major category to differentiate the acceptable use of force and space. From birth on, adults pick up, talk to, respond to, and soothe infant boys and girls differently. They play more roughly with boys than with girls and react more negatively to daughters' aggression than to that of sons (Parke and Slaby, 1983). Boys have more permission to occupy relational space and to make "shows of force" (see, for example, Björkqvist and Niemelä, 1992). Boys expect less negative consequences for aggression than girls do and anticipate different repercussions for aggressing against other boys than against girls (Huesmann et al., 1992; Perry, Perry, and Weiss, 1989). Thus boys and girls learn that different moral codes apply to their forceful behaviors and come to evaluate their own aggressive actions differently.

Children learn how force enters relational space: sometimes the stroking hand curls into a fist to bring a sharp, frightening end to predictability. While people and objects impose themselves forcefully, children also learn they themselves are a *source* of force that can affect others. Their own forceful cries sometimes bring warmth and closeness, sometimes a harsh slap that results in fear and distance. All children learn what happens when they move over, around, or through obstacles and into wider space. Over time, they notice that there are many ways to exert force besides the physical. People can be "forced" to do things by argument or peer pressure, by moral persuasion, coercion, or threat.[4] Each child learns his or her own particular variation of what it means to use force positively or destructively within the values of a family, a subculture, or a religion. The fundamental sense of being able to make something happen, of being a source of force that can have an intended effect on the world, is crucial to a positive self-concept.

While all young children will hit, push, kick, and shove, girls are discouraged more quickly and harshly than boys from learning about their physical, interpersonal force. Boys are allowed more leeway to inflict physical pain on others; girls are allowed more leeway to inflict "mental" pain (Björkqvist, Lagerspetz, and Kaukiainen, 1992). Boys' use of force is more physically and verbally direct—hitting or pushing, threatening to beat someone up (see Block, 1983; Parke and Slaby, 1983). Girls often use indirect means to affect others, such as "backbiting and manipulation of the social structure" of a schoolroom (Björkqvist, Lagerspetz, and Kaukiainen, 1992, 118). These different styles in the use of aggressive force follow expected gender themes. Boys use their bodies and physical force to establish dominance and accomplish instrumental goals; girls use words and indirect aggression to avoid detection and/or to solidify connections with others (Crick and Grotpeter, 1995). Exceptions among individuals exist everywhere—but at home and in school, girls learn very young that they cannot get away with using overt force as easily as boys can.

Children's toys also convey society's expectations about each gender as a *source* or *target* of force. Toy catalogs in the 1990s still feature pages headed "For Girls," with toy kitchen appliances, makeup and hair accessories, dolls and pink tutus. Turn to the pages "For Boys" and find soldiers and science equipment, swords and shields, and building sets. Such toys tell children that girls are to be soft, nurturing, and unaggressive while boys are to be active, adventurous, and aggressive. "Genderbender" toys, supposedly designed to offset stereotypes, were introduced in the 1993 American International Toy Fair. But consider the specific toys. Girls got a WonderWoman action doll with fluffy long hair and an unrealistic curvy figure. Her weapon to fight evil: a magic wand that dispenses bubbles. To encourage them to play with dolls, boys got trolls with names such as Battle Trolls and Troll Warriors (Wood, 1994). The myth has it that American culture today does not heavily gender-type children. The reality is that toys have hardly changed for decades.

Gendered messages about how to use force and occupy space continue into adulthood. Power and gender structure the use of space in workplaces, families, and everyday interactions in public places. Throughout history, limiting women's movement in physical space has served as a crucial way to subordinate them. The nineteenth-century attempt to define a "women's sphere" was both a specifically spatial control (to keep them in the home) and a social control over their subjectively experienced identities (Massey, 1994). The boundaries of women's proper sphere have also served as social markers of "correct" femininity correlated with a certain class and race; women outside the margins of the designated domestic sphere have been seen as "other." Thus gender stereotypes have dictated that men move out aggressively into the world while women stay in their domestic realm, even though African-American and working-class women have belied these stereotypes from their beginnings.

How a person occupies physical space reflects relations of power and instantly conveys the person's relative importance to others through nonverbal means. Today women are still accorded less space than men across a variety of social situations, including smaller physical spaces within work settings (Spain, 1992; Weisman, 1992), in conversations (Tannen, 1991), and in public spaces (Klein, 1984).[5] Anna (age 40, white, law student) reacts against men's entitlement to public space: "When I'm walking through a doorway and someone else is coming through, I'm never the person who steps back. I consider that very aggressive . . . a physical way that I express a certain kind of aggression, that I don't back off, especially if it's a guy." Without social norms dictating that, as a woman, Anna should yield space, she would never label this small act "very aggressive."

Groups continue to use spatial control to maintain power or take power from others. Today, when women try to occupy traditionally male spaces, they often encounter violence and sexual harassment. The widespread harassment of female recruits in the military is but one example. Women who invade such social spaces also encounter a policing of gender dualities that uses homophobia as a weapon. For example, the policewomen I talked with spoke of being called "Jayne Waynes," "lesbians," or "dykes." Or they were accused of wanting to be police officers only to find husbands. Attorneys spoke of a double standard of aggressiveness for women and men: "It definitely upsets the status quo when you have a whole mix of attorneys and if the men get up and holler and shout and scream, 'that's just Bob.' But, if you do that, you know the story, 'PMS, you know, she's just pregnant, she's the estrogen witch now, she's in menopause.' " Such attributions carry the message that women are not to be taken seriously. Thus, when women occupy space in ways traditionally considered male, their self-assertion is labeled not only pushy but unfeminine, lesbian, out of bounds.

Women are acutely aware of their bodies as central to their social vulnerability and power.[6]

> Here I come, in a red suit, ready to do a trial, don't give a shit about what people think and I'm not interested in dating. If they're looking for the sexual side—the men—they don't see that. I'm just saying I know what I want and I'm not flirtatious,

I'm not out to be cute, I don't have to be . . . and if you have someone walk in a room who has all those things, it scares the shit out of people. (Maria, age 32, Native American/Latino, attorney)

Male violence is a major determinant of the social status of women's bodies. The threat of violence fills the airwaves, meets the eyes, penetrates awareness at every turn until it blends into the pattern of daily life. Women know that female bodies can elicit male violence simply by their femaleness; they take male responses into account as they decide how to inhabit their space and present their physicality.

At the end of a century filled with changes in women's roles, conflicting views persist regarding the desirability of women's aggression. A long history of suppression precedes the contemporary dialogue that encourages women to be aggressive enough to make it in the world of work yet gentle enough to mother children and defuse male aggression. Since the discourse about aggression has always occurred in the male voice, the possibilities for understanding this critical issue from the female perspective have been severely limited.

Aggression and Embodied Space

Hearkening to metaphors of force and space, I found five basic patterns by which these sixty women understand their aggression: "unfamiliar territory," "pushing against limits," "a wall of self-protection," "redrawing the limits," and "standing one's ground." (I discuss the first four patterns here; for the fifth, see Chapter 6.) These patterns provide glimpses of how socialization and particular social contexts affect women's aggression and of how personal and social change occur. The patterns are not static or characterological; they continually shift as a woman steps into new contexts, as she encounters and also alters boundaries of "feminine" behavior. The patterns do not represent all women, nor are they exhaustive; each woman's pattern is her own to a degree. They do, however, follow women's use of metaphors and provide a way to enter the complex, ambiguous territory of aggression while staying true to women's reported experiences.

Unfamiliar Territory

> I'm able to show all the positive that there is in me, and yet I also know that I have to cross this line where I can also show like the negative side of me in an assertive way, and then will I be completely free. And then will I not have this fear. (Consuelo, age 24, Mexican American, student)

> For me the aggression was instead of trying to please people and continuing to just try and find out what everybody else wanted, I needed to let who I was and what I felt out. And that took some real force to do. (Lyn, age 39, white, student)

These women "know their place." Moving out of their restricted space in relationships leads them into unexplored territory and into fear. They yield to others, yet know they must "cross the line" if they are to break out of stifling confinement.

To illustrate the metaphor of unfamiliar territory, let us return to Julia, the 39-year-old white schoolteacher we met in Chapter 1. Julia has difficulty speaking up in many situations. She also struggles with major depression, an embodied feeling of being pressed down, constricted, unable to break out. She talks about a meeting in her neighborhood at which a man was "dominating and being very abrasive and insulting." She attempted to talk to him after the meeting. He started "yelling and I felt people looking at me. And then I couldn't talk and I went out to the car and I cried." The man's aggressive behavior "made me too scared to respond to him, to his attack on me. I just fled." When I ask Julia to explore her fear, she says: "I think what I'm afraid of is not being appropriate. Not knowing how my response to aggression—where that is going to take me. I think that's being in unfamiliar territory . . . being afraid of going too far and of just saying things that are destructive, not helpful."

Nothing appears more natural than Julia's apparent boundedness by convention, her fear of "going too far." This boundary line that feels personal also delimits an ideological sphere, a type of femininity. Staying within the boundary promises goodness, self-control, continuing relationships, and social order. Stepping outside and into the unknown brings dread of both chaos and her potential for destructiveness. Julia hesitates to cross into unfamiliar territory not only because she is unpracticed at confrontational conflict but also because she fears such conflict will increase distance and alienation, not lead to understanding. Also, the overt anger and loudness terrify her; they confront her with all she has learned to stifle in herself, and they carry a threat of male violence. Aggression is what "others" do, in ways that are unfamiliar and frightening.

Julia takes the risk of becoming involved with this "abrasive, insulting" man to keep up dialogue about a critical issue of community. Not wanting to increase the breakdown of communication, yet raised to believe that women should not appear angry and challenging, Julia sees no way to pursue her opposition without escalating aggression. She knows this man will not see her point of view; her moral affront over his interruption of community dialogue arouses her indignant anger, as does her sense of powerlessness to affect this interaction. She meets his dominating, angry style with tears; fearful of escalating conflict, she retreats from active community involvement.

As a line of social control over aggression, people's self-restraint makes community life possible; as a marker of "good" femininity, self-restraint hems in women's vital, authentic expression. The critical issue is how women like Julia can learn to redraw the line that affords them so little use of their positive aggression. How can women learn to push back the margins that restrict their use of positive force?[7]

Like many women who consider opposition to be aggressive, Julia was socialized for "niceness": to equate feminine goodness with self-sacrifice. She describes this model of femininity:

> It means being cheerful. Smoothing things over. It's what my mother modeled for me—being nice. "Don't say anything if you can't say something nice." And it has to do with not drawing

attention to yourself. With being selfless. With being the one to say "You can have my piece of pie." Being self-sacrificing and . . . helping guide someone away from anything that might be disturbing. Cushioning people. Being focused on their comfort, both physical and psychological.

This construction of femininity as niceness is deeply attached to inequality in relationship. It demands that a woman put her needs second to those of everyone else as she fulfills the nurturing roles of the "good wife" and mother. At the core of this image of femininity is the requirement to create harmony, or at least the appearance of harmony; its corollary is the absence of angry conflict, or at least the absence of overt conflict. Women raised in this pattern learn that others' needs come first; they are supposed to yield relational space to others. Any self-assertion is labeled selfish and, by implication, aggressive. As Julia says, "Aggression means not really putting all your focus on other people. It's either putting your focus on yourself or an issue." Actions that are not nurturing are aggressive.

Anne Campbell (1993, 20) characterizes girls' learning about aggression this way: "The most remarkable thing about the social- ization of aggression in girls is its absence. Girls do not learn the right way to express aggression; they simply learn not to express it." Actually, this type of socialization for niceness (to which not all subcultures subscribe) teaches girls to *hide* their aggression. Rather than being genuinely absent, their aggression is simply not visible because it is brought into relationship through indirect, sub- terranean channels (see Chapter 5).

Women who equate femininity with niceness and nonaggres- sion show striking similarities in their socialization and in their conflicts around self-expression. They learn that caring for others means, as Gaile (age 40, white, photojournalist) says, "kind of put- ting yourself last . . . being sure everybody was being taken care of first . . . it was an attitudinal kind of thing . . . just a sense of hu- mility." Not only does this construction of femininity enforce gen- der inequality, it continually incites anger at the frustration of nor- mal needs yet, simultaneously, demands the repression of anger.

These women also learn a "rule of harmony" that forbids direct communication of angry feelings. Ellen (age 46, white, manager) describes it this way:

> When you disrupt the harmony, you're stepping outside the boundaries of what the expectations are in this family, which is to maintain harmony and to maintain peace. So I think that the few times that I did get angry as a kid it felt as though I was disobeying a family rule and that I was somehow no longer a member of that family for a while . . . I was now somehow an alien, I was outside the family because I had broken this very clear rule about harmony.

No wonder such women fear their opposition or anger will lead to loss of relationship. In such a setting, a child's vision of relatedness can shrink to a choice between self-silencing (leading to a loss of self) and expressing feelings (leading to a loss of other). When girls do not learn how to engage in overt conflict but do learn to fear its consequences, they practice sending voice, anger, and desire underground (Brown and Gilligan, 1992). They learn to use their force to patrol and control *themselves* in order to stay within the rule of harmony.

These women learn self-inhibition and self-control through, in Julia's words, a watchfulness to avoid "being inappropriate in other people's eyes":

> I just think of all the responses I had as a child to yelling and screaming and hitting and expressing myself. And it was always to the effect that "that's not appropriate, go to your room." Just shut down . . . there's a lack of practice in being able to be aggressive in a creative way. It's like I'm afraid that I'm going to scream and cry and I don't want to do that in public. The sense of shame is part of the hesitancy, I think.

Shame is a response to others' condemning judgment. While seeing oneself through others' eyes is a normal experience and necessary to community, difficulty comes when the imagined, watching eyes are felt as always critical, when they have been internalized into a judgmental sense of *self*-surveillance which I call the Over-

Eye. This leads to a sense of *externalized self-perception* and continual feelings of shame and self-doubt even when no one else is present. Julia's anticipatory shame preempts the condemnation she expects from others for her show of "inappropriate" feeling. This shame further reduces any possibility of creative aggression.

Socialization for niceness often teaches physical inhibition as an adjunct to emotional restriction. Julia says: "When I was about seven, we would go to church and we would have to sit through the church service . . . Afterwards, there was like a social hour and we just had to sit quietly . . . we could never run around like the other kids." Julia learned to use the force of her will against her physical and emotional self, to hold still, to restrain feeling. She learned that goodness meant confining the body and the mind within tight limits, patrolled by externalized self-perception. Too closely attuned to the judgments of others, Julia expects criticism for her assertive acts. The fear of being inappropriate inhibits her from acting on the world and taking risks; her will is used for self-control.

Fear of disapproval creates a strong inhibition on a woman's ability to speak for herself. It keeps her circumscribed within a tight corral, running over the same ground without breaking out. For anger or will to escape confinement, they must "explode" in ways that seem beyond her control—"I lost it"—or must be disguised through indirect forms of aggression. Hence such women's "hysteria," seeming irrationality, and indirection. And likewise the tendency to burst into tears—an expression of angry frustration that is acceptably feminine. Julia, for example, fears that in public settings her attempts to meet others' aggression will lead to tears: "Crying in public or especially with someone with whom I don't feel safe . . . feels like an expression of helplessness. And they may think . . . 'poor thing.' It's like to risk breaking down and crying is worse than not being involved . . . I feel like I can control my screaming. I can't control my crying."

While on the surface Julia may appear to fear lack of self-control, her dread actually focuses on what tears would prove: that she is irrational and helpless. In our culture, women's tears symbolize a stereotype of female weakness and childishness. In a confrontation, tears signal that a woman's opponents have little to fear; she will not use force against them. Children's tears usually elicit protective or comforting responses; women's tears often elicit irritation, confusion, pity, or contempt. In the workplace they are often seen as manipulative. As in Julia's case, they often spring forth when a woman attempts to repress strongly felt anger, or when she feels she is violating a moral imperative to maintain harmony. In fact, tears serve as a means of expressing anger for many women. When socialized to a lack of "creative aggression," women often communicate through tears, which both they and the culture can easily misinterpret.

These elements of socialization—care as self-sacrifice, the rule of harmony, externalized self-perception, self-inhibition—lead to the significant problems these women have with engaging in conflict. In families that stress feminine niceness, fathers are often dominant, mothers submissive. Their children learn rules about the gendered use of force that are confirmed by conventional society: the submissive party engages in conflict covertly, subverting the dominant party's power by indirection (see Miller, 1976). Ellen, whose family lived by the rule of harmony, says:

> What I remember as a child is my mother losing it from time to time, just standing in the kitchen, screaming. Very frightening to us as kids, and didn't happen very often. As I look back as an adult I can see that my mother learned to manipulate and get what she wanted through other means, hypochondria for one. She's developed a whole series of ways to disagree by being sick, to disagree by being passive, and those are characteristics that terrify me. I mean I see them as kind of a maladaptive response to an environment in which conflict was not allowed.

Seeing a mother "losing it" through ineffectual screaming or through "manipulation" leads to a vision of femininity as powerless to act forcefully and clearly.

Children in such families learn to fear that overt conflict, since it is so carefully avoided, must be terribly destructive. They have no models for resolving conflict through dialogue, in which each person gets a glimpse of the other's desire so they can move forward with a clearer vision of possible resolution. Wendy (age 45, white, artist), recalls that conflict

> was unthinkable, the worst possible thing, just the worst. We lived in this old house . . . it didn't have heat upstairs. It had those vents, those little cages so that you could actually look down and hear every word and sigh and fart. So at night I just would go asleep with the pillows over my head to try and block out the sounds . . . the yelling coming from down there. I learned that conflict was hideous . . . That all conflict was bad and had a bad result and so it was to be avoided at all costs. It never led to resolution, ever. It always put people farther apart and always caused pain.

Ann (age 34, white), a physician with two young children, expresses a similar view: "It's very difficult for me to have conflict in a relationship, and it's very difficult for me to trust that if I make waves, the love that my husband feels for me won't be withdrawn." Believing that conflict leads only to pain or abandonment, these women get easily stuck in an unequal, silenced position in relational space.

Why do these women continue to follow the rules of niceness, with all the attending difficulties, when alternative models of femininity are available? In part, identification with one's mother, which includes an image of what it means to be feminine, secures the tight hold of socialization for nonaggression. These girls' mothers demanded a certain kind of behavior from their daughters, a requirement tied to love and continuing relationship. Chrissy (age 22, white, student) says: "I feel like I have to protect my mother from who I am. If I argue with her or get angry, she acts wounded, like I'm killing her and killing our relationship. She's taught me to be so nice, and now that I'm trying to change, she controls me through guilt."

Julia echoes the refrain of being bound too tightly by a restrictive mother-daughter bond:

> I have this definite sense of my mother being frightened by emotion and just keeping everything safe and comfortable and calm . . . in my college years I really struggled with eating disorders and it was associated, I feel, with shame of my sexuality. And I

felt like that was all part of feeling like my own passions and desires and emotions were out of bounds of being acceptable by my mother . . . I just started feeling like I had to protect her from who I was. And yet I had absorbed all the guilt. So my eating paralleled my sexual activity that I would just feast and then feel remorse for having over eaten. For having over felt. And so it wasn't just aggression that was muffled and smothered but it was joy too.

Aggression, linked in these women's minds with opposition, passions, and appetite, threatens not only to separate them from their mothers but to destroy their mothers. To preserve the bond and to protect the mother, they have learned to smother feelings, to squelch opposition. Their attunement and empathy, so well-developed, are not balanced by the knowledge that they can differ from others yet remain connected.

Such women's energies go into self-restriction and hiding rather than into learning how to move confidently into the world. They learn to draw lines around themselves beyond which they cannot step without being perceived as out of bounds, as too sexual, too emotional, too outspoken—*too big*. This sets women up for eating disorders and teaches them that they are supposed to occupy only a small amount of psychological and emotional space in relationships.

Twenty of the sixty women I interviewed described their adult aggression in ways that fit the pattern I am calling unfamiliar territory: fifteen white women, one Latina, one Asian-American woman, and three Chilean women. Of these, fourteen described such teachings as reinforced by religious training. Though forty-two of the sixty women had been socialized for niceness with an emphasis on female nonaggression, more than half of those had dramatically changed their attitudes concerning their aggression and were in various stages of bringing aggression into relationships in a positive and creative manner.

Many women socialized to consider any hint of their aggression as unfamiliar territory are able, in adulthood, to overcome the deep inhibitions instilled by such training. Consider the example of Wendy, quoted above, an internationally acclaimed artist. She tells a story of early personal restriction, severe depression, and an affair in which she enacted the forbidden to facilitate change. She experienced significant anorexia during her twenties and bulimia in her thirties. At the time of our two interviews, Wendy was free of depression and eating disorders and was married to her third husband.

Wendy's mother, a Christian Scientist, taught her that "we, as spirits, are the image and likeness of God, which is perfection, and so our job is to realize who we are, which is this perfection." Since, in this tradition, "anything that's not going well is because we are thinking incorrectly," Wendy learned: " 'Whatever's going on, don't make a thing about it. Just sort of swallow it all and turn it inward. Don't inflict your worries or your illness or your anger' . . . You learn just to keep a big lid on feelings." Like other women socialized to this version of femininity, Wendy learned to keep disruptive feelings out of relationship and manage them within the self. Religion reinforced the message that to do so was morally good.

Wendy's mother stayed home while her father was the breadwinner for the family. Wendy's father was gone "ninety percent of the time," and when at home was "benign and nice to us." Wendy rarely witnessed displays of his anger except at night, through the heater grate.

Contradictions swirled between what Wendy's mother taught and how she related to her children and others. "It was not okay to be angry or to express anger or what I think of as aggression. You know, it was not a proper thing to do." Yet, Wendy says:

> The model that I had in my mother was a very, very angry person and someone who felt unlovable and unlikable. What she passed off on me and my brothers was that we were unacceptable and unlikable. Sort of in all of our manifestations, whether it had to do with anger or any sort of expression of emotions, it was considered really inappropriate. So everything had to be sucked in. And anger at her—she was probably the main person in the world that I was angry at . . . —I couldn't show it to her. I had to just sort of suck it all in and figure it was my fault. You know, I was the one with the problem.

Knowing her anger was forbidden, Wendy converted it to admiring attention as a way to connect with her mother: "I spent my whole childhood . . . trying to make her happy and trying to make her feel like she was loved or something." Through this parent-child reversal Wendy learned that her own needs were unimportant, that her role in relationship was to submerge her feelings as she nurtured others like a "good" girl, in training for a future of (overtly) nonaggressive, nurturant femininity.

Such lessons explain why Wendy can call it "aggressive" simply to speak her own needs: "It is so unfamiliar to say 'This is what I want and this is what I need to have.' [How does that feel aggressive?] I have to work myself up to it with most people and so it feels aggressive. Or it feels like I'm sticking myself out there. It feels like I'm being selfish and self-centered and that I have to get what I want."

As Wendy talks about how selfishness is linked to aggressiveness in her mind, she uses spatial metaphors that portray positions in relationship:

> I guess what it [selfish] meant to me then was that you put yourself as more important than anybody else and so you had sort of this grandiose idea of yourself . . . like "Who the hell do you think you are, Wendy?" You know, that you get to say what you want, that you get to think you're so important, that you get to ask for what you want? It's something about territory . . . It's about how much I have a right to have, how much space I'm allowed to occupy, both physically and mentally or spiritually. And that if I get more space, does that mean that it takes away from somebody else's space? And do I have a right to do that? And so I have to examine every little thing to see whether it is okay for me to want this or to feel like I'm allowed to have this . . . It's better if I can just sort of sneak the space, or just occupy the space and maybe not have anybody notice.

In this vision of relational space, needs are competing: either the self *or* the other occupies the in-between. Mutual recognition of two persons, including a working out of conflicting needs, is not part of this picture.

Wendy sees her eating disorders as interwoven with depression and with the prohibition against taking up relational space:

> I was depressed probably forever. Ever since college I was doing something to move towards being an artist, and all the time I felt not good enough . . . I felt like I don't have a right to do that [make art] but I'm going to do it anyway . . . I just thought, well, I want to get skinny or be skinnier and—or keep control over stuff. But I think what it boiled down to was just feeling like I didn't have a right to occupy space on the planet, not to occupy even a little space.

Anorexia is a metaphor spoken by the body; it literally embodies the attempt to take up as little space as possible. While anorexia and bulimia present a surface compliance with society's norms for women's thinness and preoccupation with weight, these disorders also subvert commands by authorities (society, internalized parents) to be selfless and unaggressive. Both disorders are aggressively destructive and focused on self. They turn a woman's force against her own body to destroy her metaphorical wish to get "too big": they ostensibly control her "appetite" and keep her from demanding too much. In Wendy's case, her desire to be an artist, an expansive wish that requires enacting creative will and being publicly recognized, continually is mocked by the side of self that says she has no right to occupy space because she's unworthy. This conflict involves what she calls "that two-person thing or parallel lives"—which I call the divided self of depression.

How does this preoccupation with taking up as little space as possible arise? From her mother, Wendy says, she learned that aggression is "ugly, that it cuts people off and sends them away and puts distance between people rather than letting them know each other better":

> I'm thinking of the look that she would get on her face and what it would make me feel. You know, just sort of recoiling and going paralyzed in response to seeing this look on her face. I just remember coldness and withdrawal and locking me out. I don't mean out of the house but just cutting me off and letting me

know how stupid I was or how just completely hopeless. It wasn't a flaming anger . . . it was more just cold and rigid. How I would feel it in me would be like paralysis or everything just shutting down. Just inability to respond and fear, and it was like no response was possible. No response was invited. There was no way you could interact or respond to her. It was just like that was that and you're out, you're just out in the cold. You don't even exist anymore.

The shock of receiving her mother's hostile Medusa-look turned Wendy into stone. Frozen in moments of angry disapproval, she felt no way to reach her mother across a vast, frigid distance. Caught there, she would wander around her mother's perimeters, trying to find any way in from the cold.

These times of being an outcast would sometimes last weeks or months, and Wendy was always the one to "accept her back when she had sort of been unforgivable to me . . . the one to make amends and stuff." Wendy was left without a sense of what a relational violation was, or whether she had any "right" to be angry.

Anger is an accusation, a response to some perceived misdeed, a value judgment, an attribution of blame (Averill, 1982). According to John Bowlby (1973), the function of anger is to remove obstacles to close relationships. When a child must repress anger over relational injustices in order to maintain the relationship, the child's healthy anger, an anger of hope whose goal is reconnection, is replaced by an anger of despair over the possibility of any genuine connection. This anger of despair most often ricochets from its origin, a perceived misdeed by another, to turn against the self. Needing to preserve the connection to a parent at any cost, the child alters the perception of misdeed and mislabels the source of anger.

Wendy provides a glimpse of the pain she felt with her mother, who gave her so little space to be herself: "Riding in the car with her for some reason was one of the most dreaded things because it was being locked in a moving box . . . Somehow I always thought she was just watching me every second; observing me to find all the things that were wrong with me . . . I just felt acutely observed and judged." Though her mother's critical eyes were fixed straight ahead, Wendy still felt watched, as if her mother's negative judgment roamed freely over her psyche. Her protective response was to shrink to a tiny size, so as not to draw her mother's disapproving attention. She remembers "always walking this line and being really careful with her at all times." Even though Wendy is now an adult, her mother's negative eye, which she has internalized as part of her own "Over-Eye," keeps staring at her imagined faults and shortcomings, pronouncing negative judgments.

Wendy learned that aggression meant invading relational space to displace another's will, even another's thoughts. She learned to invade her own thoughts as well, to weed out angry, disruptive feelings in order to relate to her mother. The inner activity required to appear outwardly compliant to a dominant other's wishes is part of a dynamic of silencing the self that is characteristic of depressed women. Self-silencing creates the experience of a divided self: an outwardly "nice, good" self and a hidden, secret self full of rage and destructiveness. Wendy says:

> Growing up, being honest was what we were told to be at all times and yet I was probably just highly dishonest. You know, just always hiding everything and living in secret. It seemed like my growing-up life was a secret life because it couldn't be known by my mom. My first marriage of ten years was to someone just like my mother . . . and so that was all about hiding and living in secret, that whole ten years.

Expressing honest feelings, particularly anger, carried the threat of being cut off from intimacy as she had been with her mother. Yet her relationships felt fraudulent because she hid her authentic self behind a wall of pretense, trying to conform to what she thought others wanted of her.

Wendy began to challenge her pattern of silencing her self after her mother died. She was unhappily married at the time. Feeling "pulled inexorably," she began an affair with a man who embodied her own disavowed characteristics, who was "real aggressive with people and deceptive . . . angry and also real charming and passionate." Looking back on this time, she interprets it from a new perspective that has integrated aspects of self formerly walled off from relationship:

> I think it was just revolt against all of my goodness and niceness. It was all that I had ever known not to do or not to be. So that relationship was like a culmination or a volcano or something— just like jumping into the volcano and then going to the bottom of the volcano and finding out a lot of things about myself. I think about how angry I'd been, you know, to be so good and so nice and just trying to make everybody happy always and to do always the right thing for everybody else. Then finally I did this unacceptable thing that was what I wanted to do more than anything else. Just to be bad and go with a bad person. It's like I met myself finally through that and ditched Mom, like she was no longer the one that was sort of sitting on my shoulder telling me what to do and how to do it.

I ask: "When you went down to the bottom of the volcano, what did you see down there? What did you meet?" Wendy replies: "Well, sex, for one. I didn't even know about that person before. And just someone who could be hurtful and that no one would like and that everyone would reject because this person had done such harm . . . was capable of doing such harm."

Wendy cannot reunite her divided self, an inner split that has fostered depression and eating disorders, without dealing with her sexuality, anger, and power to harm others. Before, she had split off from her forceful will, channeling it only against herself. Jumping into the volcano, a symbol of erupting anger, she meets her "bad" sexual, willful self, through doing "what I wanted to do more than anything," through *enacting desire.* "I had never allowed myself to look at or to even know that was in there, the idea of me being angry or hurtful was just an unthinkable thing." Yet, she says, "it was something I had to do": "I think the compulsion was just to find out who that part of me was . . . to not just be so nice and to be more honest. That's probably been one of the major goals of my life."

Wendy felt as if her "nice" self was layered over a bad self. Living in secret, this bad self was full of its own rage and will. When people believe their core is "bad," they live a defensively created goodness in reaction to underlying aggression and hostility. Their "goodness" does not stand on firm ground but on a quagmire of rage, shame, and despair. Developmentally, there is a need to bring the secret, bad self into the open. It often erupts in ways that seem destructive but that carry their own truth: this situation is intolerable, it is killing me, it keeps me in depression. In Wendy's case, her "bad" self erupted to dislodge her angel self; change and growth occurred as she enacted the "selfish, sexual, aggressive bitch." And, as with Wendy, the rage of angels often seems to erupt through sexual affairs.

Wendy's passion for art ran like an underground stream through her life. During the times of depression, eating disorders, and inauthentic relating, she pushed ahead with her creativity, gaining recognition and confidence. Wendy talks about a painting by her grandmother called *The Gate to Nowhere*, which depicts "going through a small opening to some mysterious unknown place beyond." This visual image resonated with Wendy's desire for a way to move beyond her appointed small space. She expresses this desire in her painting: "That kind of thing is something that I just keep working with over and over and over again. You know, going through something into a mysterious beyond." Caught by the psychological power of "deep space and light . . . a feeling of distance," she incorporates such images into each piece of art, always without the presence of human figures. Art holds for her the magic of connection: "I think that's why art always drew me, because it was a way of being connected with myself that worked like nothing else would."

Through their stories, we learn that women raised to be "nice" and to "know their place" in relationships are not comfortable with such restrictions. Listening, we hear a desire for an expanded space within which to live and move, one that is not so filled with fear. The expansion, the women imagine, would bring them into closer, more authentic connection with people in ways that do not cause so much shame. It would require them to explore their psychological frontier, to go "too far" and into "unfamiliar territory" outside conventional femininity. The task for such women is to become positively aggressive: to go forward, to approach what they desire. In so doing, they can begin to increase the space within which to be themselves and interact with others.

Pushing against Limits

I was one of the first [police]women that worked the street, and the squad that I was put in was a bunch of oldtimers and they didn't believe women should be on the force. You were in a Catch-22, and that was if you went out and proved yourself, you were something other than you were, and then if you didn't, you were a failure. So you couldn't win no matter what you did . . . I had one person in particular that I went around and around with for three years and eventually put a sexual harassment charge—I was the first one, first case, along with some other women . . . It's almost like my anger emotions and stuff are what made me survive, because I was so angry at the system . . . that I thought, you know, if I give up, then that little small change that maybe I could make wouldn't occur if I was gone. (Karen, age 41, white, police officer)

Some women use their force to fight against restrictive barriers in society. Excluded from certain social spaces because of their ethnicity, sexual orientation, or gender, they fight for inclusion by experimenting constructively with aggressive behavior to see how far they can go. Such women are often perceived as aggressive by those who occupy the status quo. Their stories differ depending on their socialization and on their standing in relation to the dominant society.

Carrie (age 30, African American, social worker) uses the metaphor of pushing against limits to describe the meaning and the uses of her aggression:

If somebody tells you that door's locked, you try it anyway, because chances are you might be the one to get it open. So you always, always push. Never take no for an answer. Always push.

... Open up your mind. Make something happen. Even when somebody—now my mom always told me this . . . And sometimes I think even when they say you shouldn't be pushy, *ahhhh*, let me be the one to decide that.

Women who use their force positively in this way come from many backgrounds and from many locations in society. Their socialization does not follow as clear a pattern as does that of women who consider their aggression to be unfamiliar territory. One theme, however, unites their descriptions of childhood: their mothers' visible strength. Even though their mothers may have had little power in the wider society, these daughters saw them overtly resist devaluation and the violence that may have been directed toward them.

Carrie recounts how her mother prepared her to deal with the racist society in which she was growing up:

> She taught me my history, and I think the history—that was the best gift my mother gave to me throughout my life, was a history of where I came from and where I could go . . . I never could back it up but I *knew* it. And I was going to hold it, I didn't let go no matter what people told me, no matter what evidence they had on the matter . . . I needed a sense of pride in who I was to be happy to be black, that is very important.

In addition to this sense of pride in her racial history, critical for her self-esteem, Carrie's mother gave her the message that she had to be strong in herself, that she could not count on someone else to protect her: "I need to do, for myself, I can't depend on other people to do things for me." These childhood lessons made Carrie willing to push against doors that appear closed in order to gain access. Her strength, though individual, is part of a legacy African-American women share from foremothers who had to fight to protect themselves, their men, children, and their communities (see Belenky, Bond, and Weinstock, 1997; Mullings, 1994).

Maria, whom we met in Chapter 1, uses the metaphor of defining a large space and occupying it against forces of racial and gender discrimination. Maria is 32, an attorney, married with two young children. Her mother is Native American, her father Latino, and she was raised on a reservation. She constantly battles discrimination on the basis of her color and her gender.

From her culture Maria learned that women are strong: "In Indian country, for any woman being a woman is an asset. You are expected to raise your voice and stand up; you can be a woman and still be powerful; almost all the tribal court judges are women." Within this tradition of respect for women, who were venerated healers and wise women, sits the present reality of a culture nearly destroyed by outsiders who imposed practices such as sending Indian children to Catholic boarding schools (LaFromboise et al., 1995). Maria's mother was one of these children: "Right off the reservation, boarding schools, you know, the whole nine yards, Catholicism. I know so many Indian women my mother's age—it's a script and their daughters who are my age now, we're trying to find our place in this professional world."

Maria says that people "who didn't grow up watching their relatives beat on each other and go to church Sunday have a different yardstick of violence." She learned about violence not only from her family but also from a society hostile to her people.

Although Maria's mother was physically abused by the men in her life, she remained strong: "My mother was a battered woman, and a part of that is because she wouldn't stand being hit so she'd hit back . . . And the anger side of that is what kind of kept her being strong, being kind of angry or letting her partner know she wasn't going to put up with this." Maria says that her mother never lost her positive sense of self and continued to stand up for herself. Maria herself was never abused, and she felt her mother's power to shield and safeguard: "I always felt protected and safe. I knew that my mother would take care of us."

Maria grew up learning to deal with stereotypes about her race and her poverty: "I don't think I always had good self-esteem . . . Deep inside I was very ashamed—not thinking I was smart enough. It was always not being smart enough, not being quick enough, that whole shame that comes with poverty and alcoholism. All that did was made me more determined that I was going to achieve just as much as they."

Having now secured her place as an attorney, Maria must continually draw on her aggressiveness in order to move beyond the limited space in which others want to confine her:

> You've got to test what you're made out of, how far you're going to go, and what it feels like if you get slapped backwards. If people give you a little bit more room, what are you going to do with it? If no one ever gives you those options or lets you explore how far you're going to go, you're never going to leave the comfortableness of your own little office, you're never going to get out there and push it. You know, you need to know how to take a punch.

Unlike Julia, who feared moving into unfamiliar territory, Maria already inhabits foreign territory as a woman of color who must prove herself in a man's field and a racist society. She needs to test the limits that constrain her social movement, to explore how far she's going to go with her aggressiveness. Experiencing discrimination daily, she knows that her survival depends on pushing beyond the comfort of her appointed space and being able to take the expected retaliatory punch.

Maria encountered a number of forceful blows to her sense of self—insults, denied opportunities, exclusions—and did not give up. Anticipating a hostile response to pushing for her place in society, she seeks to clarify what she's willing to fight for and how she's willing to fight: "You just have to pick those instances that it's worth going to the mat for and risk it . . . Unless you make those decisions, go to the mat and lose, you're never going to know the perimeters of your anger or your aggression, or how to make it better or how to make it right once you've fucked up with somebody."

Change in self and society takes place through conflict as well as through cooperation. As Maria learns about the perimeters of her own aggression, her strategies of forcefulness are changing: "I'm like getting more and more terrain and I'm feeling more comfortable with it, and I realize I don't have to do some of the things or pull some of the stunts I've pulled to get me further out there, to get more in touch with that and find out what a good thing aggression can be, I can be a little bit more civil about it." As women gain confidence that they will survive in hostile environments, as they recognize their own strength, they do not have to take the offensive so often. Maria is learning to stand her ground using positive aggression and is willing to negotiate space for both self *and* other. As well, she may be changing her behavior to fit the norms of the predominantly white, middle-class profession she has entered.

Maria attributes her ability to stay true to herself (which means defying conventional norms of good femininity) to honesty about who she is and to a lack of concern about others' opinions of her:

> I think the difference between me and some other women is, I don't care if they don't like me. I'm not—I have to be who I am first of all, and it's not to say that I've just pushed through life not giving a shit, there's times where I've felt really bad about what I've done, what I've said, how I handled that . . . It's better . . . that I stay true to who I am because I couldn't live with myself. I couldn't live being some of the women that I know that are always wringing their hands that so-and-so doesn't like me and I did this and I did that.

Once Maria has gotten more terrain, she retains it through vigilance over staying true to herself, not through conformity to others' expectations.

Women's use of metaphors that signify expanding their space—getting more terrain, pushing limits—can also function as a code for talking about status and power without explicitly describing gender or racial issues. If a woman is not sure, because of her ethnicity or class, that she has a valued place in society, she may feel she has to push harder to make room for herself. A number of the women I interviewed echoed the feelings expressed by Nola (age 20), an Asian-American student: "As a woman of color, I feel I have to be aggressive in order to succeed in mainstream America. If I don't speak out or take action, I might get lost. I know this society is not set up for me to succeed . . . I have taken the initiative to act upon things that disturb me because I know if I don't take action then I can't expect someone else to do it for me."

At the same time, these women are subject to pressure to tone down their aggression in order to fit into the norms of the predominantly white, middle-class professions they enter. Aída Hurtado (1996, 379–380) describes the resulting tensions:

> The challenge for me, and perhaps for many other feminists of Color, was to bridle the anger and outspokenness—in a sense to tame it—because of its potential to destroy the person using it or to harm those who did not deserve to be hurt. My feminist consciousness, unlike that of many White women, was to *tame* my argumentativeness, to be a kind listener, to withhold the sarcasm, not to point to all illogical arguments—even when the speaker was weaker than I was—in other words to become more like a White woman with the characteristics of hegemonic femininity.

A woman's position vis-à-vis the dominant society powerfully affects her thoughts about her aggression.

Audre Lorde's (1984) phrase "Sister Outsider" captures the feelings of many women of color in relation to white society who feel they must fight for a place of equal opportunity. They are likely to see their aggression as a positive characteristic. Maria, for example, says:

> I don't see [aggression] in a negative sense, I see it as a positive attribute that I want my daughters to have . . . It's good if you're aggressive . . . I have had so many discussions with women of color who are like me and aren't intimidated by other aggressive women and almost enjoy the camaraderie that can come out of that. Whereas a lot of women who . . . were raised different from me, that's like a real negative thing, raising their voice, getting angry, hanging up . . . they really had a hard time with that.

Women's comfort or discomfort with raising their voices, getting angry, and confronting others varies with their backgrounds and with their knowledge of their own force, positive and destructive.

Clearly, some women feel freer than others to bring their will, desire, and anger into relationship. These differences are affected by ethnicity and class, though such factors never determine differences.

While in the public realm Maria and Carrie push against limits, in their intimate relationships they have had to learn how to stand up for themselves. Carrie, for example, "did not make a wise choice at all":

> Met this guy and he swept me off my feet . . . I feel like I went with this American dream that this is the way you should be and this is how it should be and I bought it . . . Until my one friend stepped in . . . and she had just had a baby and I had just had a baby . . . Then she looked at me, she said, "Wait a minute, what's going on with you?" She says, "You're fat, your house is a mess, and where is your husband?" And I just told her, "Well, he's cheating on me." She goes, "Oh, my gosh, now I've got to deal with you" . . . So she stepped in at a point in time in my life where I needed her the most and she was there and that was that strong bond that came in and she said, "You can't take this. I don't want you telling anybody what's going in your life because they'll look at you and think that you're stupid." She says, "Look how stupid you're being" . . . I mean within twenty-four hours I was like, "Okay, you know what? I'm getting a divorce. I'm not putting up with this. I'm not taking this. What is wrong with me?"

All the women I interviewed had the most difficulty standing up for themselves within their intimate relationships with men. The puzzles of aggression become most complex when a woman buys the myth of inequality in marriage and tries to adapt herself to its structure. The adaptation is reinforced by her fear of retaliation or of driving her partner away, while, most often, what disappears is her own positive sense of self.

A Wall of Self-Protection

> I had developed that tough image where I could say touch me and, and I'll kick you in the nuts kind of a thing . . . I got real

lippy with my teachers and was always trying to prove a point. Just the leather coat, tough girl thing, you know. I did hang out with some girls that liked to beat people up, but I was never really one to join them . . . I think I was scared of them, that somehow or another they would find out that I wasn't as tough as them and that they would turn on me. (Mandy, age 32, white, student)

I don't like to share my feelings. Keep it inside mainly until I get really mad, then I be talking about killing everybody. You mess with me, I will fuck you up. (Brenda, age 30, African American, unemployed)

This language—a "tough image," don't "mess with me"—conveys how these women use aggression to build a wall of protection against vulnerability. "Attitude," expressed as an appearance of toughness backed by a quick readiness to fight, exists on a spectrum. It ranges from a persona that can be put up or taken down, depending on the context, to a more permanent, defensive wall built in response to betrayals such as sexual or physical abuse. In the latter case, a woman believes that no one can be trusted; the wall is built of anger, hostility, and disappointment, kept in place by rage over violations. The wall stands as a barrier to keep others at a safe distance. Sixteen women described their aggression as a wall of self-protection: nine white women, four African-American women, one Latina, one woman of Native American/Latino parentage, and one Chilean woman.

As her 2-year-old daughter played on her lap, Gloria (age 34, Latina, unemployed) told me about her own childhood, which was filled with separation, loss, and violence. She came to the United States from Peru with her father and grandmother when she was 6, and was placed in a boarding school where she quickly forgot much of her native Spanish. Gloria remembers nothing about her mother, who remained in South America; her father "didn't tell me anything" about her. When her father remarried, "He came and took me out of the school and then he got married several more times." Gloria never got along with his wives, who, she says, "used mind-game shit" or violence. One stepmother "used to beat me up every day. There was one time when she tried to stab me with a butcher knife and then I screamed for my grandmother and then she came upstairs. When my dad came home, I told everything then."

Her father consistently chose his wife's welfare over his daughter's, so Gloria ran away at 15 to escape her stepmother's threats. She fled to a nearby home, but was raped by the son of the people who took her in. "It was the night before Christmas. He just covered up my mouth and stuff and I couldn't scream out for help. And he was real ugly and stuff. He was real dirty and nasty. I can still see how ugly he is."

This violent rape threw Gloria into an abyss of isolation and anger: "I felt lost and alone because nobody believed me. And I was living in the house where it happened so that was really bad. I hated people. I hated men mainly. So I didn't want a boyfriend. Because, see, . . . I just thought that you just kissed the boys and that was about as far as it went. I didn't know about the other part until I was raped. So it ruined my whole image of growing up as a good girl."

Gloria had been raised in the Latin Catholic tradition of virginity as goodness. Being raped robbed her of her positive identity and ripped away any hope of being morally worthy. Without any support, vulnerable to repeated rape if she stayed in that home yet having no place to go, Gloria sought protection in withdrawal: "I wouldn't let anybody come close to me. I wouldn't hardly have long conversations with anyone. I wouldn't speak to many people. Stayed out of sight and stayed indoors all the time. I didn't know what I was going to do because I didn't have anybody to talk to about it. So I just kept it all inside." She remembers feeling anger, "but there was nothing I could do about it. It wouldn't do me any good to get angry. I couldn't take it out on anyone." Feeling cut off by the shame and degradation of the rape, she thought she had been damaged beyond reach of further harm: "Nobody could do nothing else, nothing worse could have happened."

Now single, Gloria lives with her 2-year-old and her pregnant 16-year-old, custody of her third daughter, age 6, having been awarded to the child's father. Gloria used drugs, including cocaine, for a number of years and is now in recovery. She lives in an apartment in an inner-city neighborhood known for its drug activity.

Gloria presents herself as loud and tough, and in social service agencies this has earned her a reputation for combativeness. She says: "My voice and the tone of it, the pitch of it, and my attitude are aggressive." Involved with men who introduced her to drug use and prostitution and who beat her—"I've got scars on my legs and stuff from beating me up with guns and everything like that"—she has learned that no one will protect her. She must defend herself: "Everybody knows not to fuck with me . . . I'm going to protect myself to the end." She describes her "attitude" as

> a wall. A protection wall for me. See, I talk a lot of shit, I can tell you that right now. Okay? I do that as a protection for myself. When I'm scared, I can charm your ass to the bone. And I'm not talking about "Oh, you look nice today. You have a nice outfit on" . . . I'm talking about "If you put your hand on me, you're dead. It's not a problem. I'll take you out. With whatever's standing by—a heater, garbage can, whatever. It's not a problem. I'll reach out and fuck your world up." It's that simple.

Gloria learned early that people are out to hurt her; they have been doing so for most of her life. In this socialization for survival, she uses her aggression for a very specific purpose. She does not develop the ordinary feminine charm of flattery. Instead, she becomes like a snake charmer who uses sound to hold a cobra in thrall to ward off its death strike. The sound of her voice, "the tone of it, the pitch of it," raises an attitudinal shield—that of toughness. Her message warns that she intends to fight if threatened. Knowing that she must appear intimidating to avoid being hurt, she seeks to create a fear in others that outstrips her own.

Gloria says she developed her attitude "because you got to." She sketches the social context that makes it necessary:

> I've got a reputation to uphold. I got three kids. Single parent. Because, see, I can't let, just because I'm out here by myself without a man, I don't let nobody intimidate me or make me feel like I'm dirt. Because I'm not. I used to be on drugs. I used to be ass out. I used to be one of the people downtown. All the

homeless people know me downtown. The shelters know me . . .
Everybody knows not to fuck with me.

Gloria's reputation for toughness helps her survive as a woman
alone in poverty in a violent world. Her strategy of self-protection
differs strongly from strategies used by women who consider their
aggression as unfamiliar territory. Instead of seeking safety in hiding, yielding, and compliance, women who use aggression as a wall
of protection learn to take the offensive. They convey the message,
"Better not mess with me." Variations in women's aggression seem
to be based more on what behaviors are expected within specific
social contexts and which behaviors carry survival value than on
any inherent traits. In addition, women who use these radically
differing patterns of aggression often stand in very different relation to the power of dominant society and to its rewards.

Fear underlies Gloria's tough attitude, but it does not paralyze
her: "Fear is the one thing that gets your strength going, for me.
Fear gets your adrenaline running and when my adrenaline is flowing and I'm scared, I won't hesitate to protect myself in any way,
shape or form." Fear flowing through Gloria's veins fuels her self-
protective strength. Until age 15 she had positive visions of her
future—"I wasn't going to be on welfare and I was going to have a
job and I was going to be married and I was going to have a nice
house and kids. And a nice car and stuff. Didn't come out quite like
that." These dreams were destroyed; now the angry, aggressive self
protects the vulnerable self who has been hurt by others.

While the wall of self-protection that women like Gloria build
appears similar to the "street-talk" persona women in inner-city
neighborhoods use to ward off unwanted attention (Lahr, 1997),
the two are not the same. When the attitude of toughness is a
persona, the speech patterns and gestures that convey it are turned
on and off according to context. When it is a wall of self-protection,
aggressive toughness is more than speech style or a persona: it is a
defensively created way of being in relationships. Used to protect
survival, the wall stays up across differing contexts and relationships, though not usually with children.

Further, attitude as a persona is stylistic, relating more to communities of speech and socially coded behaviors than to a conviction that one will perish without the "wall." John Lahr quotes Tanasha, a 17-year-old African-American woman in New York City who is taking a speech class at the Julliard School. Tanasha uses a "black vernacular" in her neighborhood but enters another community of speech as she crosses the cultural boundary near Julliard: "In a different environment, I'm dealing with a different kind of people, so I act accordingly." She uses her fierce persona on her home turf: "For instance, I'm walking down 135th Street. All you hear is 'Yo, Shorty. Can I get you numbah? Waz'a deal wi'choo?— yada-yada-yada.' Everybody yelling at you. Trying to talk to you. And my face: I don't smile. I'm walking. Just leave me alone. Don't bother me. That's the image I'm trying to portray" (Lahr, 1997, 36).

Gloria's self-protective wall differs from Tanasha's street persona in nuanced ways. Both women use "attitude" to deal with a street culture whose rules about women's aggressive style differ markedly from those of subcultures that stress women's niceness. Both Gloria's and Tanasha's street cultures exist within a dominant society that structurally has affected their higher rates of violence through racism and poverty. But Gloria has been victimized and betrayed. She has learned that she must protect her very survival. Gloria erects her wall out of these betrayals, disappointments, and abandonments, held tight with a mortar of rage.

In order to present these patterns of women's aggression, I have had to oversimplify. Using aggression as a wall of self-protection or seeing it as unfamiliar territory does not necessarily correlate with a woman's socioeconomic or ethnic subculture. Women who have had to fight against physical and emotional violations, regardless of wealth, poverty, or ethnicity, may choose to use aggression for self-protection as Gloria does. Conversely, women who are socialized for "nice" femininity grow up in various subcultures.

The images of self in relation to other that underlie the use of aggression as a wall of self-protection are as follows:

Interpersonal premise: People are out to hurt you (I have
been abandoned, betrayed, badly hurt).

> Therefore
> I have to take care of myself because no one else will look
> out for me.
> Therefore
> my voice, my fists, and my "attitude" create a wall of
> distance and self-protection
> because
> if I am not "tough," people will take advantage of me.

Women who must fight for survival silence the overt expression of their needs for connection and love, fearing that others will perceive such vulnerability as an invitation to attack. Their experience has taught them that to do otherwise leads to disaster. They use their force to control others through intimidation, not to control themselves to appear unaggressive. Women socialized to niceness, in contrast, seek to control others' responses by silencing their own overt opposition and anger. They believe that appearing outwardly compliant to others' wishes will ensure their safety.

Gloria believes that involvement with people leads to danger and hurt, so her best bet is to be on her own:

> I don't have any friends. I'm not going to have any either. I don't socialize with anyone except my boyfriend and my kids . . . and my kids' grandma . . . See, I don't have any problems when I do it that way . . . Relationships have led to unnecessary trouble. Things I could have avoided had I stayed the hell away from these assholes. So now I just stay away from them and I don't have to be bothered. Works real well for me.

She views the most important issues in her life—how to relate to others and how to protect herself—as an either/or choice that presents her with loss on either side. On the one hand, aggressiveness allows her to protect herself but leads to isolation and maintains her feelings of disconnection and hostility. On the other, she fears that nonaggression leads to victimization or to being controlled by others. Such thinking leaves her feeling powerless in relationship even though she uses force against others.

Gloria feels trapped in a violent, self-protective mode, yet the part of self that yearns for love, closeness, and positive regard is often missed because she appears so aggressive and so tough. She only rarely lets down her wall:

> The only person that can really reach me is my boyfriend, because I know that he really cares. Other than that, no. Or my daughter, that's 16. And today at my parenting class, she was praising me about things that I didn't know she cared about. And I started crying. Well, I could say that I let my wall down at that time. Everybody was patting me on the back and my eyes was watering and stuff but I never heard my daughter talk about me in a good way before. Only in a bad way.

A social context of economic and racial inequality paired with violence against women has profoundly affected Gloria's life course and her thinking. When a personal history of abuse intersects with social realities that create hopelessness and fear, that intersection multiplies the difficulty of forming a positive vision of self. The strengths Gloria has developed to resist victimization—such as her "attitude," her self-reliance, her ability to navigate danger—often go unacknowledged by wider society, which instead reflects to her an image of a woman with little social worth.

For women who have absorbed such violence, trustworthy, loving relationships are the unfamiliar territory. As Chrystal (age 25, African American, unemployed) said, after meeting a man who offered his emotional support: "When I first met him, he said, 'I'll help you do whatever you're going through . . . If you need me there, I'll be there,' stuff—those are the things I've never heard anybody say. And a lot of people in my family say, 'He's too good for you.' " In Chrystal's experience, "It was like going to a different country when you don't know the language. I didn't want to deal with it . . . I say because he's gonna find out about me, and I guess I was almost scared that if he found out what I was used to that's the way he was gonna start treating me." As well, she was suspicious: "He's up to something, he's playing a role, he's putting up a front or something like that." Staying in the familiar territory of devaluing relationships out of low self-esteem, Chrystal perpetuates the likelihood that she will need aggression as self-protection.

The metaphors of unfamiliar territory and a wall of protection reveal that women using both these patterns of aggression envision an either/or in terms of who dominates a relationship, the self or the other. Women who see their aggression as unfamiliar territory yield to others, keeping the self tightly bound in a small corner. Those who use aggression as self-protection attempt to keep others at a distance or tightly control their access and closeness. While those who suppress and hide their aggression fear that it will lead to isolation, those who use aggression for self-protection see isolation as safety. Both patterns lack positive ways to work out conflict, but for different reasons.

Redrawing the Line

To tell you the truth, nothing feels as good as acting out—nothing ever feels as good as getting it out of your system. So some people can do that to punching bags or whatever like that, but it never experientially feels as good as when it's real . . . It doesn't always mean hitting, it just means letting it all out at that point, screaming, yelling, calling them names, you know what I'm saying, "Get the hell out of my face, you son of a bitch, and da da da da." And then the calm and quiet that happens after all of that is extremely relaxing. But I had felt like—but it was nonproductive at that point, okay, and so that's the last time that I allowed myself into it. (Sharon, age 44, Native American/white, graduate student)

One path toward learning to use force positively became clear as women told stories of personal change. For most, an aggressive act they considered destructive initiated the journey into knowing their own relational force. At times, the act was unacceptable by anyone's standards, as when it threatened someone's life. At others, the act violated only a woman's own standards, as when she transgressed an impossible moral rule never to hurt another person emotionally. Regardless of its form, committing an act she considers destructive makes a woman recognize that she is capable of harming others. She can either integrate this awareness into her concept of self or split it off through denial. Change comes as she acknowledges her capacity to do harm and chooses to use her force positively instead of destructively. Such an integration leads to honesty (rather than a false innocence about her capacities) and to taking responsibility for her actions. The resulting self-knowledge offers genuine freedom to be authentic in relationship.

Women who redraw the lines of their aggressive limits use metaphors of force and space in characteristic ways. They often speak of stepping "over the threshold," "crossing the line," going "over the limits," and the like.

Mandy (age 32, white), a single parent of three boys under 14, is studying writing at a community college. Early in her interview she contrasts herself with other women: "I see women that I perceive as being from a different social class as me . . . it's almost like carbon monoxide poisoning, you know, they're dying this real slow poisonous death because they don't get to have all of it." "To have all of it" means:

> To yell and scream and shout and be angry and not correct about it at all and just come off the wall and throw things and have all of that. I mean, it's like they get bred down to this nice acceptable size with this nice acceptable vocabulary and this nice acceptable set of behaviors, and I just don't think that I'm so unique that this wide range that I feel is limited only to me. But I think the ways that I was able or unable to control it have a lot to do with where I come from in terms of class. My family would spend weekends out on Hoods Canal, right? With all my mom's brothers, all the loggers, and they'd drive all their big trucks and they'd drink beer and we'd run around on the beach, and everybody would eat oysters and throw up all over the place . . . Then take a different class background, you know, maybe we'd go off to Martha's Vineyard and we'd drink out of little glasses and we'd never throw up. But I just don't think that human beings are that different. And I wonder where it goes.

Convinced that "a lot of my aggressive behaviors were more acceptable because of my class background," Mandy puts her finger on an important marker the dominant society uses to separate women according to class and ethnicity: styles of aggressive behavior. Women also seem to judge themselves and each other from differing perspectives regarding acceptable aggressive talk and behavior, perspectives that often follow class and ethnic lines (Hurtado, 1996; Phelps et al., 1991; Walker, 1995; Wray and Newitz, 1997). When socialized for niceness, girls learn to present less obvious physical and verbal aggression and more controlled manipulation (Brown, 1998; Brown and Gilligan, 1992; Miller, 1991), while in subcultures that encourage more open forms of speech, including anger and opposition, girls use a wider, more visible range of aggressive behaviors (Fordham, 1993; hooks, 1989, 1996; Walker, 1995; Way, 1995).

The slow death by asphyxiation that Mandy imagines for women of other classes differs from the dangers she encountered in a childhood filled with sexual and physical abuse, alcoholism and drugs. She paints a picture of a mother who has "always been a screamer, just goes from cool, calm and collected into sort of insta-rage." Her mother was also violent, hitting Mandy with shoes, hands, and words. Mandy was sexually abused by her mother's brother and felt "stalked, unprotected, and powerless against this huge man." Her parents often fought. After one incident, when "the police were there and the ambulance was there and there was blood," she found out that "my mom had tried to cut my stepdad with the butcher knife, tried to castrate him."

Mandy reenacted the violence and chaos of her early life as she raised her own young children. Now sober and in recovery from substance abuse, she talks about the importance of staying honest about her life: "Unless I have access to all of who I am, I could perpetuate a lie of a life, and I think eventually I would trip up on it—it wouldn't work." Mandy learned all of who she is from her own acts of aggression that "define the far boundary of unacceptable": "If I cross over that line, it's really unacceptable for me as a human being. But it gives me plenty of permission to make all kinds of mistakes. Not necessarily the gravest of errors—to really hurt someone or to kill someone or whatever. But it definitely gives me permission to make lots of mistakes and not beat myself up with them." Instead of "knowing her place," Mandy occupies her space, a space expanded by honesty and experience.

Her new sense of freedom relates to knowing the line between acceptable and unacceptable aggression:

> If I drew the line at raising my voice, then I would probably go crazy. But if I put the line out there further and say, "Okay, to really hurt someone's body, to really damage them physically is unacceptable to me," then I can do a whole lot of stuff. Stuff like standing up for myself. I can say, "That is completely unacceptable to me." Or, "It's not okay that you do that to me" . . . And a lot of people won't cross those lines, but because that line for me has been way farther out here, I will.

Mandy ran into the boundary line of the unacceptable when she nearly killed her first husband. At 24, with three young children, she and her husband were both using cocaine and drinking heavily. He was also shooting heroin. "We were both really, really messed up, all our needs and our survival stuff, home, food, money, all those things were messed up because of our addiction . . . throw in a couple of crying babies and you've got the seeds for a real mess." Her husband would often disappear for weeks at a time, leaving her no money. "My attempts to control him were usually fairly violent. I liked to push him, shove him, talk, you know, tell him what a piece of shit he was, what a rotten father he was."

One night after he had been gone several weeks, Mandy saw him outside in a strange van. She went out to get his paycheck: "He handed me ten dollars and he was just fried." She took the money into the house and hid it.

> He came in the house, a fight ensued, we were into it verbally, and I was so pissed off that I started picking things up and throwing them. He bent over to pick something up and I threw this big ceramic Buddha and it caught him across the back of the head. Well, the neighbors by this time had called the cops . . . So the police came . . . by the time they put him in the cop car, he was bleeding profusely, and I had fractured his skull. Instead

of going to jail he ended up going to the hospital, and they cut his skull open and pushed this piece of skull back out where it belonged.

Mandy felt "really upset that I was capable of nearly killing somebody." The act brought her to the "far boundary of unacceptable," an edge of wasteland, regret, and pain, and propelled her to reconsider her life. Within three months, she began treatment for substance abuse and ended her marriage.

For Mandy the Buddha was both an aggressive weapon and a source of clarity that led to healing. In her words:

> One of the poisonous assumptions that keep women in the place of victimhood is believing that we are not aggressive. I think that, for me, it would have kept me stuck for a lot longer than it did . . . My victimization of sorts, throughout my life, kept me stuck. And it wasn't until I was able in some ways to be violent and to act violent that I had enough energy or motivation to move out of the stuckness.

Mandy redrew the map she had formed in a childhood filled with victimization and a sense of powerlessness. Reconfigured by the knowledge that she, also, was a source of destructive power, this new map allowed her to move from seeing herself as a helpless victim of stronger, harmful forces to taking charge of her life.

Mandy protects the space within which she can be herself through honesty. The line she continues to cross, the one she refuses to be limited by, is the boundary of conventional good femininity. To continue being honest she must call on her "dark side": "For me to tell the truth as unpolite or unpretty or, you know, all those woman words, me telling the truth isn't all those woman words, you know, it is my dark side. It's the brashness and the boldness and, my dark side doesn't wear high heels. She wears cowboy boots and big hiking boots and she doesn't really care what people think."

From this place that defies convention, Mandy says: "I know who I am, all of who I am. I don't have any denial about the things that happened to me or the things that I caused to happen. I don't deny or reject any of those components, and I wouldn't say that that's necessarily the dark side. But being able to tell the truth about it requires me to access my dark side. It requires me to be really fearless in the face of others." Telling the truth is not done in "high heels"; it is not necessarily feminine. Truth defies gender norms and does not care what people think.

What Mandy calls her "dark side" defies convention and carries danger to the status quo. Once a woman moves outside the bounds of authority, she can engage in positive, creative acts that help transform herself and the culture, or in destructive, hurtful actions.

Mandy's newly enlarged sense of self is threatened not only by potential relapse into drugs or alcohol but also by the model of selfless, good femininity, which might pull her back into pretense and jeopardize her hard-earned sense of self-worth. This threat comes when she experiences the enticing draw of the conventional "good woman's" life:

> There's a woman who watches my youngest son, and she's a, you know, really nice lady, she lives in a beautiful house on a nice cul-de-sac . . . She's married, her husband's just peachy. They have two brand-new cars in the driveway, and she's so nice and she has a Bible study at her house every Friday. And when I'm dealing with her, I really put myself aside, you know, my strong self, my self-full voice, and I try and be nice. And if I spend too much time around her, I go home and inside, I just kick the hell out of myself. I say things like, "Why couldn't that be you? Why aren't you like her?" But I would suffocate. I know that now.

This woman's picture-perfect existence presents the dominant image of how Mandy should look, what she should own, and how she should act to gain social approval. Spending time in "good woman" space activates Mandy's critical Over-Eye, the internalized eye of the culture, which decrees the importance of social class and the "right" way to be a woman.

When Mandy sees herself through this Over-Eye, it says things like "Why couldn't that be you? Why aren't you like her?" The side of self that talks back—her "self-full voice"—knows where her strength and value reside. She has gone to the furthest reaches of existence with fear and violence as her companions. There she learned about her capacity for destructiveness. To keep that knowledge integrated, she must oppose an idealized vision of femininity that denies women's aggressiveness and against which she appears flawed. This vision tries to prevent her from staying with the truth wrested from her experience—that she is capable of destroying others and herself but chooses not to.

Mandy's story illustrates that the move from powerless victim to powerful agent comes, in part, from owning one's aggressive force and choosing to exercise it positively rather than destructively. As Mandy redrew the line that defined the far boundary of the unacceptable, she moved from using her aggression as a wall of angry self-protection to envisioning ways to use it to create a positive life:

> When I was 13 and the abuse was still keeping going on, and I'd found a release in drugs and alcohol, I learned how to smoke and spit and swear and do all those things. I just pretty much point-blank let those people that were hurting me know, "Don't fuck with me any more, I'm done with you, you can't hurt me any more." Now I'm claiming my power as best I can . . . It's all interconnected, the sexual abuse and the people that my abusers were married to, and what kind of women they were . . . and what kind of woman I can be. So for me to keep going in this vein and keep working to be self-supporting and keep going to school to be able to get the kind of job that I want, . . . that's about claiming my power as a woman. It's about me using my aggression in a positive way.

Women's Bodies in Women's Minds

Women's experience of their own bodies is affected by their sense of men's aggressive potential and by their own socialization to de-escalate aggressive interactions. In adulthood, changes in a woman's felt bodily strength can affect the pattern of her aggression and her sense of self, as I found by following metaphors of force and space.

A triad of images—physical weakness, lack of aggression, and fear—link together to keep women from asserting their positive strength. Women fear not just male power but also their own weakness—and their own strength. Lisa (age 43, white), who teaches women's self-defense classes, describes what happens when women must break a board by striking it with the edge of their hand: "Most of the time, when women are fearful, it's that they won't be able to do it, or that it will hurt them. This one woman told me that she didn't want to do it because she was afraid she'd find out how strong she was. She was used to being taken care of and depending on people, and if she found out how strong she was, it would change her life."

For a woman who has always assumed she is weak, discovery of her strength may challenge not only the familiar fear but the very structure of her life. Why do many women avoid behavior that demonstrates their positive interpersonal forcefulness, their self-reliance, even when they face no threat of direct retaliation? How does the avoidance of experiencing and using one's strength relate to culture and to the female body?

Feminist scholars have shown that the body works as a cultural sign, a symbol of biological sex that carries gendered meanings. Historically, physical frailty, signaling an absence of hard work and a need of male protection, was one feature that distinguished white upper- and middle-class women not only from men but also from women of color and working-class white women. Femininity was also associated with weakening the body through practices such as footbinding and corsets, which disabled women's ability to move forcefully, much less to fight. Current practices of surgical enhancement often require periods of extended convalescence. Physical "weakness" in women enhances men's appearance of greater physical size and strength, reinforces women's sense of vulnerability to men's violence, and contributes to women's feelings of emotional weakness.

While today's ideal of femininity includes the possibility of physical strength, that strength—the slim, muscular body—serves as a new standard of beauty that has spawned an epidemic of eating disorders. This strength is most often portrayed by the media as mastery of one's own body, as sculpting one's form into a desirable shape, or as an escape from traditional roles of mothering and nurturance (Bordo, 1993). Its role as a new means of sexualization and subordination is less obvious. The media rarely show women's physical strength as leading to assertiveness at home or work, or as a means of self-protection. Sports is the one area in which the media portray female physical strength being used to attain goals other than beauty and male attention.

Women often are socialized to believe they need men to protect them from threats ranging from muggers and rapists to snakes and spiders. Lisa says: "A lot of times in attack situations, women think there'll be this other person there who will help them. I even have a friend that's a nurse and her husband's an attorney, and he's like 'I will take care of her.' Well, where are you forty hours a week, you know? And why is it so threatening to think that she could take care of herself?"

Our culture does not commonly regard the female body as a source of force, either self-protective or hostile. Part of the threat presented by a self-reliant woman is that she challenges assumptions about gender and strength. Women often get the message that they imperil not only relationships with men but their very lives when they depart from the cultural script of strong man, vulnerable woman. The assumption that women are physically weaker than men (and will back down in confrontations) interlocks with the belief that they are naturally less aggressive than men. Both work to inhibit women's discovery of their own physical and emotional strength and replace them, instead, with fear.

How do individual women learn to experience their bodies as weak and vulnerable? Physical and sexual abuse are known to have devastating consequences, including viewing and treating one's body negatively (Herman, 1992). Another common pathway, less brutal than physical attack or sexual abuse, also leads to bodily fear, as Lisa notes:

> I actually grew quite disconnected from my body because I had
> a very overly protective father who wouldn't allow me to do
> anything like ride a bicycle. And I did so few physical things I

was actually diagnosed by the time I got into junior high as having some kind of problem, so I didn't even get to take PE. I very rarely did anything physical with my body that a normal kid would do. My body's always been something that's been very hard for me to use, the fear of falling, the fear of being hurt that comes along with not knowing how to use it.

Like a partially lived-in house whose locked rooms fall into disrepair, much of Lisa's unexplored physical self became unusable to her. Forbidden to explore her body's capacities, Lisa came to regard "it," this vital vessel of self, as a source of danger. Her disconnection from her body and its strength was brought about by her socialization for female nonaggression, carried to the extreme by a controlling father.

Experiences of being preyed upon by men added to Lisa's feeling of physical vulnerability. She vividly recalls being "almost kidnapped" on the way home from kindergarten. When she was 13 a stranger accosted her and tried to drag her into his car, leaving her "afraid to do the simple thing of walking to the neighborhood store by myself." Several years later her mother divorced her father and "went away quite often and left me alone on the weekends." During those times, "someone tried repeatedly to get into the house." "I would panic and freeze," Lisa says: "I had a telephone by my bed, and I couldn't even call for help. It started off the first time just at the front door, and later the person got braver and braver 'til they would go around the house checking all the doors and windows, even with my dogs in the back yard. And the police figured it was somebody who knew that there was no man in the house."

Lisa, like many other women, absorbed the message that women without a protective "man in the house" are likely targets of male violence. This sense of vulnerability unless a (protective) male was by her side followed her into adulthood. She remained "afraid of being hurt and of freezing. Unless you've done that, you just don't realize how to just be frozen like that is so powerless."

In women's narratives, shifts in their emotional/psychological ways of interacting with the world are often initiated by physical acts that lead them to challenge their physical limitations and their fears. Such experiences carry psychological power by creating an embodied sense of self as a source of force and strength. Lisa's story serves as an example of how the feeling of being weak in relationship, a form of subordination, changes as a woman gains a sense of her physical strength.

When Lisa was 37, her husband took a job that required travel. Still terrified of being alone in the house, and hoping to lessen her fear, Lisa signed up for a self-defense course. In the course, women learned moves to disarm attackers. Each woman in turn had to step into the circle to fight the "mugger": "It's a real face-your-fears type of thing . . . The male muggers attack you and you fight back, and they do not go down until they feel that you have delivered a knock-out blow or punch."

When Lisa, who had "never had a sense of my strength or what it felt like," discovered that she was "able to go through my fear, to feel capable and confident about protecting myself using my body," she began to perceive men differently: "I would walk by guys and think, 'Oh, he doesn't look as big and as scary, or his face is really small, or it would be really easy to do this or to do that technique on him.' It was just as though they weren't so powerful and I was so weak. I felt more competent and more capable of defending myself, and that there were areas where I could fight back and be effective. And it wasn't so one-sided." Once she knew she could defend herself, Lisa's rigidly gendered view of strength crumbled. She began to see men as individuals instead of as projections of her fears. Watching other women break through fear, seeing them deliver knock-down punches and learning to do so herself taught her that she could occupy physical and emotional space in a way that no longer required her fear, victimization, or submission.

Lisa's new sense of her physical self carried over into her relationship with her husband:

One night . . . we were both in the bathroom just kind of kidding around. And my husband was kind of coming at me, kind of tickling, and I was like, "No, I don't want to do this." And he came at me; he just wasn't listening really. And all of a sudden I just took a posture, and I just said, "Look, I don't want to do this." And he just stopped dead in his tracks and he looked at me. And the relationship changed.

Lisa is not sure what occurred in that moment: "It was like he realized that I was really powerful in some way, either through the body language, or through what I was saying because I had taken this class. He really felt differently toward me." Asked what was different, Lisa replies: "It shifted to—it was just equal . . . it was the shift that I was strong in what I was saying and that he knew I could stop him."

By taking a stance of physical readiness, Lisa proclaimed that she owned her body, and that she was ready to back up her words with physical force. She met her husband's will with her own, saying that her desire was as important as his. Instead of meeting her assertiveness with retaliatory force or emotional distance, consequences many women fear, he stepped aside to give her will room to hold sway. Their relationship became more equal: "It kind of shifts, I think, almost from parent-child to equal-equal, because it's like if you're playing around with a kid and you're going to tickle them, you can just do it." She moved to adult status in the relationship.

From the outside, this shift in power relations between Lisa and her husband is barely discernible. As she says, "It's not that my husband's an abuser, he's a really nice man." The most important change takes place in Lisa's subjectivity, a change that grew out of her new sense of her body's force and that, in turn, led to an actual shift in power relations. What had seemed a static and stable aspect of her self since childhood—the lack of any "sense of my strength or what it felt like"—kindled her resistance in adulthood. Such minute shifts in power provide evidence that, as Foucault (1977) argues, resistance arises at the site of domination. The power relations that make Lisa feel subjugated exist both internally and externally: an awareness of the threat of male violence, an internalized sense of male power, lack of development of her own physical strength, a felt sense of weakness. Yet this array of internal and external forces did not leave her frozen and oppressed, a perpetual victim, but led to her active resistance.

Subjectivity is shaped not only by social practices but also by bodily experience, and is deeply inscribed with cultural messages about power and gender. By physically challenging her socialized "weakness" and paralyzing fear, Lisa changed her felt existence. Learning that her body could be a source of force and strength brought changes she had never anticipated.

Conformity to norms of feminine compliant behavior may also, ironically, lead to an emerging consciousness, a movement to new strength and energy (Bordo, 1993). Blythe (age 42, white) took up weight training because her domineering husband demanded that she improve her body: "He brought a set of weights from Sears . . . and said, 'Come on, we're gonna do this.' I did what he told me to do, because I was used to doing what he told me to do, right?"

Blythe had "never been able to do any kind of athletic pursuit, I'd never been able to run with my kids or hike or do anything . . . I'd been afraid of taking risks, I had been afraid of challenges." Along with the sense of her body as a "little butterball" that she cautiously, shamefully inhabited came the psychological effects of this embodied self: "I was very much victim oriented, I was very nonaggressive, very intimidated, rather shy a lot, fearful of a lot of things, had very, very low self-confidence, very little self-respect."

Change came about through physical and emotional experiences that challenged these long-standing psychological orientations. After weight lifting, Blythe began working out at a gym, skiing, and running, and finding pleasure in her new physical competence. When her youngest child started school, her husband insisted that she find a job, and again she complied, though she had always wanted to run a daycare center in her home. Emboldened by her newly discovered physical abilities, she decided to join the police force, a decision that flouted every aspect of her socialization for femininity: "Traditionally our behavior is enforced to be meek, to be polite, to be serving, you know, our fathers and our brothers and stuff like that. In the police department, we get positive enforcement in another direction." Coming from a background in which "there's like a little bubble around people and you don't touch people unless you know them very, very well," she had to learn the rules of space and force that go with police work. Her new job, she says, "dramatically changed my relationship with my husband, with my family, just really turned things upside down."

When Blythe entered the police force of a metropolitan California city in 1989, she was the only woman in her unit. At that time, the majority of male police officers held traditional, stereotyped views of women as the "weaker" sex and treated them accordingly. The treatment included sexual harassment and unequal opportunities for promotion.

Blythe also had to confront the "power of masculinity within the organization of policing" (Spillar, 1991, 15). This male view—the macho, gun-wielding officer fighting criminals—fosters the use of excessive force. According to the Christopher Commission, convened in the aftermath of the beating of Rodney King in Los Angeles in 1991, "female LAPD officers are involved in excessive use of force at rates substantially below those of male officers . . . The statistics indicate that female officers are not reluctant to use force, but that they are not nearly as likely to be involved in use of excessive force" (Report of the Independent Commission on the LAPD, 1991, 88).[8]

Blythe's narrative is filled with accounts of male officers' assumptions about her weakness, the harassment she received, and her tactics for overcoming such obstacles. She countered her colleagues' belief that she would not be "aggressive enough" by "pendulum swinging, from being super nice to trying to fit in with the guys and trying to build a reputation." Now she has found a "middle ground that works," "a point where I [am] confident of my abilities." Asked when she feels the strongest, she talks about

control, but not a facade of control with everything actually really boiling around underneath. It's deeper, it's understanding the situation, understanding myself, understanding what my options are, where my parameters are, and making very clearly focused decisions. It tends to relate a lot visually with weight lifting . . . there's that feeling of challenging and of marshaling everything: this is the direction I'm going to go in and I will do this. I'll do whatever I need to, to get this done, but this is my choice. I will get this bar up. I will put everything I've got into this, and there's that feeling, it's controlled, the bar is not bouncing. This is exactly the path that I'm going to take. It's not quick, but it's persistent.

The metaphor of marshaling her forces reveals how Blythe's body is in her mind. She evokes her felt physical sense of gathering all her strength to overcome difficult obstacles, to lift the bar, to deal with the barriers to her as a woman in police work. The force she musters fuels the steady exertion of will she needs to pursue a profession so antithetical to her socialization. The use of force and control leads to clarity of purpose, not to domination of others.

Blythe says that weight lifting changed her sense of self:

Weight lifting for me was the first thing—it was something that I could control and I could discipline myself. And I could see results. I had always been afraid to try things up until that time, . . . afraid of challenges. And here was something that I could determine the outcome of, depending on how hard I was willing to work . . . And then I would succeed and it was so exciting and it was so rewarding and I could see the changes in my body . . . It was like, if I stick with something I can succeed. Well, if I can succeed in this area, maybe I can succeed in this other area.

Learning, on a physical level, about her self as a *source* of force gave Blythe a new sense of confidence and control.

At work she gained equal footing with the men by using a language they could understand. One day, at a party, a colleague was giving her a "hard time." Having learned that "you have to play tough sometimes," she "finally told him to shut up or I'd hang him over the banister."

He made some comment about me not being able to do it, and he grabbed my arm—he didn't realize that I was a weight lifter— and he let go really fast . . . It was something he could respect, weight lifting is something that's a traditionally male thing. They know what it takes to build that kind of muscle. He knew

what I must have given to do that, and it was like, the relationship just switched, very, very much.

Later in the party this man taught her how to defend herself from
a certain kind of attack, and still later he "tested" her by asking,
"What are you going to do if somebody comes at you like this?"
"I pretended I was hitting him with my flashlight, and he says,
'Fine, you can back me.'[9] And it was like I had crossed some sort
of bridge, I had been tough enough and didn't back down when he
was harassing me. I threatened him, I had some muscle to back it
up, and I was talking tough, and it was like, 'Okay, now you're in.
This is the way we do it.'" Once the word was out that Blythe
could stand up for herself with a strong body, she was accepted as
an equal. Yet she did not mimic the male style of policing; she
changed its practice to accord with her values and her less confrontational, authoritarian approach.

Power relations were also changing at home as Blythe began
to see herself as someone worthy of respect and as she continually
overcame internal barriers of self-doubt. A turning point came one
day when she stood up to her husband, who "had, not very often,
but had physically assaulted me. He was very dominating in the
relationship, was very controlling." On an otherwise ordinary day,
Blythe got home from work and began telling her kids to do their
chores. Her husband said, "Oh, leave them alone, you're always on
them."

> I didn't back down. See, for the ten years or more before that, I
> had been really scared of him . . . I had never talked back to him
> before. He was really angry, he was yelling at me. He picked up
> the phone, threw it at me, I dodged part of it, but I had a pretty
> good bruise on my stomach after that. And he was getting up
> and he was walking toward me across the room, and I knew he
> was going to clobber me . . . And I thought, "If I back down now
> in front of the kids, what are they going to think of their mother
> for the rest of their lives? I refuse to live this way anymore" . . .
> I've never been more scared than at that moment. And I said,
> "Look, whatever you're going to do, you better do a good job of
> it, because as soon as you're finished, I'm going for the phone,

because if you lay a hand on me, I am going to call 911." And I said, "You will be in jail within the hour. I will take the kids and you will not know where we are when you get out." And by that time he had come up so he was inches from me, far closer than we would ever normally be in talking. He was so angry . . . he was just shaking.

In this moment full of potential violence, her husband "ended up leaving the house and was gone for a couple of hours." And "that was the last instance that we've ever had of that. He has never—so that was over six years ago. That was the big shift in our relationship."

Blythe now feels like a "different person": "I am learning to respect myself, and I demand a certain amount of respect in return. I won't accept anything less. I refuse to be a victim." She paints her changing sense of self with force metaphors that portray her as actor rather than as acted upon: surmounting hurdles, making things happen. She now requires that others share the space of relationship with equality and with mutuality. All this started with deferral to her husband's request that she begin weight training, which led to her new embodied sense of force. From that kernel of change grew an effective, positive self that engages with others on equal ground. Blythe's expanding self, much like a root seeking water, pushed its way through the barriers of inequality and social roles to arrive at a place where she feels free from fear and self-restriction. The courage that it took for Blythe to accomplish such growth cannot be overestimated.

Of the sixty women I interviewed, eighteen described experiences similar to those of Lisa and Blythe, in which gaining a new embodied sense of strength leads to a changed sense of self in relationship. Their stories make it clear that subjectivity is prone to change through the body and that patterns of relating are affected by one's sense of one's own bodily force.

Today, few girls are forbidden physical activities as Lisa was. On soccer fields, in gymnasiums, and on playgrounds, girls learn their physical strengths as they bump and grapple with other bodies, flip over vaults, or push their limits through swimming or running. Does participation in competitive sports make them more assertive interpersonally, more able to compete in the work world? The answer is more ambiguous than we might hope.

Women's interviews reveal a sharp distinction between areas where competitive aggression is sanctioned, such as sports, and areas where expectations for women's nonaggression still hold sway, such as intimate relationships and many workplaces. Three women, ages 17, 20, and 21, illustrate that the lessons learned in competitive sports—you can be strong and aggressive—do not necessarily carry over into intimate relations, which are governed by very different rules of gender and power. All three grew up strong and athletic with a felt sense of their own physical powers. Yet all three have been unable, so far, to bring their positive aggression into their intimate relationships with men.

Let us listen to the words of one of them: Patricia (age 20, white), nicknamed Pete. The captain of her university crew team, she carries herself with a confidence that conveys her strength and her positive sense of her body. When asked to describe her aggression, Pete immediately turns to sports: "I row, and so when I think aggressive, I think that's a time when I'm really pushing myself to be as aggressive as I can, just, no holds barred . . . We lift a lot of weights, we run a lot of stairs, we do a lot of aggressive workouts . . . I'm actually thinking aggressively when I'm rowing; that's what's on my mind."

Pete carries this positive, pushing-herself-hard aggression into areas that are less welcoming to women's forcefulness than team sports. She is a geology major in a university department that has few female professors to serve as role models. Pete has learned to use her voice freely as a student: "I like hearing lectures, but a lot of times something'll come up that I feel real strongly about . . . I approached a geology professor about him using 'he' all the time when referring to scientists, and it's gotten to where I don't really have a problem doing that kind of thing." She also easily stands up for herself in other public situations.

Pete rides horses alone on the back roads of rural Washington, and at some point she began to fear becoming a target of violence. Rather than accept restrictions on her freedom, she decided to carry a gun.[10] Asked whether learning to shoot made her feel more secure, she says: "I don't know if that necessarily makes me feel a lot safer. It makes me feel a little bit mixed that way, like, 'Well, I have this, this power.' But, on the other hand, 'Wow, I've really brought a lot of danger into my life.' "

Guns are supposed to equalize any difference of physical strength between victims and attackers. Yet victims' guns are often used against them. Pete now stores guns for her relatives; there are "probably a dozen" shotguns and handguns in the house she shares with her boyfriend. Their presence evokes a fleeting fear that "crosses my mind":

> Oh, you know, the funny thing that is very weird to me? I've actually had a fear of my boyfriend threatening me with a gun. And he's, the best I can tell, a pretty nonaggressive person . . . A lot of times I go to bed before he does, and actually I'll have that thought that if he gets angry, he could—and that's a real scary . . . I've only thought it a half a dozen times, but it scares me. That's something else that it's brought in, that fear, whether it's irrational or not.

Though Pete may have little to fear from this boyfriend, the culture of male violence against women supplies the vision that creates her unease.

In sports and academics Pete's competitive aggression is regarded as prosocial, elicited and rewarded; she has few inner conflicts within these areas. But in intimate relationships different patterns of socialization, interpersonal expectations, and value judgments govern her aggression. The white middle-class values in which she was raised regard a woman's aggression as selfish and destructive, even when it takes the form of merely opposing a partner's will, pressing for her desires, or showing anger. While Pete's aggression has been socialized for active expression in sports and academics, it has been socialized to disappear from view in relationships with men.

With her boyfriend Pete takes care not to appear angry, not so much because she fears his retaliation (though the thought is obviously there) as because she fears her own anger and anticipates his negative judgment: "I feel like if I ever came to the point that I was raising my voice to him, that he would just be like, 'I don't want to deal with this, this is totally out of line.' I can't imagine myself just raising my voice a little bit, I can't imagine myself getting a little angry, all I can imagine myself is just being *very* angry and lots of yelling and you know, very dramatic."

Though Pete does not conform to images of traditional femininity elsewhere in her life—she carries a gun, she goes where she wants, she confronts authoritarian professors, she is physically very strong—within the gendered space of intimate relationship she conforms to the myth that women are not aggressive. She fears that displays of anger will take her across the line of good femininity and lead into unfamiliar territory. She imagines only the extremes of anger—either keeping it completely under wraps or being "very angry" and "yelling." In four years she has raised her voice only once with her boyfriend. By not bringing her anger into dialogue, she is setting up conditions for a divided self: a good, unaggressive self that tries to please her partner and keep him close, and a hidden, angry, rebellious self that undermines her "goodness." Following rules of relationship that exclude her anger, Pete helps create a structure of relationship that is sure to stifle her.

What explains this disjunction in behavior? Clearly, socialization to the image of "good femininity" as the way to make and keep an intimate relationship shapes Pete's actions with her boyfriend. Conformity to this image is enforced by a lurking fear of male aggression: "if he gets angry, he could . . ." Another reason for the disjunction between her intimate and nonintimate behaviors is Pete's fear of her own destructiveness: "That's a large reason that I don't want to have kids . . . because I'm fearful that [anger] is maybe something that I wouldn't be able to control." She relates an incident that led to this decision:

> I took my friend's two kids up to campus in a truck, and on the way back it started snowing, so the roads were getting icy, and I was tense. And they were doing, you know, kid stuff, laughing and stuff, and the one girl said something that was slightly,

maybe I'd asked her to do something, and she kind of said "No" or something. And I reached over and I didn't actually hit her, but I just stopped myself probably within a inch of—I mean, when that happened, it just scared me, I was like "Urrg! what have I done?"

Pete knows the power of her physical self, the force she can bring to bear on another person, and fears its harmful potential. Entering adulthood and encountering the contradictory images of womanhood—be strong and forceful, be anything you want, but be sweet and nonthreatening to your partner, be nurturing with children—she has yet to discover the perimeters of her aggression. Because her anger feels so opposed to nurturance, she is convinced that she would "be overly aggressive with children, from the little bit I've been around them." Pete fears her destructive force, and tries to keep it absent from close relationships. She both removes the possible trigger for its expression (she will not become a mother) and tries to suppress it entirely (she will not raise her voice with her boyfriend). The myth that women are not aggressive in the roles of lover and mother collides with the image of women as aggressive competitors in today's world to create deep conflicts for women who attempt to do both.

In the land I am exploring, no true north can be found, no one point on the compass that we all call aggression. In the absence of such agreement, I have used metaphor to enter the complexity of this human experience and to examine women's perspectives. Following the trail of metaphor as it reflects both the particular self and wider cultural norms has led me to consider the different maps society hands men and women to guide the use of force and space. Following selected metaphors has also revealed patterned ways in which women bring their force into relational space in a society that says they should restrain their aggression. And the metaphors have led me to consider the body's role in women's patterns of aggression. Women's use of metaphors of force and space, which varies with social context, clarifies the culture's role in shaping the many forms their aggression takes.

As a woman enters adulthood, her socialization regarding how she can use force to occupy space is tested by the world. Sometimes her use of force fits with the world, sometimes not. Perhaps a prejudiced societal hand checks her move into social spaces because of her ethnicity or social location, and she decides to push for more space. Or perhaps she decides to yield, which carries a different set of consequences for her and society. If a woman's socialization has taught her to shrink from opposing others openly, her adult development may include the task of challenging inner barriers more than that of confronting outer limitations. Or a woman who uses her force destructively may encounter negative consequences and perhaps spend her time relearning how to engage with others in positive ways. Throughout, the crucial factor that shapes a woman's aggressive behavior is a dynamic *interaction* between her uses of force in relational space and the responses of others to those acts.

3

Why Not Hurt Others?

In their narratives women make it clear that they harbor aggressive feelings much more often than they commit aggressive acts. When asked what keeps them from acting on their feelings, they usually say they don't want to hurt others.

> I think because I was so hurt for so long, I don't want—I just don't want anyone to hurt. I just would never hurt anybody . . . whether people intentionally hurt me or it was unintentional or it was direct or indirect, it doesn't matter. The pain is still so deep . . . I wouldn't want anybody to go through it. I just feel like the pain and the hurt sets them so far back; you can't move forward. You're stuck in a place somewhere. (Kim, age 34, Filipina/Danish American, social worker)

> In my own personal life, I don't want to hurt people. You treat other people like you want to be treated. It's not nice to deliberately set out and hurt other people. It's mean spirited and you don't like it when people hurt you so why would you hurt somebody else? (Jodi, age 35, white, corrections officer)

> In my ethical/moral world view, the worst thing that you can do is hurt somebody else. Consciously hurt somebody else. (Cassondra, age 34, white, artist)

On the basis of their past experience, these women strongly identify with the hurt that victims of their aggression would feel. All the women I interviewed voiced this concern to avoid hurting others as they explained why they refrain from committing aggressive acts.

Carol Gilligan (1982) named this wish to avoid harm a morality of care and found its basis in a sense of connection with others that is more characteristic of women than of men. Empathy, the capacity to identify with and understand the feelings of others, provides the foundation for morality and for harmonious social relations. Basic tasks of establishing and maintaining positive ties with others are impossible without empathy. Lacking empathy and moral concern, the most violent, brutal sociopaths act in ways we consider "inhuman."[1] When aggression arises from the inevitable clashes of living together, empathy puts the brakes on its expression, usually transforming hatred, anger, and hostility into acceptable behavior that does not destroy others.

Women are generally assumed to be more empathic than men, either by training or by nature. Across almost all cultures, women rear children and are involved in nurturing, supporting activities, while men's roles lead them to develop other interpersonal characteristics. The cultural narrative presented in movies, TV, books—everywhere we turn—says that women, not men, are and should be concerned to prevent hurt.

If women are more empathic than men, it is easy to conclude that their greater empathy explains their lower levels of aggressive behavior.[2] But this may be too pat an answer to the question of how and why women subdue their aggression, an answer too rooted in stereotype and in the moral virtue society expects of women. Women do hurt others, at times with clear vision and at other times blindly. Though their aggression differs from men's in socially constructed ways and is often less physical, it causes harm.

The same three women whose words open this chapter also describe instances in which empathy steps aside:

> I don't mind hurting him, and I can admit that openly and freely without a doubt and without any guilt. (Kim)

> I was feeling very aggressive and I wanted to hurt him every bit as bad as I was feeling. And part of me was going, "That's really not fair because you didn't tell him." I mean, it was like saving

it all up and going boom! And I think that's a real rotten way of fighting with someone. But I did it anyway. (Jodi)

Three separate times I hit him, I slapped him in the face . . . it was just pure heat, pure fury. I have gotten that feeling with him often enough. I wanted to hurt him. I really wanted to hurt him. I wanted to take away any sense of well-being he had about his actions. (Cassondra)

This vital tension between the ideal and the real, between a desire to avoid hurting others and the inescapable fact that we do hurt them, runs through everyone's life. Without acknowledging such tensions, accounts of women's psychology may idealize women's goodness and reinforce the societal myth that they are not aggressive.

The sense of interconnection and empathy that underlies an avoidance of hurt is present in many women's narratives. Leigh (age 44, white, Buddhist teacher) expresses a particularly strong sense of interrelatedness: "It's like when you touch that place of that deep inner connectedness, why would we want to do anything to hurt anyone? I mean hurting you is no different than hurting me or hurting my son. It's no different than hurting yourself, or hurting God, or hurting the universe. It's war, it's no different than that at all."

When this sense of connection, filled with moral empathy, is brought from the spiritual plane into a culture that glorifies individualism and competition, its forms lose their purity. Women's empathy has been shaped by inequality, by the requirement that they be caretakers for men as well as for children (Miller, 1976), and by the threat of violence. Empathy, which involves the ability to keep one's own feelings in view while also responding to another's feelings, is difficult when one has been taught that attunement to another's feelings requires submission to the other's will (see Benjamin, 1988). In this case, a woman's empathy becomes one-way; that is, it extends to everyone but herself, particularly if she believes that to avoid hurting others she has to put others' needs before her own.

Both Carol Gilligan (1982) and Nel Noddings (1989) consider the imperative to avoid hurt a moral principle to which men and women should adhere: "Real evil—moral evil—occurs when some agent causes such pain or fails to alleviate it when he or she is clearly in a position to do so" (Noddings, 1989, 99). Noddings ties women's moral concern to avoid hurt to their history of caretaking: "Because female experience has been so often and so intimately confined to persons for whom we must care (or for whom we do care), the feeling should arise in us that we *must* relieve pain when it is in our power to do so, and certainly we must not inflict pain unless we have an excellent reason" (ibid.). When such a statement is placed in a social context in which women are required to take care of men as well as children, and which includes a prohibition of "selfishness," we can begin to catch a glimpse of the complexities of women's thoughts about avoiding hurt. Such a context affects their feelings about when and how to alleviate pain, and about whose pain deserves the most attention.

While "real evil" may come from causing pain or failing to alleviate it when one can, pain itself lies on a spectrum from minor disappointments to torture and death. In relationships of inequality, in which empathy means responding to others' needs first, women find it difficult to discriminate between "evil" injury to others and mere disappointment of others' unrealistic expectations.

Thus another problem with the explanation that women's empathic wish to avoid causing hurt makes them less aggressive resides in the ambiguity of language. "Avoiding hurt" does not always mean what it appears to say. To understand the various meanings and maskings carried by women's language of "not hurting," we must understand its links with a culture of violence against women and with women's social roles. Not all avoidance of hurt is based on empathy and connection.

Mediators of Women's Aggression

In conversation, when someone says "I don't want to hurt anybody," people rarely respond "Why not?" The claim not to want to inflict hurt is usually accepted as morally adequate, with no need for further explanation. In fact, "not hurting" can act as a verbal mask obscuring a more complex reality. As a mask, "not hurting" presents a beautiful visage—an empathic concern for others—but it conceals unarticulated feelings such as fear, self-interest, and shame. It protects as it hides: the mask of "I don't want to hurt anyone" configures a woman's appearance to accord with a moral norm that is required of her gender more than of men. From the inside, the mask obscures the wearer's vision of the inequities and myths that work to stop her from taking action in the world.

We cannot just rip away the mask and find the "real" person behind it. No clear divide separates the real self from the false self; in a sense we *are* the self we present to others. Much of women's wish to avoid hurting others is real and authentically moral, but it often hides a complexity that affects women's aggression.

Going behind the language of "I don't want to hurt others" to ask "why not," I found six relational images that mediate women's aggression. In order of the frequency with which they appear in the narratives, they are: a fear of retaliation, empathy, responsibility for children, wanting to be different from past abusers, avoiding negative self-judgment, and a belief in cosmic retribution.[3] These images, which are formed out of past experiences, work to inhibit aggression by bringing to mind its potential consequences for relationships and for oneself.

As I examine these mediators behind the mask, I am not questioning the moral goodness of the wish to avoid hurt, or its crucial importance for society. My purpose here is to look at the complex meanings of this language and its links with social factors. As part of women's caretaking roles, the broad injunction to avoid hurt functions to control much more than destructive aggression. It also works to inhibit women's positive assertiveness, including their action and their voice.

The Iron Rule of Fear

Fear of retaliation, the expectation of being hurt back physically, emotionally, or economically, is the most common reason women offer for curbing their aggression. Arliss (age 27, white, student) puts it this way: "As far as that extreme physical aggression goes, I know that I have that deep inside me and I don't have a fear of releasing that. I have a fear of the consequences that it might entail. I think that's what keeps me in check."

Fear of retaliation was felt by almost all the women I interviewed, including those with the most power. It ranged from concern about retribution in the workplace for a "too harsh" tone of voice to fear of being killed for physical acts of aggression, including those committed in self-defense. That women abused as children or adults would fear physical retaliation for aggressive acts is not surprising—but women from all backgrounds spoke of this fear. And yet it was not voiced until I asked "Why didn't you hurt him/her?" Forty-five of the sixty women explicitly said, as they described specific incidents, that fear of retaliation was their most basic reason for not wanting to hurt others. Twenty-nine of the forty-five had been abused as children or adults.[4]

Fear of retaliation pervasively and subtly suffuses women's descriptions of why and how they stop their aggression. Gaile (age 40, white), a photojournalist who works for a metropolitan newspaper, reveals that a fear of being hurt back has become entwined with a desire to avoid hurting others:

> I say nasty things to people. I will point out weaknesses. I will blame or . . . just verbal assault. In the sense of probably finding a weakness and pointing it out . . . just saying something that's going to hurt somebody. It's more toward men that I have practiced that kind of venomous, assaultive kind of—I've thrown a glass through a window . . . I have thrown things or I have broken something . . . But I haven't ever hit anybody or driven my car into the side of their house or poisoned their cat or anything. Because I am super sensitive to people's feelings, I really am . . . I think it's a self-protective measure. I'm not going to hurt anybody because I don't want anybody to hurt me. It's kind of a "do unto others" kind of thing . . . I think there's a real part of me that just—I toe the line because if you don't you might get in trouble.

Though Gaile does not succeed in avoiding "venomous, assaultive" harm, she stops what she considers unacceptable aggression. Her restraint is guided by the underside of the golden rule: "I'm not going to hurt anybody because I don't want anybody to hurt me." This should be called the "iron rule," given its utilitarian nature and its powerful grasp on women's consciousness.

Constance (age 50, white), a respected politician, also worries about retaliation. Here she talks about whether or not she will campaign negatively:

> Part of me says I don't want to say something about that person even though it might be true. But I think it's more than that. I want to protect myself. I don't want to get hit back. And then I have to tell myself, "You're going to get hit anyway." But there's a part of me that says I don't want to do something to them that's going to make a reaction definitely to come back to me . . . I really don't like to say something bad about somebody. But I think it's more that I don't want it to come back at me . . . but that is sort of related to being the first one to step out aggressively.

Constance is discussing negative campaigning, but if taken out of context, her language portrays avoidance of a violent encounter. Images of retaliation and the need for self-protection spring to her mind when she considers actions that might hurt someone else. For her, as a woman, to be the first to campaign negatively would violate unwritten rules. She can protect herself if she is under attack, but she cannot attack without provocation. She fears the political consequences of being seen as a "bad," self-interested woman, and she also fears what the potential retaliation may prove about her. We hear little concern about the opponent she may target with the negative campaign, and a great deal of concern about the possible consequences she herself may incur.

When we listen to women's fear of retaliation, we should consider it in the context of centuries of violence against them. Women's bodies have been used as spoils of war, as proving grounds for masculinity, as targets of frustration and hatred. Women have learned to create a camouflage of appeasement, stillness, silence: don't draw attention to yourself, don't say much.

These obviously self-protective actions slide into invisibility behind the injunction "don't hurt others," a form of talk that hides the unsettling recognition of their fear of retaliation for overt opposition.

Women's wish to avoid hurting others is based on fear as well as on empathy. This leads to a major dilemma when the requirement for positive self-assertion conflicts with the need for safety. Women stop their forceful actions, not only destructive ones but positive ones as well, out of fear of consequences. Julia (age 39, white, teacher) describes the conflict between self-assertion and self-protection: "It's like a rock with many faces—it's not wanting to be hurt, it's not wanting to offend, it's not wanting to not do justice to my thoughts by not being articulate. It's not wanting to be inappropriate and dismissed. It's like being in a bind where to be true to myself, I need to act and speak, but to protect myself, I'm afraid to do that."

Women's need for safety is real. This need strengthens the moral mandate not to hurt others and helps build firm boundaries beyond which a woman fears to step. This fear feels intensely personal, as if the forces that silence a woman's voice derive from personal anxieties or lack of confidence. In fact, the fear of retaliation operates as a powerful form of social control within women's subjectivity, often hiding behind the language of "don't hurt others." The corollary, "because you may get hurt in return," goes unspoken but is implicit.

The Complexities of Empathy

Twenty-six women talked about inhibiting their aggression with empathy; twenty-one of these had been physically or sexually abused. They described empathy as running in two directions at once: forward through imagining what the victim would feel and backward through identification, through remembering their own experiences of being hurt. One does not actually have to witness another's pain in order to experience forward or anticipatory empathy: it is imaginary, expectant, immanent, and foreseeing. Retrospectively, identification runs through one's own memories of being hurt (or through memories of loved ones, especially one's mother, being hurt emotionally or physically).[5]

A number of abused women echoed what Anna (age 40, white, law student), who was sexually and physically abused as a child, says about why she stops her own aggression: "I think it has a lot to do with what I grew up with, just the level of harm that I saw. The battering situation, my stepfather hurting my mother and the sense that there's something really awful about harming someone."[6] Anna's empathy has been elicited and honed within a context of brutal inequality. This learning has affected her understanding not only of who gives out hurt and who receives it but of what feelings she does not want to cause in others.

Anna knows that words can be a powerful weapon:

> And because the abusive situation included these incredible yelling, screaming, angry, harsh, terrible things being said, I think for me it's like that was at least as difficult as actual physical harm. To be this little kid listening to the most horrible things and taking them so literally . . . So that they were saying the most awful things and that was as hurtful as hitting someone. So [I have] a real strong sense that it's as bad for me to hurt that way as . . . to physically abuse someone. If I go around being abusive with language, it's almost equal to being abusive with force. Because it is a force.

If Anna leans toward hurting someone, she remembers her own childhood; identifying with her potential victim's pain stops her physical and verbal aggression. Though breaking the cycle of abuse requires more than just empathic identification, such empathy provides a necessary base for all other steps (Putallaz et al., 1998).

Angie (age 25, Native American/Latino, unemployed) has rarely been physically aggressive, even though her life has been filled with violence against her.

> I don't like to hurt people. [Why not?] I think it's growing up in an abusive home. Because me and my sister always used to get

spanked with anything my mom could get her hands on. But I
didn't get it as bad. My sister always protected me or she would
jump in front and take the beating and keep me in the corner
. . . I just don't believe in abuse. I told myself—even before I got
pregnant with my kid—that I would never abuse him. Not the
way my mom done us.

The strength of Angie's identification with the pain her children
would feel stops her hands from imitating her mother's. Psychologically, she takes on her sister's role of shielding her children from
abuse, but she is unable to extend such empathic care to herself.
So long treated as an object of others' aggression, she turns her own
hostility against herself as well.

Emotional empathy, based on identification with the pain potential victims would feel, is a strong mediator of aggression in
many abused women's narratives. Empathy appears to offset aggression in any particular instance only when a woman identifies
the prospective pain of the intended victim with her own past suffering. The image (what psychologists call the cognitive schema or
mental representation) of past hurtful interactions (with their re-
membered affect) interrupts hostile action.

When empathy is role based, in contrast, aggression itself
comes to be defined in an overly broad way. Much of what women
call hurt is not a moral issue, but is a gender-role issue that has
become moralized. From the perspective of the traditional female
role, departing from nurturance and submissiveness can be considered as hurtful to someone else. As Lisa (age 43, white, self-defense
instructor) says: "We're taught very often that we shouldn't hurt
other people and that we should be nurturing and kind and we
should do all these things which are contrary to what you need to
do when someone's trying to hurt you." Lyn (age 39, white, student)
reveals this kind of "role-based empathy" that defines stepping
out of a subordinate caretaking role as aggressive. She describes
an incident in which she challenged her husband of seventeen
years:

I just really confronted him in a really angry tone of voice and
very firm, you know, and then got really embarrassed about it

at that point . . . I had always felt that I should respect my husband. And respect from me meant never calling him wrong and never confronting him in front of the girls and never saying anything bad or negative about him, not ever, to anybody else in the world. So I felt like I had really done a terrible, aggressive thing.

In the narratives, both types of empathy are present as mediators of women's aggression: emotional empathy that identifies with the pain of others and role-based empathy that defines hurt as departing from the female role.

For the Children's Sake

A third relational image that stopped women's aggression was envisioning their children being motherless. Twelve of the women I interviewed explicitly mentioned the importance of subduing their aggression to stay alive and/or out of jail so they could raise their children. Gloria, who uses aggression as a wall of protection (see Chapter 2), mediated her aggression by thinking of her child: "See, a year ago, even less than that, I would have beat the daylights out of the person who did this. But due to the fact that I only had my daughter for less than four months in my custody, I wasn't going to jeopardize my freedom to go to jail for some stupid ignorant SOB."

Angie fears losing custody of her son more than violent abuse from her husband:

We made a mistake and we both started drinking together. And he just—I didn't answer him so he started kicking me in my ribs or something. And my son tried to stop him and he just threw my son across the room . . . And it got to the point to where I just—yesterday we were arguing. I was in the kitchen cleaning up and he got me so mad. There was a knife in the dish rack and I was just waiting for him to come around that counter. I was so mad at him. I was getting tired of it. And then I started thinking, "Dang, where would I be, in jail." And it wouldn't do no good for my son.

All the women I interviewed whose lives were disrupted by poverty, violence, and substance abuse mentioned stopping their physical aggression with thoughts of what the consequences would be for their children.

Police officers, whose work puts them at physical risk, are another group who articulate a concern to guard their own safety for the welfare of their children. Karen (age 41, white) speaks of this issue:

> I've been an aggressive police officer my whole career, and I'm not afraid of getting involved . . . My change came when my daughter was born. Before then, well, when I came on the department, I was one of the first women that worked the street . . . My daughter, I've got a 3-year-old, and I'm a single parent on top of that, by choice, but once she came into my life, it's like everything made sense. Priorities changed. I got out of patrol, I wasn't the cowgirl any more, because I really wanted to come home at night.

The image of what would happen to their children without them leads women to curtail their own risk-taking aggressive behavior. Though made explicit only by mothers who live or work in physically risky situations, the relational image of their bereft children may work as a frequent mediator of women's aggression. The biological and emotional imperative to stay alive to nurture their children may help explain women's avoidance of physical aggression.

Being Different from Past Abusers

Some women who have been abused mention, as a deterrent to their aggression, a determination not to be like those who hurt them. Deborah (age 41, white, police officer) says: "I've watched people act out what their parents do. For me it was almost like 'I swear I'm never gonna be that way,' and so, for me, it's mostly keeping it inside and suppressing the aggression that I feel and trying to find alternative ways of dealing with it."

Anna also resolved to differentiate herself from her abusers: "It was real conscious—when I was growing up . . . I wouldn't say the things these people said. That was real conscious. I wouldn't hit people, you know, 'I won't be like you, like what you are is really awful and I will not be awful.' " Many abused women have formed identities based on being different from those who harmed them, and this determination not to be like their abusers works to halt their aggression.

Avoiding Negative Self-Judgment

Women also stop their aggression by imagining how it would make them feel about themselves. "Don't hurt" operates as a standard of moral self-evaluation, and violations of it cause negative self-assessment. Such thinking is evident throughout the interviews, revealed by statements like "If I stoop to hurt someone I lose my self-esteem." Social expectations about gender and goodness also contribute to this standard: women often judge themselves harshly when they disappoint cultural expectations about "feminine" behavior.

Cosmic Retribution

While revenge is personal, retribution on the cosmic scale means that some greater force will keep things in balance. A common theme is presented by Karen: "I believe in karma, I believe in what goes around comes around, and I know he'll get his. 'I know he'll get his because you don't do that kind of stuff' . . . I told myself that." This belief lets a woman's desire to even the score move out of her hands and into a spiritual, interconnected realm where larger powers will take over.

As well, this sense of a connection with a larger moral order keeps women from committing aggressive acts for fear that those acts will come back to them. Carol (age 32, white, biologist) says: "He was just so cruel to me. He definitely brought out the anger in me. And I remember thinking, 'What can I do to him . . . do something to his vehicle . . . hope he dies in an avalanche.' But then I would think to myself, 'No, don't wish that because that's bad karma.'" Many other religious and spiritual beliefs also affect women's inhibitions about harming others, as we will see.

Schemas of Aggressive Interactions

While the six mediators of women's aggression can be listed separately, in a woman's thought they are never found in isolation. Each image, such as a determination to differ from one's abuser(s), is inextricably linked with at least one other. A woman's schema of aggressive interactions is composed of her unique, idiosyncratic combination of these mediators.

Within a woman's schema, I most often found a concern about hurt entwined with at least one of the other mediators. For example, Lynnea (age 32, white, social worker) says she avoids aggressive acts because she does not want to hurt others. When I ask what is wrong with hurting somebody, she replies:

> Well, hurt is a terrible—you know, what we perceive hurt is. It's a sad, heartwrenching emotion. To hurt is an awful feeling and I don't want it imposed on me. So I don't want to impose it on others. To hurt someone is such a negative act. What good can really come by it? I think if you're around someone that hurts you all the time you just come to despise that person, and I don't want anybody despising me in life.

Avoiding hurt is tied with the concern that if you give it out, you will get it back. Empathy is not an isolated cognitive/emotional concept. In thought, it is linked with other critical aspects of the social world.[7]

Women understand their aggression as a dynamic, relational interaction that includes both the initiation of an action and its consequences. They see themselves as instigating aggressive actions with destabilizing, chaotic effects. They picture action and reaction at the same time; yet, much like a person who yells fire in a crowded room, they have little sense of being able to control the outcome. Women's schemas of aggressive interactions usually include this element of chaos, including the fear that she who initiates the aggressive action will suffer most in the resulting chaos. This element of unpredictable negative consequences (chaos), so prevalent in women's narratives, may arise from awareness that a woman's aggression interrupts dominant social expectations and opens the door to retaliation. Central to this feeling of inevitable chaos is women's sense of vulnerability: give it out and you'll be hurt back.

Take Jessie (age 34, white), a single mother on welfare raising two young children. Jessie's schema of aggressive interactions has been affected by the severe battering she experienced in two relationships, and also by her socialization to view her own physical and emotional force as unfamiliar, forbidden territory. Jessie avoids conflict, which she calls aggression, a pattern she learned as a child. Avoiding conflict leads to "not being able to stick up for myself. I'm always apologizing even though it may or may not be my fault. It's like, 'Okay, I'm sorry. That's fine.' When, you know, I shouldn't have said I'm sorry. It wasn't my fault."

I ask Jessie for an example of her inability to stick up for herself:

> I had a problem with a neighbor borrowing my phone all the time, and she made a few little long distance calls and it came up to $10, $15, $20 after a month. And she kept promising she'd give me a couple bucks, couple bucks. Finally, instead of just saying no, I told her when she came to me, I said, "I'm sorry. They turned my phone off. I can't call out. I can only get calls in." I can't just say no. I have to, you know, I make up some type of an excuse to pad it instead of just being "no." And not abrupt about it but just saying, "No, you can't use my phone right now" is like a negative thing. So I like cushion it and pad it. Give it a story behind it.

This need to pad the truth in order to avoid any direct confrontation comes from a number of factors. Not only was Jessie never taught any way of engaging in constructive conflict ("I don't remember any fighting, I don't remember any anger"), she also learned to silence disruptive feelings ("I keep them to myself, I clam up"). As an adult in abusive relationships, she learned that showing any opposition to another's will led to terrible brutality and endangered her life.

But Jessie does not point to these reasons in exploring why she doesn't stick up for herself. Rather, she says she thinks that saying no reveals "me being mean . . . not being able to give somebody what they wanted or needed, not being able to help": "Being a mean person is having to say no, tell somebody no. I feel mean when I have to tell my son no, he can't watch this TV program, he has to go to bed . . . I guess it feels—mentally it feels aggressive to me and so that's why I tried to pad things and make them not so mean or aggressive or negative."

The meanness Jessie perceives in telling someone no is far distant from the "real evil" defined by Noddings. Yet the sense that she is inflicting pain—being "mean or aggressive or negative"—when she says no trips her up each time she wants to assert herself. And she fears such meanness might lead to a situation in which her phone-borrowing neighbor would "be mad at me and retaliate in some way, whether she takes it out on me, whether she . . . takes it out on [my son]. Something that wouldn't be fair. Something that wouldn't be right."

Let us trace the logic of Jessie's schema of aggressive interactions. She wants to be able to "give somebody what they want or need," to attune herself to others' needs rather than to oppose others. Bringing her own force or agency into relationship is what she understands as "mean or aggressive or negative"; goodness and harmony require her to yield, to disappear. She also thinks opposition causes chaos in relationships: she is certain the other will retaliate, but she cannot predict in what way or with what virulence. To avoid such chaos and retaliation, she must submit to others' wills; she has no sense of her personal force to affect relationship. Thus, in Jessie's schema of aggressive interactions, "meanness" is equated with preserving herself (which includes opposing others at times), and is considered certain to trigger retaliatory meanness. Her schema requires her to yield to others, but hides such self-effacing inequality behind a morally tinged language of "meanness."

Jessie judges her actions through others' eyes. Her externalized self-perception guarantees that she will feel powerless until her own eye ("I") claims a perspective on her experience. Further, if Jessie risks self-definition through opposition, she must face her lack of attunement with the other, that is, her separateness, which carries deeper fears of isolation, negation, and death. A woman who has been violently abused, as Jessie has, may be particularly fearful of opposing others. In Jessie's schema of aggressive interactions, she can be safe and good only if she never openly opposes other people.

The schemas that mediate women's aggression center on how to act in relationships to avoid hurt to self and others. Within these schemas, in varying combinations, are the specific relational images, such as fear of retaliation, empathy, and so on. Because the mediators are always mixed with talk about avoiding hurt, determining how they affect women's restraint of their aggression requires further exploration through three extended examples.

Inequality and Avoidance of Hurt

In order to see how the language of "not hurting" masks complex ways women mediate their aggression, let us listen to Deborah (age 41, white). The first woman on the police force of her city, Deborah has been an officer for fourteen years. When she was a child, her parents physically abused her. In one incident, her father hit her, leaving bruises that made it impossible to wear a formal dress to her junior prom. Her first husband, too, was violent and "hit me around." Deborah left him.

I ask Deborah: "What do you mean when you say you try not to hurt other people?" In reply, she first voices a generalized, moral prohibition against hurt, phrasing it in terms of how women feel: "I think that's two issues. Obviously you don't want to hurt somebody, hurt their feelings, hurt their emotional state, and, physically, I think women don't want to hurt other people." Then she goes behind the mask of "obviously you don't want to hurt somebody" to consider what hidden factors inhibit women's aggression: "On the other hand, I know a lot of women probably would act out more aggressively if they didn't think they'd get hurt worse back, until they reach a point where it doesn't really matter any more. They're acting out aggressively because they are so angry it really doesn't matter that they get hurt or get killed." As a police officer, Deborah sees the consequences women face when they dare to throw off restrictions on their anger or aggression. In acting aggressively, a woman not only abandons care for the other; she must cast aside concern for herself because of the probability of retaliation.

In her own close personal relationships, Deborah says, "I never would be physical": "If I got physical, I know I'd get hurt. You know, most of the time the people that you get angry with are people that are bigger than you, and I didn't want to get hurt. I never hit back at my dad." Here Deborah ties the inhibition of her aggression not to concern about others but to her awareness of physical vulnerability.

I ask what she did when she got angry: "I usually held it in. I cry. I'm a good crier I think (laugh). I always have this feeling I need to take care of myself and no one else was going to do it for me and so I was going to have to take care of myself. And I always have the need of taking care of everybody else too, for whatever reason. Usually I go on the back burner and take care of everybody else." Deborah takes care of others while her own needs simmer with slow, unexpressed anger. She learned to do this in her early relationships, when anger was seen as a sign of disobedience. As Elizabeth Spelman has written, "There is a politics of emotion: the systematic denial of anger can be seen as a mechanism of subordination and the existence and expression of anger as an act of insubordination" (1989, 270).

Deborah explores how her background has contributed to her wish not to hurt others. From childhood on, she learned to take care of other people. The power relations that direct her caretaking are present in her narrative but hidden behind the mask of "not hurting": "I think that also, being raised as a caregiver and always taking care of men—I had two sons and a husband and my father— I mean, always taking care, and I'd just have to walk here and there making sure I don't walk on too many egos. And I can't say what I want to say because I don't want to hurt their feelings. So I have to couch it, you know, between this and that."

What is the danger that leads Deborah to wander in a land of "here and there"—to silence herself, her voice caught "between this and that"? She says she avoids speaking because "I don't want to hurt their feelings." But we are left wondering how much of her caretaking is a strategy for self-protection. Women in battering relationships clearly silence themselves in attempts to prevent male violence. But fear of male aggression is a concern of many women, not just those who have been abused. As we learned in Chapter 1, part of gender ideology is a quid pro quo: a belief that a man will restrain his "natural" aggressive, sexual nature in exchange for the woman's love and submissive caretaking. Deborah focuses on avoiding hurt and "taking care" because doing otherwise would break this implicit contract, and thus would leave her open to the threat of reprisal.

Other women I interviewed also feared that if they departed from compliant caretaking their partners would become aggressive. Unlike Deborah, Lyn (age 39, white, student) never worked outside the home until she divorced her husband a year ago. Lyn was abused as a child by her religious mother, who harshly punished her for any infractions of goodness. At age 22 she married a doctor and, from the beginning, silenced any disagreement:

> It was like the first thing he said to me, and it registered in my brain that it was wrong and I should say something but I didn't. He said, "Well, I make the money and you take care of the kids. That's our role because you have the baby." I knew that was wrong and I wanted to say something but I didn't know what to say, you know, and I was already into, "Well, he's the male and he's obviously smarter than I am and I'm worthless." So by the time I figured out something I could say, which I don't think I ever did, it was too late.

Any feeling of anger Lyn has over her husband's domination is undermined by her feeling of being "worthless." Her felt lack of worth originates not only in her mother's emotional and physical abuse but also in a culture that tells her a doctor husband is worth more than she, a mere woman without a college degree.

Like other women who see their own aggression as unfamiliar territory, Lyn experiences a conflict between what she calls aggression and her belief that she should be nurturing. She calls it aggressive and hurtful to put her thoughts "out in front of people." As she explores why she thinks this way, Lyn takes us behind the verbal mask of "not hurting" to reasons based on power rather than on moral concern:

> I always assume it is hurtful because I'm saying it . . . if I say something, if there is more than me in the room, they have another opinion and their opinion is better than mine. Therefore if I say something, they're going to disagree with it. So it's going to be hurtful because they want to do what they want to do. And since I'm supposed to be nurturing, I'm going to hurt them if I say something that's my own opinion. It is hurtful because the other person doesn't get their way. And disagreeing sets up fights, which are not ladylike, which means people won't like you anymore.

The logic of Lyn's thinking is clear: any relational position other than "nurturing"—submissive attunement to others' needs—is hurtful. Opposition, with the outcome that "the other person doesn't get their way," is cast as a moral issue of hurt. Further, veering from "ladylike" behavior leads to isolation: "people won't like you." Since Lyn's schema of aggressive interactions includes no notion of how to engage in healthy conflict, and since she both fears and disavows the hurt that she thinks attends conflict, she submissively disappeared throughout her marriage. She feels so little entitlement to relational space that she shrinks to invisibility by self-silencing. She explains her disappearance in the "moral" language of hurt: "I'm going to hurt them if I say something that's my own opinion."

Lyn says: "It is not nearly as hard for me to talk to women . . . and say what I need to say. It is harder with males."

I don't know what their reaction is going to be to what I say because I am not used to saying things that haven't already taken into account what they need. I always say it in a way that will not hurt them, you know. I have not done that very much, so part of it may be fear of how it is going to affect them. They might literally be destroyed in some ways spiritually or they might go off and commit suicide.

At the time of the interviews, divorced for a year and back in school, Lyn is beginning to question her deference to men: "I still feel fifty percent that men are more knowledgeable and authoritative and all that stuff, but I thought ninety percent before." I ask: "Why would it be harder to hurt someone who is stronger and more—?"

More authoritative and worth more is probably what I would have said. More than—because the other side of [my husband] always degrading me was his terrible sense of inferiority and me having to build him up. So my best ploy if he was humiliating me was to try to say really nice things about him to stop him from humiliating me. So there is a real convoluted sense of need to take care of, but they're worth more.

Lyn's compliance reinforces her own sense of worthlessness as she sees herself submissively accepting humiliation. What kind of fear restrains her from breaking out of this prison of degradation, one that her own silence about issues critical to her life has helped to create?

I ask, "So if you hurt them, what?" As Lyn goes behind her own statement of not wanting to hurt, she finds that the threat of violence directs her caretaking:

One just flashed into my mind: they will hurt me. If you don't do the right thing, if you don't clean right, if you don't raise the kids right—then I get smacked. I mean, the comments start coming about how irresponsible, how—I don't even remember all the words. It's not that I have to protect them, it's that I have to treat them very well or they'll hurt me. That is a part of it. It

has something else to do with, you do not hurt because it is not
right to hurt the person you are supposed to be serving.

Until this moment, Lyn had not tied her wish to avoid hurting
others to her fear of emotional and physical retaliation. Here again,
behind the mask of a moral concern not to cause hurt, we find the
quid pro quo of gender ideology based on inequality: a woman's
compliant nurturing staves off a man's "naturally" aggressive nature. For many women, inequality and fear of violence are core
elements in the relational images that mediate their aggression.

Returning to Deborah, the police officer, consider further how
the language of not hurting masks other mediators of her aggression. Deborah talked about trying to change her work schedule one
summer in order to complete college. Even though she had seen
the police force "bend over backwards to allow a lot of officers get
their masters degrees and finish their B.A.s and not even blink an
eye," her supervisor would not give her an answer.[8]

> The second time when I went back in to say, "Well, now, what's
> going on here, I need to register," I was told, "Well, this might
> really impact how you do your job." And I said, "No, Jim," and
> I told him, "There's this officer down there in patrol that you
> have bent over backwards, you have taken his school schedule
> and worked his patrol schedule around it, and I've never asked
> you to do that, the whole time I've been going to college I've
> been going on my own time, and I find out what my work sched-
> ule is and I plan my classes around it. I'm asking you for this
> six-week period of time to be flexible so I can graduate." And
> he was upset that I challenged him on that. *[How do you know he
> was upset?]* Because his jaw locked and he said he'd let me know
> later, he'd think about it.

Analyzing why this incident bothered her, Deborah resorts to
the language of hurt—yet behind it we hear her concern that her
supervisor may retaliate:

> When you make somebody feel uncomfortable, I don't like to
> do that, that would hurt somebody's feelings, that I challenged

or just put him in an awkward position, you know, so I try not to do that. *[Why don't you like to do that?]* Because I won't get what I want (laughs). Simple. You get more with honey than— what is that saying? And it's because it's the way I was brought up. Be a good girl and try not to hurt people's feelings, and I never really questioned it. It's just I know that if I'm nice to people and respectful of their feelings and do my homework, then I usually can end up getting the end result that I went in there to get, without having to play games.

Deborah denies playing games, but her "good girl" behavior is precisely that—a strategy to get what she wants from someone who holds power. Her language of hurt presents a surface appearance of traditional "good" femininity while it obscures a number of critical issues.

First, the strategies she adopts are shaped by stereotypes of gender and realities of power. Within the hierarchy of the police force, in an office where she is the only woman with rank, Deborah cannot afford to challenge authority directly. Placing the practical issue of achieving her goals into a language of hurt obscures the power realities of the situation; it casts hierarchical/power issues as personal issues. Her language makes it appear as if *she* is the one who causes the problem: "When you make somebody feel uncomfortable, I don't like to do that, that would hurt somebody's feelings." She makes herself accommodate to existing power structures by labeling her actions in moral, interpersonal terms—as hurtful.

Second, the language of hurt casts the issue of challenging power into a question of feminine character. Challenging the status quo goes against the injunction to "be a good girl and try not to hurt people's feelings," the essence of "nice" femininity. "You get more with honey" expresses the social reality that women whose superiors are male usually are rewarded more for niceness than for self-assertion and are punished for overtly confronting injustice and unfairness. The language of hurt coerces the self, which wants to be good and remain safe, into avoiding actions that might be seen as insubordinate.

Speaking more about her strategies, Deborah returns to the language of hurt and, this time, reinterprets its meaning:

I have a lot of ideas that I think would help make this organization flow, but I'm not in a position to bring them forth to, let's say directly to the chief. I do it right by the book and I go to my supervisor. I would probably hurt other people's feelings if I took my ideas straight to the chief. *[How would you hurt them by doing that?]* Well, because I would sidestep them and misuse protocol. We were all at a "supervision for women in law enforcement" conference and I heard the highest-ranking person talk about how she didn't go into the bathroom and urinate with these other assistant chiefs and so she was left out of a loop of an area that—you know, the decision was made in the bathroom, okay, so that's a source of frustration for me. I know that if I start stepping out of those fuzzy boundaries and stirring the bucket and causing the waves—maybe it's not hurting people's feelings, it's more of a challenge to their authority.

Though the boundaries delineating power are getting "fuzzy," they are still intact. When women step outside these boundaries and into unfamiliar territory to challenge male authority, they upset the clichés: they "stir the bucket and cause the waves."

Deborah is considering initiating a sexual harassment suit on behalf of herself and other women in the police force. In discussing it, she again masks power issues by the language of hurt:

I am not a malicious person, I try really hard not to hurt anybody, but obviously when you have to make a choice and the choice is like to bring this complaint forward or not, somebody's going to get hurt. *[When you say "get hurt," what do you mean?]* Well, they're going to have their own personal career challenged, they've got to deal with what's going on in their home life when they go home and tell their wives that they're being investigated, and they're going to lose time off, which is going to impact their livelihood, their reputations, whether they're going to get promoted even any further, or going to be held as a credible person . . . *[So for that specific situation, how would you hurt them?]* Oh, just hurt their feelings, I suppose, because I wasn't very respectful, which is silly in a way, because I know if a guy walked into the commander's office and said, you know, "This is what I want da-da-da-da," they'd kind of have that guy thing. But if I walked in and went, you know, I'd be challenging him and his ego, and it's not an appropriate way for me to get what I need to get probably.

As she casts bringing a sexual harassment suit into the language of hurt, Deborah steers away from consideration of violations of her own rights to empathic concern about the hurt her actions would cause to others. She worries that bringing the suit would prove her to be a "malicious person" and could bring retaliation. Finally, challenging male authority—not being "very respectful"—would hurt commanding officers' feelings and would not be "appropriate." While empathy is clearly an aspect of her wish to avoid hurt, it is deeply entangled with other issues and other mediators of her behavior.

Deborah's use of the language of hurt reveals it as a powerful form of social control over women's consciousness. Talk about avoiding hurt is also a narrative about power and its exercise. Such talk functions rhetorically to control aggression as a woman attempts to persuade herself and others of her intent to avoid harm. The wish to avoid hurt draws both from the highest human ideals and from women's history of subordination. Often it works to contain women within boundaries that are drawn as much by power and gender as by genuine moral concern; it stops not only women's harmful acts but also their positive aggression, which is necessary for self-development, action, voice, will—for their freedom. It can give women a "moral" understanding of why they should not act on the world and can confine them within a safe space of pseudo-goodness. Through the language of "not hurting," fear masquerades as a moral concern while differences in power and avoidance of retaliation remain hidden.[9]

Fears of disapproval and reprisal that hide behind the verbal mask are not focused only on men's responses; they extend to women as well. In fact, women police one another around behaviors that might be perceived as hurtful. For example, Mary (age 43, white), a psychotherapist who works in a large agency, describes a staff meeting at which she voiced her opinions about how a room would be decorated and who would get to use the room for group meetings: "I felt I was very aggressive in claiming that territory for mine, but I also was monitoring the other people, and there's another woman there that I just perceived was kind of feeling stepped on." Asked why she doesn't want to be perceived as one who will step on others, Mary says:

> I feel like, these people don't like me especially, because I tend to be pushy and aggressive, I'm told I'm pushy and aggressive by other women. And so I try and think to myself, "Well, that's not a good thing to be." I mean I also realize that women often view other women who are assertive and aggressive as *bad*. And so my imagination or reality said that if I get on her bad side then what's going to happen is that it's going to come back to me . . . she could go to another person and say, "Oh, that Mary is a pushy and aggressive bitch, blah blah, and we don't like her," and I'll get blackballed. That was my fear.

Worried that other women will judge her behavior as aggressive and will retaliate by giving her a bad reputation, Mary closely monitors her actions. She continues to push for space but tries to stay within limits acceptable to other women. Her schema of aggressive interactions reveals that she sees action and reaction at the same moment, and that she fears her aggressive actions easily lead to social ostracism and punishment. Constance (age 50, white) also monitors her aggressive behavior, trying to weed out any that might be perceived as hurtful and lead to a negative reputation. Constance is a legislator in a western state that elects only a handful of women. By aggressive women, Constance says, she means women with a "sharp tongue": "a tone of voice that may be short, a quick answer on something—a tone of voice." I ask her what a sharp tongue does.

> I think it irritates. I think it puts up the fences and a wariness that this may not be friendly territory. But watch what you say . . . because someone may come back at you. What I see is that you don't get anywhere if nobody agrees with you. And if you

make everybody angry, nobody agrees with you. And in the closeness that we work in the legislature, you get reputations very quickly about what type of person you are.

In a sense, the legislature is like the small communities in which people lived their lives for centuries. Everyone knew each other's business; speaking out was dangerous, especially for those low on the power hierarchy. Veering from clear rules for acceptable behavior resulted in punishment. One penalty for women in seventeenth- and eighteenth-century Europe was the "scold's bridle," a metal cage that frames the head, featuring a spiked iron bit that pushes into the mouth and penetrates the tongue and two spikes that pierce the cheeks (Walker, 1983). It was used to control the tongues of women who cursed a man, gossiped, or spoke in ways people did not want to hear. A sharp-tongued woman risked retaliation for departing from approved female behavior. Constance's watchfulness over a sharp tongue that, she says, irritates, puts up fences, and creates a wariness, carries this social history.

As we have seen, hidden social aspects affect a woman's perception of when her own behavior is hurtful and therefore aggressive. Many women socialized to be nice label as hurtful any action that opposes another person, any action that is not nurturing, or anything that challenges male authority. Also, others often mislabel a woman as aggressive when she departs from submissive, quiet behavior.

Talk about avoidance of hurt is powerful because it has one foot in a genuine moral concern, strengthening its credibility, and another foot in women's subordinate role. It stands within a sense of interconnection, where the experience of continuity with others prevents destructive acts toward them; it stands also within a culture of inequality and violence against women. Sometimes a woman's actions are hurtful and should be stopped; sometimes the judgment that an action is hurtful is based on the shoulds of women's roles and needs to be overthrown. Distinguishing authentic from role-based concerns would not matter except that so many women stop themselves from acting with positive assertion out of fear of perceiving themselves, or being perceived, as aggressive.

Calculating Hurt

Women also mediate their aggression through calculating the costs of hurting someone to determine if doing so would be worth it. Comments like "it's not worth it" and "it cost me" indicate a weighing of costs and benefits. This pragmatic approach to deciding whether or not to commit aggressive acts appears explicitly in twenty women's narratives; it reveals how the factors that mediate aggression (the costs) are weighed against what one woman calls the "momentary satisfaction of getting back at someone who has hurt me."

In these pragmatics of hurt, we see how social elements affect estimates of costs. Let us listen to Jean (age 46, white, potter), the mother of a 16-year-old daughter, who left an abusive marriage and is now in a committed relationship with another woman. She clearly believes that aggressive behavior always carries a cost, a lesson she first learned, as do many girls, through fear of her physical vulnerability:

> Situations would arise where my 9-year-old instinct would be, "I'm going to zip in there and punch him in the face." I don't remember being counseled against doing that. I remember being asked to think about what that would lead to . . . think about well, let's see—A leads to B leads to C. Probably the end result was, usually since I was kind of smaller than a lot of people, I'm going to get myself pounded . . . So it's sort of like you can do aggression if you want to but there's always going to be a cost.

Jean talks about the price she anticipates for acting in an aggressive way as an adult:

> Well, let me tell you a dream and maybe you can understand what it costs. In my dream, I'm realizing that something is wrong with my mouth . . . there are these sort of bony structures growing out of my jaw and it's beginning to wear on my lips and it's getting kind of sore. But I'm still able to eat and really nobody else has noticed. And then . . . this thing just gets completely out of hand. Just totally appalling. It feels very bad and it's also

just completely repulsive to look at . . . But all the time, I have this sense of "I will be able to cope with this." And so I'm trying to hold in whatever it is I'm trying to hold in. But all the time, the people around me have seemed to have no awareness this is happening.

She gives her interpretation of this dream: "My feeling about aggressing on somebody, which I would probably do verbally rather than attacking them physically, is that I would be so appalling that I won't be able to function in the real world. When in reality, the only person who's even realizing that there's something appalling going on is me."

Dreams come to us to re-create the world from the inside out, relying on metaphor to represent inner experience. In Jean's dream she becomes monstrous, not in others' eyes since they cannot see her self-alteration, but in her own experience of self. The venomous tongue that she must bite carries such toxins that it disfigures her mouth and jaw. Why must she hold these feelings in rather than share them with others? How can they alter her self-experience? I ask Jean to tell me more about what she perceives as the costs of taking action:

I divorced my husband of nineteen years in '92. And it was because of feeling that I just had tried long enough to find ways to communicate many different things with him that he simply couldn't hear. I gave up . . . He has been aggressive verbally for a very long time and physically for a pretty short time against me. And I would like to return that in a way. But I think . . . that it will cost me more to do that than it costs him to receive it.

Without models for how to use her anger positively, Jean follows the traditional female script—she must simply hold it in, with deforming consequences to her experience of self. When anger escapes, such a woman can feel she "lost it" (that is, lost self control). She denies the legitimacy of her feelings and redoubles efforts to contain and silence her anger.

The perceived costs that restrain Jean from hurting her exhusband include the fear that she would become just like him:

> I would like to hurt him now. I would like to bring him to the point of really physical fear. And I would like also—I would like to do that in front of, say, his father. So he would experience not only physical fear but the humiliation of being brought to that point by another person who is supposed to be supportive, loving, whatever. Yes, I would. If I thought it would get me anywhere. And also—now this is a thing that I do in my head all the time is to kind of pull down the lever that pulls up the sales tag—what's that going to cost? It's going to feel real damned good initially but what will it cost? I suspect that it would cost me a lot more than I want to pay . . . I'm thinking in terms of what would it cost me mentally to do that. What would I think of myself after I had done that? I think that I would think that I had joined ranks with him. That I had really become Michael or a part of Michael or like Michael . . . And I just don't want to be like that.

Jean's anger is clear. But as she calculates the costs of acting on it, she emphasizes her unwillingness to do anything that would make her identify with a man whose tactics she despises.

Trying to learn more about how Jean inhibits aggression, I ask, "What's wrong with hurting somebody else if they hurt you?"

> I think initially it would be so satisfying. I think of daughters who've been raped by their fathers or young women who've been beat up by their boyfriends just for the fun of it . . . Just visiting pain and suffering on that person would be so satisfying. But . . . that is very, very short lived and then you must live with your actions. And if you have joined the . . . forces of evil then you've joined the forces of evil, at least for that moment you did. [And evil is what?] Well, it's real, real complicated. But one thing evil might be is visiting hurt and pain on somebody when you really didn't have to. When you really knew there would be no gain. When it was simply for kind of a momentary high from the revenge. But you really know that if you put that action into the cosmic river you're just adding to the violence that's already out there. There's plenty of it.

Echoing Nel Noddings (1989), Jean considers unnecessarily hurting someone to be a moral evil. She stops herself from acting on her strong desire to hurt her ex-husband not out of empathy with the hurt he will feel, but out of dread of becoming like him. She also recognizes that her revenge will reverberate beyond her and Michael to add to the violence that pollutes the "cosmic river" in which we all swim. These three elements factor into her calculation of the costs of hurt.

When Jean talks of "the forces of evil," she invokes powerful imagery of a dualistic battle between good and evil, imagery that has supported countless wars and political and social movements. This apocalyptic imagery unconsciously shapes the way people— whether or not they are religious—experience their own anger and aggression (Pagels, 1993). Jean here applies it to her own internal conflict. The forces of evil, *wanting revenge* ("visiting hurt and pain on somebody for . . . a momentary high from the revenge"), battle the forces of good, *avoiding hurt*. The price of taking aggressive action is too costly for Jean's sense of self and for the larger, interconnected whole that her actions affect.

Overt aggression by a woman is also a cultural transgression— threatening not only to the social structure but also to the mythology that separates women into demons and angels. If an angel suddenly turns into a demon, punishment can assume apocalyptic proportions.

I ask Jean if hurting someone else would ever be justified. In reply she talks, not about what context would justify hurting someone, but about an insight she gained when she left town for a while "so that I would not have to interact with Michael at all if I did not choose to." Her insight was about a kind of hurt that alters relationship—a way of hurting that does not fall into the familiar categories of perpetrator and victim:

I think there are many, many ways to hurt somebody . . . I realized that the most hurtful thing I can do to Michael . . . is to simply say, "For me, you don't exist." And I'm not able to accomplish that quite yet with Michael because we have a child in common. But the day will come when I am able to say, "For me, you don't exist." And I think that will be much more hurtful to him than me punching him in the face or kneecapping him or having somebody who's really big go over to punch his lights out. But where I want to be . . . is, on that day, I want to not care what his reaction is.

Learning that distance from her ex-husband gives her some control, Jean begins to decide how to channel her feelings of hate, revenge, and anger. She does not plan to transform her feelings of hate and anger with love (a way endorsed by religion and particularly prescribed for angry women). Nor does she plan to inflict hurt by verbal, economic, or physical means. Instead, she plans to do "the most hurtful thing I can do": to kill the relationship. She will completely disconnect from her ex-husband, condemn him to a kind of death by exclusion. This act of purposeful withdrawal, while self-protective, feels so harmful because it ends a relationship that has been central to her life.

This way of inflicting hurt reveals Jean's schema of aggressive interactions: increasing the distance and isolation increases the level of harm. To retaliate with aggressive words keeps connection; *to disengage completely is the worst kind of aggression.*

If disengagement is the worst kind of aggression, why is it acceptable while other forms are not? Jean explains:

> I suppose because it's sort of Gandhi. Passive. Stepping aside from the hurtling object rather than trying to absorb it—simply step aside and let the person hurtle over the cliff themselves. And in that way I can kind of go, "Well, I guess you went over the cliff. Gee, how satisfying for me. But I was not the one who pushed you." I can step away and say, "You know, I maybe could see it coming. I maybe even told you about it. But I'm not responsible for you going over the cliff." If I stand there and help push, then I have a part in having helped the guy go over the cliff.

Though Jean invokes Gandhi, her form of passive nonviolence does not sound like his teachings, which advocated a willingness to absorb violence while actively working against it. In this scenario, she will leave her ex-husband to himself, to let his own emotions and actions carry him off the cliff—without absorbing any of them herself. This passive retaliation requires her not to care what his reaction is when he realizes that, for her, he does not exist. The scene she sketches evokes fairy tales and epics of the gods: she stands aside while the vengeful demon, blinded by his own fury, hurtles off the precipice.

Jean's fear, expressed earlier, that she might become like Michael raises the question of how one becomes—or avoids becoming—what one opposes. Hate, hostility, destructive thoughts, fantasies of retaliation—these are "brink" emotions; they bring one to a place where things easily slide into their opposites. In this territory, it is easy to become what we oppose without being aware of the transformation. Focusing on how one is *not* like the instigator makes it easy to lose sight of other, more subtle ways it is possible to cause harm. Brink emotions carry a grave danger of self-deception, of becoming like the hated one who abuses or hurts others. How does a woman who is determined not to be like those who hurt her become an aggressor? Alternatively, how does a person who has been the victim of hurt avoid hurting others in turn?

Wondering about such questions, I ask Jean about her relationship with her current partner, Lacey. Changing from a male to a female lover would seem to present many possibilities for escaping old patterns, particularly of dominance and submission. With Lacey, Jean says, she feels as if she has become Michael at times. In their marriage Michael repeated a pattern from his own childhood, in which "Dad is going to talk so we all get real quiet and we listen. And whatever he says is kind of law and you certainly don't argue." If Jean attempted to turn his monologue into a dialogue, he would get "very angry" and say, "Don't interrupt me!" Jean was never "very able to change that kind of exchange"; instead, she became "a little better at not interrupting." This pattern followed the well-known conversational rules that reflect male dominance (Tannen, 1991).

This pattern in her marriage, Jean says, made her "more irritated at being interrupted too than I used to be." She sketches an interaction with Lacey that alarmed her:

Lacey asked me a question, I began to answer it, and then she interrupted and said something—as I recall was kind of off the subject of getting the answer that she had requested in the first place. And so I attempted again, she interrupted. I attempted a third time, she interrupted. And I just said, "I *want* to finish the answer!" (hitting fist to hand). And again, I think many times . . . I think my face looks very angry. I think my voice is very tense. I think probably the lines around my mouth are real unhappy looking. And she was very, very surprised. It just shut her down. I mean, no interaction for several minutes. So at first I was feeling like good, at least you're being quiet now. And then I kind of realized . . . that she had lost interest in what the answer was. She was busy trying to keep herself together. So I went away for a few minutes and then I came back and said something like, "I hurt your feelings, didn't I?" And she really was crushed . . . She didn't know she was doing anything irritating. I apologized and then said, "I really could probably think of a more pleasant way to ask you to just let me finish the answer." So, you know, I'm trying to relearn patterns. It's not the easiest thing I've ever done.

While Jean's actions may not seem earthshaking (hitting fist to hand, demanding to be heard), they lead to her partner's withdrawal from interaction. The connection between them, for the moment, breaks. To Jean this incident brings a startling new awareness: she has the capacity to act like her husband; she too wants to control and dominate.

In male-female relationships, issues of dominance most often are dictated by gender. But in intimate relationships between two women, the partners have to work out dominance together, and they may find themselves sliding into ways of behaving that they associate with maleness. Jean has discovered in herself a capacity to engage in what she identifies as male aggressive behavior:

I think I feel like I am—oh, I don't know, what's two steps away from monstrous? But really, I feel like I have danced around into Michael's position. Like we're all in this huge circle and there's a multitude of roles to play and we're all constantly turning and Michael's here—and Michael and I are always opposed—but as we go around the circle, at some point I'm going to end up where he was. And I think I'm constantly kind of fearful of that. That one of the reasons I was with Michael is because I'm like Michael, which is not a real pleasant thought. I don't want to be like that. So I think when I do stuff like that, there's sort of a physical feeling of queasy, or tension in the stomach. And kind of like when somebody shines a flashlight on some little piece of mirror that is connected to you.

Jean finds that she has danced into her former husband's role and position in the circle of possible selves. The aspect of herself she sees reflected in the mirror of Lacey's eyes is the dominating potential she was able to project onto her husband during her marriage. As her behavior mimics Michael's, she sees that the good woman and the woman who is "two steps away from monstrous" have the same face. Both attitudes, if they become one-sided, are destructive. For Jean to recognize as her own a quality detested in her ex-husband requires great courage. But if she had continued to disavow the quality, it would have manifested itself in disguised ways.

Many women, longing to be loving and good, have turned the mirror to the wall so they never see their own dominating actions. Living with men who embody aggressiveness, not wanting to be like those who cause hurt, they split off their destructiveness and project it onto masculinity. This appears harder to do when in relationship with another woman. Viewing aggression in the context of women loving each other brings the issue of a woman's own dominance and aggression into stark relief.

Such reflection as Jean engages in is dangerous. Looking at oneself realistically may mean risking death: "The death may be actual: people take their own lives out of desperation from what they see. Or it may be symbolic (no less real): it may be the death of the image of yourself in the world, a dying to what you have been" (Hall, 1980, 221). Jean dies to the image of what she has been throughout her life, the "good" woman who "took it" from a man and so remained innocent and unaggressive herself. In her new relationship she must take responsibility for her own anger, dominance, and controlling tendencies.

Jean has moved from denial to consciousness and choice regarding her own aggression. As she changes partners, she changes her images of her relational force. From feeling as if she has no personal force (so that her way of dealing with her husband's emotional abuse is to become "a little better at not interrupting"), she progresses to recognizing her own potential to use her force in ways she detests. This awareness leads to thinking about positive ways to use her force: about how to bring her will into relationship without dominating her partner.

Love Doesn't Have to Hurt

Clearly, women from all backgrounds get angry, want to retaliate, feel like hurting others. It is not hard to understand how women who grew up with loving relationships can stop their aggression, but what about women who have been brutally abused? What schema of aggressive interactions does a woman form when she has been a target of sexual and physical aggression throughout her life? Having learned to bond with others in traumatic, violent ways, how does she change her pattern of connecting to others through aggression?

I met Latisha (age 32, African American, unemployed) through a group for lesbian battered women. She was married for seven years to a man who often beat her. Since her divorce she has been involved in a series of violent relationships with women. Two of her children, ages 9 and 7, live with her. The oldest, age 12, is in foster care because of her neglect of him through drug and alcohol use.

Latisha had one of the most violent childhoods of the women I interviewed. Born an identical twin, she was the second-youngest of eleven children. She received little nurturing from her mother, whom she describes as either ignoring the children or "always gone." Her father often beat his wife and daughters. Even after her mother remarried, Latisha's father came over regularly and "disciplined" the girls:

> My dad used to always tell us girls, "If you get pregnant before you finish school, I will stomp that baby out you." And like I say, when he make threats, it's not, "Well, I'm saying this to

scare you." When he said he was going to do something . . . I was real scared of my dad. I remember my twin sister called when she was running away and he went and got her, drug her out the house where she was at, and brought her home, and he beat her and beat her. I don't know how he did it, but when he finished, it's like, his initial, "F," was in her thigh, and then, "Well, I should go into my truck, and get my gun and shoot you." And that's when, from then, I thought . . . I have to make sure I do nothing . . . And he wasn't even living with us, like I said. My mom called him. And I felt like, she can't protect us . . . she let him come in here and do this to us.

Latisha found no protection from the adults she depended on; they were the very ones who threatened her existence. Society also failed her: through the racism that daily affected her family and her life, through economic structures that kept her locked in poverty, and through social mirrors such as schools, welfare, and social services that reflected her as undeserving and underclass. Abused from birth, Latisha learned that connections with others occur through channels of anger, aggression, and hurt.

Though Latisha's father and older brothers abused her, she could not fight back. She learned, instead, to turn her anger against herself: "If I do anything to anybody, it's gonna be me. You know. I'm so used to cutting on myself or either punching the wall. Because I turn it all in on me." Self-cutting can be understood as a physical and psychological reenactment of trauma-based relationships with the abuser (Miller, 1996). If children learn from parents that injury, love, and care are associated, then attempts to self-soothe, to reduce unbearable feelings, can occur through self-injury (Suyemoto, 1998). Self-mutilation also creates a way to convey and control anger, anxiety, or psychic pain that cannot be verbally expressed to others; it is used to decrease dissociation and post-traumatic symptoms. Further, childhood sexual abuse is associated with self-mutilation of the kind Latisha describes (Briere and Gil, 1998). Most of all, Latisha's self-cutting is her way to communicate the unspeakable. As Judith Herman (1992, 1) explains, the "ordinary response to atrocities is to banish them from consciousness. Certain violations of the social contract are too terrible to utter aloud: this is the meaning of the word unspeakable." In place of uttering words, Latisha carves her pain on her body.

Toward men Latisha was not aggressive, but toward other women she used knives, fists, kicks, and whatever was at hand: "I fought a lot, in junior high, and high school. Fist fight. Other girls. I hate to fight more on guys than girls. I was more of a tomboy then . . . I used to look for fights, really . . . it's like I was waiting for something. I'm not gonna go approach them, but I'm waiting for somebody . . . to come approach me. It's like I'm on guard." Though Latisha does not specify why she "hates to fight more on guys than girls," she follows a pattern that is common around the world: women attack other women far more often than they attack men. Further, her avoidance of men as targets probably stems from her expectation that men will retaliate with escalating violence. Not only in our society, but worldwide, women get the worst of it in male-female fights; those who initiate fights with men often end up severely beaten (Burbank, 1987).

We might wonder if a close relationship with her twin offered Latisha an oasis of connection in her family. She says no:

> Me and my twin sister, we used to fight. I mean, fight-fight . . . I have a scar somewhere (points next to her eye), where she put a nail in, where I had to go to the hospital, cause this nail went through. And then one other time, she knocked me out. And I remember sending her to the hospital one time. So, I guess I do have aggress—but it wasn't intentionally. It's like, I got tired of her beating up on me, and one day, I just grabbed a bottle and I broke it. "If you come near me, I'm going to cut you" . . . But it wasn't that I . . . I wasn't going really—just like, "Leave me alone." You know, that maybe she would leave me alone if I was to—you know, and she, I guess, she thought I was going to throw it away or whatever, and she come charging at me, but she ran into it. That's the kind of fighting, I guess that's what I was used to, you know. And us being brothers and sisters, that's how we used to fight . . . but the way we did, you wouldn't think we was related, it was out for blood when we fought each other.

Latisha describes a kind of fierce fighting with her siblings that is characteristic in families where children are physically abused

(Leavitt et al., 1998; McCloskey, Figueredo, and Koss, 1995). Their fights seemed unrestrained by any bonds of family or loyalty, so she never felt safe. The furor of arguments even makes it difficult for Latisha to assign blame, yet she never fully excuses herself. Clearly, her schema of aggressive interactions includes an image that violence is part of intimate relationships and that love hurts.

Latisha got pregnant at 14 and ran away from home, fearing her father would kill her. She moved across the country to live with her grandmother. At 15 she gave up her first child for adoption, then took to the streets, drugs and alcohol, and prostitution—a pattern often followed by survivors of sexual and physical abuse.[10] During that time she attempted suicide twice, feeling she had no reason to live, no connections with anyone in the world. The birth of her second child, when she was 20, "slowed [her] down" and gave her a reason for wanting to stay out of prison. She married, had two more children, but was regularly beaten by her husband. She was also heavily involved in substance abuse. At the time of our interviews, she was in recovery and was beginning to feel less isolated.

Latisha ties the change in her behavior to two events: the birth of her son when she was 20, and her desire to kill her abusive husband, which led her to a new understanding of the link between love and hurt: "I'd start to worry, sometime we be arguing, and I would look at something, and the back of my mind, have the thought, pick it up and hit him. But I would never do it. And then it gets to the point where I had started sleeping with a knife under the mattress on my side. Because in my mind, it was like, he had one more time to lay a hand on me . . . he was dead." During the last beating, she says:

> I broke loose from him and I picked this bar up and I got to swinging and it's not like I swung it one time, it's like I just kept swi—I couldn't stop until . . . all that anger was out. It scared me. I could have killed him or really hurt him, you know. And it really scared me. *[Did you make any kind of decisions, or come to any ideas about what you would do?]* Well, I told him that was it. Told him he didn't have to leave, I was leaving. I said, "This marriage is not worth it if it, if it comes to that." Because in my

head, I got to the point—I had never fought him back during the whole abuse. So I, it have to stop, and I start thinking the only way is to, was to kill him. And I go, "That's not the only way." So I, actually, I check myself in the psych, on a psych unit after it happened. Because I, I was scared. It's like I wasn't myself. I guess it was really more for safety reason.

In this critical incident, Latisha saw herself as ready to kill, and was frightened for herself and for her husband. Though she had fought many times before, this episode differed in its intensity and in the destructive force she used. As she stepped outside the lines that defined her acceptable limits and felt completely out of control, she experienced a loss of identity severe enough that she went to an emergency room and asked for hospitalization. She was "scared . . . I wasn't myself."

Latisha talks about why her physical attack on her husband was a critical turning point: "I don't believe in hurting nobody. That's really, that's what it is. I guess because I know how it feel to be hurt, and I wouldn't want to inflict it upon nobody else. That's really what it is. I just don't want the next person to really feel what I went through. In my mind, it's always, I would never turn out to be a abuser." At this pivotal moment, Latisha's picture of herself suddenly shifts: the images projected on her internal mental/emotional screen match those of her brutal attackers. Fearing she is capable of inflicting the same kind of hurt that she herself has suffered, she places herself in a safe setting so she can do no harm.

Latisha learned from her family that love is linked with hurt: "I can never remember once her [mother] saying 'I love you' . . . Or either, my dad. Well, actually, no, I take that wrong. I remember when my dad used to whup us. He said, 'Only reason I'm doing this is because I love you.' "

Such expressions of love have to be put into social context. In the family in which Latisha was raised, loving was mixed with attempts to survive, with being spread too thin by poverty and by dehumanizing treatment from the dominant society (Fordham, 1996). Latisha's parents were abused by their parents; in a well-known pattern that characterizes family violence, cycles continue from generation to generation (Putallaz et al., 1998). Rage over violations by family and society sits close to the surface, needing little provocation to erupt into violence. It often takes family members as its targets.

Familiar with this kind of hurtful love, Latisha initially accepted it in her marriage. Victimization and inequality were central components of her image of intimate relationships, just as they were central to her schema of aggressive interactions: "I used to always think when my husband used to beat me up, he loved me. And then, I guess I started, I got to the point where I thought, 'Love don't have to hurt.' So, it's like, you can really love somebody, without hurting them. You know, so that I can really love my kids without hurting them physically, or emotionally."

I ask Latisha what led to her realization that love doesn't have to hurt. She replies:

> I had started going to a domestic violence group. I was in a relationship, and I guess I kept hearing it over and over. You know, if you love somebody, you wouldn't hurt them. And then I started seeing that in me. It's like, I guess I do love people, because I try, I try my best, not to hurt them. But it's like, when things build up, I still wind up hurting them. Because I attack them verbally. So. And then I kind of found myself, I was doing that with my kids. I'm guilty of a lot of emotional abuse, yeah. That I wasn't aware of then, but now—I was hurting them more emotional than physical. Kind of was doing the same thing to them that my mom was doing to us . . . And also, abandoned them, like my mom did me. You know? And that's due to alcohol and drugs, so. I guess too, a lot of my growth of knowing how to love is part of getting into treatment too, drug and alcohol treatment. I saw a lot of things that I was doing to my kids, that I said I wouldn't do. And today, I try not to. You know. Still, there are times I might find myself—I guess too, why it's different. I talk to my kids, and I tell my kids, like, "If you feel like I'm, I'm doing anything, if I'm hurting y'all . . . tell me, because a lot of time, I might not think I am."

In a reexamination of the bonds of love, Latisha looks at her relationship with her children and sees herself doing the very things that were done to her. She begins to rework her relational images to recognize that she not only receives harmful force from others, she also gives it out. Once she becomes aware of herself as an agent of harm, she looks at her relationships to see where she is hurting others. She takes a deceptively simple lesson, that love doesn't have to hurt, and uses it as a guide for how she wants to love: "If you love somebody, you wouldn't hurt them."

A longing for the closeness and absence of hurt she may some-day attain in her relationships, paired with intimate knowledge of how she has both been injured and injured others, now restrains her from aggressive acts. The change in her understanding of love involves a reworking of the most fundamental aspects of her world, including her patterned ways of interacting aggressively and her identification with her internalized mother.

Latisha moves from blindness about critical aspects of her own aggressive actions to conscious awareness and control over them. She makes a number of critical changes as she recognizes her own aggressiveness: she begins to empathize with her children on the basis of her own experience with her mother; she asks how her children feel, wanting to know when she hurts them; and she takes responsibility for her past violations of her children. The courage this requires goes unsung; it is the most powerful shift that she has made in her life.

Latisha is also reexamining how to communicate painful, angry feelings in ways that are not destructive to herself or others:

> I'm starting to notice a lot of my feelings that, in the past, I never did. And it's like I kind of want to—the next person to hurt with me. I said [to my counselor], "Them thoughts are there, you know . . . And also there's a lot of anger there." I said like, "I just want to lash out at the next person and make them hurt too, because I'm hurting." But I said, "But I'm not, you know." So I said, "It's just the thought there. It's like, you know, misery love company." I'm hurting and so it's like, I want some-body else to hurt with me. But I told her, I said, "No, and I know, two wrongs don't make no right."

Following what she learned in childhood, Latisha attempted to connect to others through pain. This kind of aggression—"I'm hurting so I want somebody else to hurt with me"—occurs when a person feels trapped in feelings that are too terrible to bear alone. The pain of such disconnection generates hostility and rage. Until recently, Latisha did not know how to share these feelings in any positive way. For her, one way of connecting with other people was to drag them into her territory of emotional pain and isolation by making them hurt as she did.

While women raised to see aggression as unfamiliar territory fear that hurting others will increase their isolation, Latisha and other women raised in violent families often see aggression as a form of connection. As Latisha explicitly says, hurting others creates a link to them through shared pain. As she works on changing this deeply engraved schema that equates aggressive interactions with love, she also must learn a new way to create intimate, sharing relationships with others. She must bring these feelings of pain, disconnection, and anger into relationships positively.

Latisha's narrative is filled with reminders to herself that she must learn how to stay with her painful feelings, how to cope with them in ways other than dulling them with drugs and alcohol:

> I just remind myself that, you know, I have to deal with these feelings. I keep telling myself I don't want to go back to dealing with them the old way . . . I refuse to go back to alcohol and drugs . . . I guess it's like, I could go ahead and suffer, and get it over with, so I could start living life again, or either I could just continue—eventually, I'm gonna die, from either the drugs or either killing myself. You know, and I don't want neither one of them . . . So I just tell myself I'm gonna have to deal with this pain, though I don't want to . . . The one reason why I never wanted to deal with none of it is because I always thought that I was gonna have a nervous breakdown, I wasn't gonna get my mind back . . . And when I started hearing that from other people in my group, I thought, "Well, hey. It's normal. I'm okay." Now I know that other people feel that way, so it's like, you know, there's nothing wrong with me . . . I really don't want to

talk about it, but I really need to . . . It's the only way I'm gonna
deal with it, is feel it.

Suffering that was never brought into relationship isolated Latisha,
making her think she was crazy because the depth of her pain
often overwhelmed her. In this passage she looks squarely at her
choices—die from despair or drugs, or learn to experience her feelings and to share them with others through dialogue.

Latisha's interview took place in the midst of a major reworking of her schema of aggressive interactions, including her understanding of how to connect with others. With the new understandings that she voices here, she may be able to move beyond the kinds
of violent relationships she has been involved in all her life. But
only with support for her insights and for her emerging behaviors.
She had turned to intimacy with women to get away from violence—"I always thought a woman would be nurturing more"—but
changing the gender of her partners offered no protection: "And
all the women that I've been, had the relationships with since I
came out, always been some kind of emotional or physical abuse."
Latisha's task, to disentangle love's ties with hurt, requires not only
personal courage but the kind of support and community she is
gaining from her battered women's group. This group both provides emotional support and presents new images of attachment
and new ways to share feelings. It offers guidance in how to follow
her hope that love doesn't have to hurt.

4

THE RAGE OF DISCONNECTION

All the women I interviewed used judgmental words such as "bad," "mean," "worthless" to evaluate themselves for acts that they thought had hurt others.

> I always feel like I am a really mean person . . . Then I'm going like, "Who really am I? Am I this nice person or am I this really mean person?" And then I'm like, "Who is, you know, what is my true personality?" (Consuelo, age 24, Mexican American, student)

> I'm bad. I'm left with I'm bad. He's leaving because I'm bad . . . I'm angry, and I'm violent. That's what's bad about me . . . I'm not a real cuddly person. I've been hurt a lot physically, sexually, and I don't, I mean I can be pretty cozy, but I don't want to hug all the time . . . I don't like to be held. So I was bad because of that too. (Cassondra, age 34, white, artist)

> Oh, I felt horrible . . . I felt *bad*. I mean, I was just saying like, "God you're just a worthless piece of shit, you're fat," and all those messages that came from growing up years, I mean emotionally, it's still there. (Mary, age 43, white, psychotherapist)

Aggressive acts are always value-laden. They carry the actor's inner judgment about their legitimacy; they incur evaluations by others regarding their harmfulness and the motives of the aggressor. Often the justifications and judgments are stated in moral terms; they may be self-serving or self-condemning and based on any number of norms or beliefs. Once a woman formulates a moral justification for an aggressive act, she can use it to provide a rationale for moving beyond ordinary social constraints.

Women's moral language about their aggressive acts, particularly their justifications, offers insight into the complex reasons for destructive aggression. Why can some women physically injure another person while others condemn themselves for mild verbal opposition? What kind of moral reasoning justifies a knifing or a fist in the face? At the other end of the spectrum of aggressive acts, what moral standards condemn angry fantasy or legitimate self-assertion?

The Aggression of Despair

Destructive aggression arises out of the psychological pain of disconnection from others. Such aggression seeks to alter painful feelings and bridge separateness by affecting those from whom a person feels disconnected. Hurting those who are perceived to have caused the painful feelings is also an attempt to gain some sense of control when one feels powerless. In women's accounts, their harmful aggression derives from loss, the threat of separation, shame, obstacles to fulfillment of goals, or other dangers to their self-concepts.[1]

Physical violence aimed at hurting others is the most forbidden form of destructive aggression. As mentioned earlier, I am not considering child abuse; the following descriptions all pertain to acts of aggression toward peers. Of the sixty women I interviewed, thirty-nine described using physical aggression against another adult for reasons other than self-defense: twenty-eight of the thirty-six women who had been abused and eleven of the twenty-four women who had not been abused. Eight women, all of whom had been physically abused in childhood and some also in adulthood, habitually resorted to physical aggression when angry.

What happens in that mercurial moment when feelings—of anger, shame, or abandonment—translate into acts of destructive aggression? Insight into such moments comes from listening to women talk about the reasons for their acts intended to hurt others.

Each woman who used physical aggression destructively spoke of feeling she "didn't care" about what happened to herself or others. The anger was so despairing or the shame so intense that she no longer cared about the consequences of destructive actions, including retaliation. She had nothing left to lose.

It's when I feel powerless that I get violent. Totally. That's what it's about. There was just no stopping myself. I knew that I was being irrational, I knew that I wasn't in charge, and I didn't care. I wanted to hurt him . . . I didn't care whether he thought I was a bitch. I didn't care whether I thought I was crazy anymore, I didn't care anymore. I said, "I'm gonna go and I'm going to be absolutely insane and I don't give a shit anymore. Because it's totally justified. All of it. And you can think I'm a bitch, absolutely." (Cassondra, age 34, white, artist)

When I got older there wasn't too much [my mother] could do except for yell at me, because I became physically aggressive towards her. My stepfather was sexually abusive to my sister and I, and we had told her about it, and she refused to believe it. I can remember getting into an argument with her and telling her that I didn't respect her and shoved her up against a wall and told her that she was trash for marrying my stepfather and stuff. I think I got to the point where I didn't care anymore. I had had enough of her and her attitude . . . So it didn't bother me that— I didn't have as much to lose. (Arliss, age 27, white, student)

And people be bending over backwards to be nice to me and I be nice to them and then all of a sudden, oh, I guess I just go off. But I guess I just got that thought where . . . "I don't care if you got problems. Fuck your problems, deal with mine." That's the kind, I don't know, it's the like I-don't-give-a-fuck attitude, you know. That's how it is. (Vanessa, age 37, African American, unemployed)

These women link their not caring to their destructive acts. How does "I don't care" work as a moral rationalization for acts of aggression? Empathic care, the capacity to put oneself in another's position and to understand that person's perspective and feelings, underlies moral concern and prevents harmful actions. The despair of not caring about what happens to self or other opens the gate to a terrain that lies beyond moral, social, and personal safety concerns. It removes ordinary self-restraint and risks physical violence.

Women who have been severely abused as children and who habitually resort to physical aggression give us some clues to how not caring relates to destructive acts. These women learned their way into the human family through violence. They have experienced an absence of care from those they love and trust and have felt abandoned and betrayed. Not only has the mutual emotional attunement between self and other that teaches empathy been interrupted, their images of how to attach to others often include physical aggression as an aspect of intimacy.

Additional obstacles to the development of caring about self and others include poverty, drug and alcohol use, witnessing violence between parents, and parental mental illness (Chase-Lansdale, Wakschlag, and Brooks-Gunn, 1995; Puka, 1994; Goleman, 1995; Jaudes, Ekwo, and Van Voorhis, 1995). Perceptions of injustice, including racism, also create hostility when no recourse seems available to right them (Brownley, Light, and Anderson, 1996; hooks, 1996). When these factors are added to childhood abuse, they create powerful barriers to care and trust.

When women with such backgrounds encounter situations that are emotionally threatening or shaming, they can resort to early lessons: they abandon the moral requirement to care either for themselves or for others. Such women are at risk for repeating such patterns unless positive relationships and caring communities offer new models to offset this early learning (Chase-Lansdale, Wakschlag, and Brooks-Gunn, 1995).

The interviews reveal five reasons for using aggression destructively: as a way to connect despite the loss of hope for a positive relationship; as a way to get even or settle a score of betrayal and hurt (usually called revenge); as a last resort, when no other means of affecting others appears to work; as a compulsion to act over which a woman has no control; and as a strategy of survival.

A Way to Connect

Some women use destructive aggression as a way of maintaining connection when they have lost hope for a positive relationship. John Bowlby's (1973) distinction between an *anger of hope* and *an anger of despair* helps us understand how destructive aggression can become a substitute for positive connection.

Threats to a significant relationship arouse anger that can function in a positive way to remove obstacles to closeness. The goals of this "anger of hope" are to restore relationship and discourage the loved person from going away again. Acts of positive aggression arising from an anger of hope include positive confrontations to "clear the air" so mutuality can be reestablished, and initiating conflicts to restore fairness and respect. An aggression of hope requires a belief that one can communicate and be heard, and that anger and conflict can have positive benefits to relationships.

The anger of despair often arises from a feeling of being powerless to restore relationship, or when hostility over separation has replaced the bonds of attachment. Anger is transformed into destructive aggression when its positive function, to protest and repair a disrupted relationship, cannot be expressed clearly and directly. The aggression of despair does not function to restore good relationship; it has lost hope that reunion is possible. Instead, the rage of disconnection propels a person to cross the gulf of separation by destructive means. Even though rationally the person may know the relationship is over, emotionally it feels like destructive connection is better than none.[2]

Cassondra (age 34, white, artist), was recently left by her partner, Kevin, after a year-long relationship. She has a son, age 4, from a previous relationship, and at the time of the interview she was not working. Cassondra was raised in a chaotic, violent family and was sexually and physically abused. Her parents both used drugs, especially speed:

> They were very young, and they would booze it up all night with their friends, and I'm sure they felt like shit all the time. So their tempers were totally out of control . . . The phrase I remember hearing most is, "I'm gonna get the belt, I'm gonna get the belt." And so when they'd get really angry, one of them would go get the belt, one of my father's belts. And it wasn't like this controlled, "You're going to get a spanking now because you've been bad." They would just be totally out of control, and they just would whale away on us.

In childhood, Cassondra's basic needs for love, comfort, and stability were frustrated, arousing her healthy anger and self-defensive aggression. At the same time, the abuse would have led her to feel worthless, weak, and helpless to change her parents' behavior. To avoid the danger of punishment, she had to repress her healthy hostility and anger, leading to a sense of ever-present threat, nameless anxiety, and diffused hostility. Such children direct repressed hostility toward the self, increasing their feelings of worthlessness, shame, and fear (Horney, 1937; Miller, 1981). For Cassondra, the wider culture echoes the family message that her anger is dangerous: it must be repressed or it goes out of control. In addition, though her family continually incited anger, she had no models for positive ways to bring anger into relationship in order to resolve disagreements or restore closeness. She rarely even knew what she had done to anger her parents. Repeated punishments and fear transformed her anger of hope, which Bowlby called simple aggression, into an aggression of despair.

Following a pattern common among adolescents whose parents use drugs and are abusive, Cassondra turned to drugs herself as an adolescent, hitchhiked often, was sexually assaulted, and jumped in and out of many high-risk situations. Yet she kept looking for positive ways of being in relationship: "From the time I was about 15 . . . I knew that there were other possibilities, other ways of being in the world, and being loving was one of those ways of being that I wanted to be. And I just decided that I was going to be that. So I've worked really hard. I work hard all the time. I'm working against being [my parents]."

Kevin's leaving aroused an anger of despair. Convinced that she would never have a loving relationship, she was engulfed by intense shame, the sense that her very self was unlovable. "Shame is intricately connected with social separation and threats of abandonment—responses to alienation from others" (Scheff and Retzinger, 1991, 65). Anger at Kevin is mixed with shame at her own inadequacy that, she thinks, drives him away: "I just felt deficient, I felt violent. I wanted to be this really loving person, this really loving, giving woman. And I was made to feel that I was anything but that." Anger quickly becomes rage at herself and at him as she confronts the reality that the relationship is ending.

On his way out the door, Kevin informed Cassondra that he loved someone else. She felt powerless to bridge the disconnection in any positive way; her despairing anger leapt across the gulf that had opened between them: "I needed to be with him and confront him. I needed to connect with him. I needed to connect with him, if only in a totally destructive manner." His announcement felt like a negation of her very being and cast her into a void of isolation and abandonment. To affirm her existence and her power in a situation where she felt none, she wanted to affect him, even destructively. Doing so helped ward off the sense that she did not matter, that she did not exist.

Cassondra's rage of disconnection led her to destructive actions against herself and against Kevin. She physically wrestled with Kevin to try to stop his leaving, attempted to intercept him and his new girlfriend, and took a number of other actions that only increased her humiliation and hopelessness. She tried to reduce unbearable feelings through self-harm; lining up her pills, she took enough tranquilizers to get "fucked up" though she did not want to kill herself. She also tried to overcome her escalating shame and rage by taking positive actions—connecting with friends and doing artwork.

Cassondra's childhood was a rehearsal for the aggression of despair. Despite this early learning, she continued to risk loving, guided by her vision that there were "other ways of being in the world, and being loving was one of those." But with Kevin's abrupt departure, her childhood schema that equates love with hurt took over. Destructive connection felt better than no connection, and also sadly familiar.

The emotional logic that supports using aggression to connect destructively can be summarized as follows. Perceived abandonment leads to unbearable feelings of isolation and shame that one has driven another loved and needed person away. The intense shame and rage threaten to overwhelm a woman; often she has not learned to name these feelings or to communicate them in ways they will be heard. She also easily experiences the loss of other as a loss of self; she combats the loss of self by acting out the kind of destruction she feels is occurring to her. Trying to harm the other person externalizes the psychological experience of being destroyed; it offers some brief sense of control over self and other. Destructive aggression offers a way to connect overwhelming psychological pain, including the shame of feeling unloved, with the person perceived to have caused the feelings. Or, such feelings can be deflected onto another person so that they do not have to be borne alone, in isolation.

Revenge

Women describe using their destructive aggression to get even or to pay others back for betrayal and hurt. The moral justification behind retaliation is *lex talionis*, an eye for an eye, a tooth for a tooth. Betrayal arouses intense anger and fear, creates loss and shame, and diminishes the sense of self. It shreds understanding, slips past reason, and undermines trust to consume mind and feeling with a desire to get even. Betrayal is a central theme in the narratives of women who use destructive aggression.

Myths of betrayal, which dominate the Western mind through central stories of Judeo-Christian religion such as Adam and Eve or Judas's kiss, show that betrayal can be an opening to wisdom and growth or can lead to life-denying forms of response. Such negating responses to betrayal include revenge, denial of the value of the relationship with the betrayer ("I never loved him anyway"), cynicism, paranoia, and self-betrayal (Hillman, 1975). In self-betrayal, one subverts or forsakes oneself, takes revenge on oneself.

The link between betrayal and the rage of disconnection is clear in Chrystal's life. I interviewed Chrystal (age 25, African American, unemployed) three times over a year and a half. She was involved with the Seattle Birth to Three Project and was taking steps to regain custody of her three children. By the third interview she had moved to new housing and her children were to join her the following month. Confused about her aggression and fearful of its repercussions, Chrystal was actively working to understand the sources of her anger and why she would "go off" and physically attack someone. (While she had this difficulty with other adults, she never abused her children; she had lost custody because of neglect caused by drug abuse.)

Chrystal tells of being betrayed by her father and her grandmother and links it to the direction she has taken in life. At 14 she left her maternal grandmother's home, where she always felt a "gap in between" herself and her cousins, and moved across the mountains to her paternal grandmother's home, where her father lived. Her father had been in prison for years, and Chrystal did not know him. She was eager to reconcile with one of her parents (her mother was using heroin and lost on the streets) and find a place where she belonged.

> When I first moved in, it was the nighttime, and [my grandmother] said, "Chrystal, make sure you lock your door." I'm like, "Why I got to lock my door?" And she would always come and knock on my door and say, "Chrystal, are you all right?" and stuff like that, and she did it for like three nights in a row. And then one day she said, "Chrystal, you want to go to church with me?" I said no . . . "I think you ought to go, just come on. Well, I'll take you and drop you off at your [great-grandmother's] house," and I said, "No, I'd sit here and talk to my dad." And she said, "I don't think that's a good idea."

She interrupts her narrative at this point to look at me and say: "I guess you could already tell he tried to do something that was, you know, not natural." She moves immediately to her reaction: "And that really hurt my feelings. But what hurt my feelings most was [my grandmother] didn't tell me. She *knew*. She knew it might happen."

Her father, Chrystal continues, "said, 'I don't want you, I don't want you as a daughter, I want you to be my woman.' And you know I'm only 15 years old. And when she came back, you know, she wouldn't look at me. It was like *she knew* because he had did the same thing with his sisters. But he had physically attacked them." Chrystal felt abandoned by both these people from whom she longed for love and protection.

It was almost like she was trying to protect me, but she put me through it too. Why didn't she just come out and tell me? Because she didn't want me to leave. I tried to stay, and I told him, "No, you're, just stay away from me, I just want to be with my grandmother." But even after that I would lock my door every night, and I don't know how he got in but he got in and he was trying to—you know—and I know that she heard me yelling, I know she did. But I found out I had to leave after that. *[So you had to basically fight to protect yourself?]* Um-hmm, and her room was right next door to mine, and it hurt me. That's when I really felt, you know, like nobody's gonna take care of Chrystal, don't nobody care.

Chrystal could not understand why her grandmother, who was kind and solicitous, did not protect her: "It was almost like I felt betrayed like she wanted this to happen or something." With no one to help her, Chrystal escaped her father by fleeing, leaving "my clothes there and everything," and running through the night "all the way to my great-grandmother's house."

For 15-year-old Chrystal, this betrayal thrust her into what felt like an unprotected universe. It undermined any hope of secure connection or trust, leaving her to fend for herself. Betrayal carries a sting of negation as Chrystal absorbs the poison of knowing that her father wants to use her for his own purposes and that her grandmother will not protect her. She learns she is expendable. This negation is like an emotional death as Chrystal is confirmed as one who is alone.

One way for Chrystal to communicate her despair and rage, to connect her experience with others, is through destructive aggression. When she attacks and sees the effects on another person, it affirms, at the very least, that she exists. A momentary feeling of control replaces painful feelings of nonbeing. Women who have felt betrayed and hurt by others often attempt to ward off such feelings by reversals of who does the hurting.

Seeing that others had abandoned her, Chrystal abandoned herself. After this episode she began heavy drug use: "I used to get real depressed because I felt like nobody cared about me. Then when I found drugs it was like, you know, when you're getting high you don't think about things, things don't bother you. But then it increased my anger." Though Chrystal does not mention it, her anger and depression are increased by the realities of racism and poverty that she, like many African-American inner-city adolescents, sees in her future (Hawkins et al., 1998). The many images of material wealth and happiness that leave her out of the picture only increase her sense of betrayal, this time by society.

Trying to numb her pain through drugs, Chrystal moved more and more deeply into a rage of disconnection. She developed an aggressive, violent self to protect the caring, vulnerable self that had been betrayed. She cannot bear to leave her vulnerability exposed or unprotected, because doing so may lead to more shame and negation. Aggression defends against the dread and anger of disconnection, yet she feels trapped and further isolated within it.

Chrystal is at a different point in her life now. The advocacy program she is involved with has given her a positive relationship with another woman who cares about how she is doing and who helps her deal with the social service agencies that oversee her life. Love for her children and the determination to avoid betraying them as she was betrayed keeps her away from drugs and in her treatment group. These connections are enough to give Chrystal hope that she may be able to form relationships based on positive interactions rather than mediated by drug use and violence. She knows that her chances for strength and growth lie in positive relationships within which she can learn how to express her feelings and be respected: "When I talk about things, it's almost like being on the outside of yourself. You can see things you can't understand, you wouldn't see just by thinking about them."

A Last Resort

Women also describe resorting to destructive aggression when nothing else seems to work. A person who has little sense of relational force—who feels no one will listen, or is convinced that no other kinds of behavior will affect others—may turn to aggression. Mandy (age 32, white, student), who is in recovery from drug and alcohol abuse, presents this view of aggression:

It's like, you say things over and over and over or you try something different to make something work. It wasn't like violence or my anger was my very first choice, you know? . . . I think that people get down to the wire, I know that I got down to the wire, that talking wasn't working and, all the other shitty skills that I had, it didn't matter how many great meals I cooked or how many goddamn laundry piles I folded, things in my life were still out of control. And so I think for me it was a real lack of any other way to deal with the ways that I felt.

But the aftermath of destructive aggression, for most of the women, was moral self-condemnation. Recalling the incident in which she fractured her husband's skull (see Chapter 2), Mandy says: "I was feeling really upset that I was capable of nearly killing somebody. That was really frightening to me. I didn't want that to be in me. It wasn't nice and it wasn't good, and it wasn't all the things that all my life I felt like I hadn't been able to live up to."

Passivity in Aggression's Activity

In their moral justifications and condemnations of their destructive aggression, women often convey the feeling of being taken over by something that compels them to act. They feel passive in the grip of a powerful force, as if swept away by an irrational, unknown aspect of self.

I drove over to his house and I just kind of walked in, blasted his door open, woke him up and I scared him . . . I don't remember a lot of what I said because I was totally, I was not in charge at the time . . . There was just no stopping myself . . . It's like panic but it's not panic. It's like being on a drug, when you believe that your mind is engaged on a normal level. I mean you really think that you're being rational. But you're not . . . You're actually making decisions and they're just really destructive decisions. (Cassondra, age 34, white, artist)

When I get mad I might be crazy for a little while because I really don't—it's almost like I don't know what I'm doing and I don't—it's like another person's taking over. (Chrystal, age 25, African American, unemployed)

It's like you don't have a choice, it's like on you and you just react, and that's how I reacted in that particular incident, was reaming on him because I was really upset. *[But did you make some choices at that time?]* Oh no, it was totally involuntary. I mean, it was like I had no control over it, I just did it. (Karen, age 41, white, police officer)

All of a sudden, I just go off . . . I go off and then I feel bad and I say, "Now why did I say that to that lady, that lady ain't done nothing to me, well why did I call her a bitch, I don't know that lady," you know. Whatever it is inside me comes out; it's like an alien or something . . . it's like I'm supposed to be, um, shit, evil and I'm not evil, I'm not an evil person. (Vanessa, age 37, African American, unemployed)

Even though these women are carrying out aggressive acts, they do not experience themselves as in charge. Instead, they feel passive, as if " 'it' made me do it." This "it," a feeling of being compelled by something else, reproduces a dominant cultural view of aggression as an "impulse" within us that must be controlled and managed. Such talk directs attention away from the interpersonal aspects of aggression and locates the problem within the self. As they talk about being taken over in this way, women often call their behavior "crazy."

When women describe losing control, they conform to Western culture's construction of female aggression as a sign of both weakness/irrationality and powerful, destructive force. Talk about losing control and being compelled by some kind of force implies that something untamed and unruly is taking over, something that presents a threat to order. As these women fail to "control" their aggression, they observe themselves both as subject to the feeling of rage and as the one who was unable to control it.

Catherine Lutz has found that women talk about the control of emotions, such as anger or hate, more than twice as often as men do as a proportion of the total speech each produced in interviews.

Women's discourses of emotional control offer "evidence of a widely shared cultural view of the danger of both women and their emotionality" (Lutz, 1990, 71):

> When cognition outreasons and successfully manages emotion, male-female roles are replicated. When women speak of control, they play the roles of both super- and subordinate, of controller and controlee. They identify their emotions and themselves as undisciplined and discipline both through a discourse on control of feeling. This construction of a feminine self . . . includes a process by which women come to control themselves and so obviate the necessity for more coercive outside control. (ibid., 74)

When a woman has lost control, she particularly needs to offset the need for "more coercive outside control." One way to do so is by interpreting the episode as a momentary lapse in which she was taken over by something else: to speak of her actions as "not me." The "real me" would never do something so destructive. Denial that one's "real self" was in control is also a way to avoid taking moral responsibility for injurious actions.

The "it," that force that takes over, seems to compel action. Mark Johnson calls compulsion "one of the most common force metaphors that operate in our experience": "Everyone knows the experience of being moved by external forces, such as wind, water, physical objects, and other people. When a crowd starts pushing, you are moved along a path you may not have chosen, by a force you seem unable to resist. Sometimes the force is irresistible, such as when the crowd goes completely out of control; other times the force can be counteracted, or modified" (1987, 45).

Not only do people feel compelled by external forces, they also experience feelings as internal forces. Histories of relationships, particularly of parents' use of force, affect whether adults experience themselves as passive in the face of internal forces (their feelings) or as the source of force and action, as in "I made that happen."

Women who feel passive as they act aggressively cannot tolerate painful feelings of disconnection brought by anger and shame.

Such feelings were continually elicited within their families of origin, but were never brought into connection positively. In adulthood, such feelings reawaken layers of pain; when the psychological pain is too intense, the observing self can become paralyzed while emotions, experienced as overwhelming, trample over the self. Compelled by the force of these feelings, a woman attacks: she is both actor and acted upon. As Cassondra says, "It's when I feel powerless that I get violent." To resist being "swept along" by feeling requires powerful activity, including relearning how to bring painful feelings into relationship.

A Strategy of Survival

Many women who use aggression as a wall of self-protection (see Chapter 2) feel it is a necessary defense against a dangerous world. For Brenda (age 30, African American, unemployed), "fighting back" is a tool of survival in a world filled with violence:

> At the age of 14, I left home and I got with my oldest two kids' father . . . And then we was together for six years and we went and got our own apartment and he got to drinking alcohol. Hitting on me, abusing me . . . I'm the kind that I fight back, though. You bruise me, we're gonna bruise each other . . . Do I look like I'd let somebody just hit me and say boo-hoo? I'm not that one. I'm not that one. Uh-uh.

Brenda never portrays herself as a victim, but as a fighter and a survivor. This sense of being a strong woman who survives violence is a legacy carried by many African-American women who have overcome a negating society and personal traumas (Painter, 1995; Higgenbotham, 1992; Palmer, 1983).[3]

Brenda presents her world as threatening, with danger located both within her marriage and in the society around her. She worries about her children in such an environment: "I want to see my kids, man, to grow up to at least see 30. At least my age! Because when I grew up my parents wasn't worried like I'm worried now, they wasn't worried about me making it to age 30. Because back in those days, back in the Sixties, it wasn't like it is now. I mean, hell, I could walk to school all by myself, you know. And now you can't even do that . . . this world is too rough."

Social location has more to do with Brenda's use of aggression as self-protection than any other single factor. Trapped within an economic and social context created by racism and pervaded by violence, she avoids victimization by building a wall of aggressive self-protection to guard a vulnerable self. Brenda describes herself as "crazy" when she resists her first husband's violence—but her craziness is effective: "He hit me in my head about thirteen times, blows straight to the head, and I wouldn't go to sleep and I didn't fight him back. I didn't do nothing . . . The next morning I got up crazier than a crazy bat woman. I got up and said, 'Man, wake your butt up and get the H out of my house! Don't you never come back!' It's over and we ain't been together since."

Brenda does not present her aggression as "out of control." On the contrary, she uses aggression for self-protection and to gain the upper hand in specific situations. Whether or not she will fight in a given situation "all depends" on "who's bothering me" and "what the scene is." She describes another incident in which she chose to be aggressive, and calls it "crazy":

> I went on a warpath about a week ago. People were taking my house over as a drug house and I got my baseball bat and I started breaking up my tables in my house. They said, "Oh, we won't leave." I called the police. "Oh, you won't leave? Yeah, you will." I took a big bucket of water and poured it over the floor. Took the coffee pot, threw it in there. Broke it in the bathtub. Took the iron and threw it through the window. I was moving anyway, but they said they wasn't gonna leave. Betcha they got up and left. My kids wasn't there but I have to do that to get peace in my own home? And it makes me go crazy. It makes me do crazy things like I'm crazy. But I'm not crazy. People just taking advantage of me because I'm a woman . . . I had to go off, tear up things in my house just to make people leave.

In this situation, Brenda *appears* to lose control in order to gain control. Her use of aggression involves assessing her situation and then acting in ways that look crazy and out of control, but that are strategic.

Her act involves three elements. The first is *attempting to use means other than aggression:*

> I tried to come in and ask them very nicely. "Well, you guys go back home. You guys have partied long enough. I'm ready for me and my kids to come in, you know. Can you guys leave?" "I'm not going nowhere. I'm going to sit here and sell drugs." I mean, that kind of talk. It was just crazy talk.

The second is *protecting herself and her children from a dangerous situation:*

> I left and took my kids because the police could come kick this joint in and take my kids. Me and my kids got to leave our own home? . . . And then come home the next morning, they still there and tell me they ain't gonna leave and I just went off . . . I didn't want to hurt them. See, I have to look out for my kids. I could have hit them and hurt them and killed them and then I'm gone to the penitentiary. And then there my kids are, no-where to go. So I just, I did it a different way. "Oh, yes the fuck you are. Oh, yeah, you are." And I just went berserk.

And the third is *asserting yet disguising control through "crazy" behavior:*

> Anybody walking around with a baseball bat beating up their furniture that didn't do nothing, innocent furniture, that is like a crazy mood. Shit, I mean for real (laughs). They'll be thinking that when I go off, "What's wrong with this crazy bitch?" They'll say "This girl is crazy! She need to be in a nut house." Because I make them think I'm crazy.

To dismiss Brenda's display of aggression as merely destructive and irrational is to overlook its strategic intent and its context. She sees her actions as an attempt to take control, to cope in a situation that offers few choices.

Researchers have not investigated how women determine when to "go off" or "lose it" for an intended effect, or how they use "irrational" aggression to control others. We need to ask whose control a woman is losing, what control she is attempting, and how she is disguising control through her behavior. Following the cultural construction of women's aggressive anger as illogical, researchers have not searched for the logic within women's strategies of acting "crazy."

Brenda's strategy of acting crazy with destructive aggression is intended to get people out of her house and to harm only furniture. But it also harms her when, resorting to these tactics, she is arrested for disorderly conduct and destruction of property, goes to jail, and continues to see herself as marginalized and powerless. Her rage of disconnection increases as her goal, to protect her children, backfires when they are placed in temporary custody of relatives and beyond her safeguarding reach.

Brenda's use of aggression is not an issue of personality or character; it has been shaped by powerful social forces. Her ability to stop relying on aggression as a survival strategy requires both individual and social action directed against the oppressions that influence her life. She cannot fight these large structures alone; she must transcend these imposed barriers by joining with others to struggle against them (Robinson and Ward, 1991), to make her fights liberatory instead of self-destructive. As of now, Brenda does not share her rage of disconnection and her powerlessness by talking about them with anyone. Instead, the hostility that comes from such feelings surfaces as aggression: "I don't like to share my feelings. Keep it inside mainly, until I get really mad, then I be talking about killing everybody. Then I be wanting to kill everybody."

Without a positive community that can help her honor her strengths and communicate her feelings in undestructive ways, Brenda will continue to feel such a rage of disconnection. She will teach her children the aggressive strategy she sees as necessary for survival, even though she wants a better future for them. Programs such as the Seattle Birth to Three Project and "public homeplaces" are essential for connecting with those "who have been cast as Other and excluded by society" (Belenky, Bond, and Weinstock,

1997, 162). As Bernice Johnson Reagon, singer and activist, has written: "Often when you come up in an oppressive culture, you question the importance of your very existence; you have to search for courage to express yourself. You have to talk to yourself so that when you speak with your voice, it is your heart, your mind, your eyes, your living, that supplies the text" (1993, 24, quoted in ibid., 39). Before she can overcome rage, Brenda's voice, heart, and mind must be brought into positive community with others.

Aggression Directed toward the Self

What happens to the despair of disconnection when it does not find overt expression in attacks on others? Some women keep their aggression out of relationship by turning it against themselves: by suppressing or internalizing their angry, destructive feelings. Do their narratives reveal the same moral themes as those of women who physically attack others?

Sherry (age 17, white, student) is a wrestler. She defies the stereotype of women's reluctance to fight others, and she enjoys feeling her body's power: "I liked to be strong, to be tough, you know. You go in there and you take control and you show you're in control by how you move; you look strong and you feel strong and that shows." She describes her philosophy of "toughness": "You never, ever, ever quit . . . Like, 'I don't care if you hurt me. It doesn't matter because I'm still going to beat you.' "

But when Sherry steps out of this sport and into a relationship with a man, different rules apply. They tell her she must keep her frustration and anger out of relationship and, in some way, manage them herself. She lays out a scenario that will test these rules: "I got all ready to go somewhere with my boyfriend and it took me a long time to get ready, I mean like an hour and a half. It's not a big deal, but when you do it and you get makeup on and you do your hair and you get on a nice outfit. And you feel good and you're like ready to go somewhere and you brush your teeth and all that (laughs). He didn't show up."

She summarizes how she managed her feelings during the three hours she waited for him:

I was so angry I just, for a while I just sat and watched TV and just felt depressed basically ... And then I had something to drink, you know, which is a common thing. You know, that helps a little bit. But you see, I didn't have enough to get drunk or anything because there wasn't enough there. But, so that was better but, see, then it just turns to depressed, not because I drink but even before that really. I was only really mad when I talked to him on the phone.

I ask what she said on the phone, and she replies: "There's that warning to remind me 'Don't say too much,' you know. Because at the time I'm mad. Later on I'll say, 'I really wasn't that mad, it was just the heat of the moment kind of thing.'" After the phone call, she "stopped thinking and I decided to have a drink. Because I was trying not to for a while, to drink at all. And it had been like a few days, which I was proud of, and then I just didn't think and I just did anyway. I just said it doesn't matter, it doesn't matter at all. So I did that and I ate something, yeah, I eat when I get depressed, you know."

The voice that justifies what Sherry calls "self-destructive" drinking and eating "bad stuff" says that "it doesn't matter." Keeping her feelings out of relationship, she begins to enact them in ways that she condemns:

It's not good to eat late and when I do that I feel, it's like so stupid. It's so hard on your system and then in the morning you always feel stupid ... like, "Damn, why did I do that?" Especially if it's something fattening ... And I have such a sweet tooth so I'll just pig, you know. Then drinking, of course, is self-destructive. I mean, that time I only had one drink because that's all that was there, but normally if there had been enough, I would have just—

I start to ask a question: "You talked about a philosophy of being tough, 'don't let anything get to you.' There's a real clear delineation of when you do that, in wrestling, and yet it is hard to hold to that philosophy—"

She interrupts me: "Well, in a way . . . it's like I have to do it, I have to eat or whatever it is to deal with it. And then after, it won't be as bad." Like women who talk about being "taken over" and having no choice but to use destructive aggression, Sherry feels compelled to act by her feelings of powerlessness and anger. Rather than convey her anger directly, she numbs herself with food and alcohol to soothe the harshness of her boyfriend's reminder that she is expendable. By using herself as a target for her rage of disconnection, she keeps her aggression out of relationship.

I ask what her behavior does for her:

> Well, if I'm eating, it's something that tastes good and makes you feel good a little bit. It's kind of just like a drug, you know. Especially if it's sweet or something, it's just, it's good, you know. It's something to do, for another thing. Because you can't really concentrate on anything else. And then for drinking, that definitely alters you so you don't feel as bad, I guess. I mean it sounds so pathetic. It's not like I go, "Oh, if I drink this." Well, actually sometimes it is. I don't know. Sometimes it's really definite like "God, I'm going to drink this because it'll make me feel a little better." Sometimes it's just like all of a sudden I'm in this mood to drink for no reason at all. And I just don't think at all, I just do it.

In wrestling, Sherry defies gender stereotypes and is resourceful, smart, and self-confident. In her love life, she sits and waits for her boyfriend for three hours, dulling her anger in self-destructive ways.

Gender rules powerfully affect Sherry's way of dealing with her anger. As Catherine Lutz (1990) argues, there is no avenue for a woman's expression of anger that will not be considered irrational. Sherry's schema of aggressive interactions also includes a fear that she will lose her boyfriend if she does not suppress her anger. She finds herself in a bind. She is angry and wants to let him know it, but "there's this warning, 'Don't say too much.'" She wants to maintain their relationship, but does not want to be treated thoughtlessly and disrespectfully. Her solution—to be angry but to keep it out of relationship by numbing behaviors such as drinking, drugs, or eating—is a form of self-silencing.

Women's images of how to make and maintain safe, intimate relationships often lead them to silence certain feelings, thoughts, and actions (Jack, 1991). Anger is a major aspect of self that is silenced. This self-silencing contributes to a decline in self-esteem and feelings of a "loss of self" as a woman keeps parts of herself out of relationship. While the goal of self-silencing is to protect a relationship from angry, aggressive interactions that may threaten closeness, the reality is that self-silencing leads to disconnection, hostility, and depression.[4] Sherry says her eating and drinking are something to "do" to assuage her depressed feelings. She does not recognize her behavior as a way to keep anger out of relationship, which, in turn, *creates* the feelings of disconnection and depression.

Women also report turning their destructive rage against themselves as a way to hurt another person. Mandy (age 32, white, student) gives an example:

> I was coming to some awareness that I've got this kid and I've had a marriage and a divorce and now I'm living with this guy and he's quadriplegic . . . I was taking care of him, and I was in love with him, but his physical limitations weren't allowing him to love me back. And not just physically, but psychologically, emotionally, he wasn't able to love me. And he felt guilty about that. And I came home, and I just wanted to cry and let it all out, and he said, "Just get the hell away from me." And it was like a gigantic rebellion of my lifetime. I picked up a bottle of Valiums; I knew he was in no position to save me, you know, he couldn't reach the phone, he couldn't get out of bed, he was like absolutely powerless to do anything over what I could do to him. And so it was almost like this act to get back at him for his not caring about me. I picked up a bottle of Valiums, drank the whole thing down, finished it off with a bottle of Jack Daniel's and kind of stumbled around the house for a while, and laid down to die.

This double-pronged attack, directed against both self and other, was a raging protest against the one-sidedness of their relationship.

Her self-harm carried anger about what she yearned for but feared she would never have, about the devaluation of her in his command to "get the hell away," and about the failure she felt her life represented. This moment entered her psyche's hall of mirrors, reflecting to her images of similar contemptuous dismissal from past relationships—with mother, father, abusers, schools—that judged her as worthless. She struck against herself as well as against her partner and all the people he represented. He would have to lie there, unable to move, and watch her vengeful death.

Though Mandy was saved by someone's chance visit, she suffered a coma and kidney failure. Since that narrow escape she has come to realize that others are not the source of her aggressive anger. Rather, the rage arises from the disconnection and devaluation she has felt since childhood. She sought solace for that rage in substance abuse and in fighting, which only increased her sense of isolation. Mandy's brush with death led her to reinterpret what her anger signals, and warned against dealing with it through alcohol, indiscriminate sex, or attacks on herself or others. She is learning not to fear her anger but to use it as a force that stimulates the green of growth.

Not all women who keep anger out of relationship and turn it against the self do so through such extreme self-harm or through numbing behaviors such as overeating, drinking, and drug use. How do women silence or suppress their anger in less overtly destructive ways, using what moral admonitions? Consuelo's narrative offers some insights.

Consuelo (age 24, Mexican American) immigrated to the United States with her parents when she was 3. She grew up with five brothers and three sisters in a family that struggled with poverty and acculturation to American life; her parents still speak only Spanish. Consuelo has been married seven years to another first-generation Mexican American who is a laborer; they have a 5-year-old son. She will soon graduate from a university and is the first woman in her family to earn a degree, as well as the first in her Latino community. She has just taken a job with a state social service agency working with migrant workers.

Concerns about aggressiveness, selfishness, and her "mean-ness" are central to Consuelo's life as she struggles between two cultures: "During my teenage years . . . my father was following the traditions from Mexico. So it was like in our home it was Mexico. But yet I went outside the home, and I went to school and I saw that it was different. So that's where my aggression came from. It was like, it doesn't have to be this way, you know, my friends don't live like that so why should I?"

By her "aggression," she means that her father's controlling behavior "would make me angry." His attempts to raise a daughter in Mexican traditions using force and restrictions created in her a fear of authority, obedient behavior to ward off punishment, and continuing anger: "When I was growing up my father would be very limited to the time that I could go out, and so I had to be back on a specific time. And if I wasn't there then he would get angry. And then if, like say I went to the store on the corner, and I felt that it was longer than he had given me, then I would start feeling this fear."

By controlling Consuelo's physical space, her father effectively restricted her emotionally. The grip of fear that compelled her childhood obedience tightened in adolescence. Her father's power was embodied in her fear of being "hit by the belt. So then I better behave and do whatever he said." While her father's hitting was not frequent, his yelling was, and Consuelo's fear inhibited her voice, blocking expression of anger. Caught between obedience to her parents' expectations and her own need to grow and change as an adolescent in a bicultural world, she fell into depression: "It would make me angry the way he was overprotective. But there was nothing I could do so I would just keep it inside, and then I would just become depressed. And so I just—I guess that's what I learned, was just to seal off my emotions and become de-pressed."

Consuelo silenced her anger because she perceived no other way of relating that would allow her to maintain connection with her father, her family, and her culture. From her culture she had learned *respeto*—respectful, submissive behavior toward those in authority (Ginorio et al., 1995). She saw no exit from this sealed-off room of negative emotions: "I also thought about running away and then I thought, well, where would I go. And then it all was suicide, but I believed that if I commit suicide I wouldn't go to heaven, so then, suicide was out. And then running away was out, and talking back to my dad was out. So that would just get me deeper into my depression."

Looking to her mother for a model of how to express anger and will in relationship, she saw a clear pattern of male dominance and female subordination: "[My dad] didn't take her into account for family decisions, like you know, if there was a car to be bought or a TV to be bought he didn't like say, 'Would you like this one' or 'Which one would you want to buy,' he just would go out and buy it. He basically just did all the decisions on his own. And my mother was just there, and so if she got angry she was just, she really wouldn't say much."

Like many Mexican American women socialized to be submissive toward men (Shorris, 1992; Vasquez, 1994), Consuelo must learn assertiveness herself as an adult. Unassertiveness has been found to predict depression and other psychiatric symptoms in Latinas (Napholz, 1994), not only because it affects intimate relationships but also because it interferes with attempts to cope with hostile or demeaning environments in the wider culture.

Now working and about to graduate from college, Consuelo has challenged many of these assumptions regarding her role as a woman, and she has a more egalitarian relationship with her husband. But her central inner conflict, the one she struggles with "daily," elicits her self-judgment using moral terms: How assertive can she be without being selfish and mean? Stepping out of cultural norms of *familiarismo*, which places the extended family above the self, and *marianismo*, the sense that she should have to suffer and bear it, brings conflict and anxiety.

The issue of her "meanness" has surfaced strongly at home since her brother and sister-in-law, with their three children, moved in with Consuelo and her husband. The arrangement was supposedly temporary, but after eight months of looking for work they have not found anything, and it appears they may stay indefinitely. Within Consuelo's culture, this arrangement is not unusual, as extended family members are expected to support each other emotionally and materially (Ginorio et al., 1995). She states her dilemma: "Right now I'm caught up in this thing between like my rights and sharing. It's like, how can I be both? Be sharing and yet still have my rights, or like my protection."

The tradition she was raised in says: "You need to share and . . . you need to love your neighbor and, you know, help others. So that's basically what helps me from being really aggressive." Yet her feelings do not comply. Forbidden, "mean" thoughts flood her, like "God, I wish I could just take them and throw them out of my house." We hear her inner dialogue:

> If I get angry with somebody there's just all these thoughts, "If I could just do this, if I could just do that to them, if I could tell them," you know, just all these things that run through my head. And then I stop and I say, "No, that wouldn't be right." And I just let it go and forget about it . . . I always say, oh, you know, "God forgive me, I really didn't mean to say that." You know, but then I always think, "Well, you thought it!" "But I didn't mean it!" You know, and part of me is saying like, "Yeah! Yeah, let's do it!" And this other part of me is saying, "Stop thinking like that."

Consuelo uses moral admonitions to oppose and suppress her aggression; self-opposition creates a deep fracture in her experience of self. From contradictory positions, her divided self argues over how to judge and what to do with her angry thoughts. As of now, she keeps them out of relationship by this kind of self-inhibition through self-judgment.

Though it feels intensely personal to Consuelo, her inner division about aggression reflects the differences between her two cultures' perspectives on women's roles. Her opposing selves speak radically different beliefs about how she "should" act in relationships, one grounded in traditional Mexican culture and the other situated in the liberalism of a university campus. Consuelo's divided self argues about whether she has a right to voice her opposition and her will, to be what she calls aggressive. Aggression's presence, even in her thoughts, challenges expectations for "good" feminine behavior, a goodness that requires its absence. As she renegotiates her feminine and ethnic identities, conflicting moral judgments around her aggression dominate her inner dialogue.

From the outside, to others, Consuelo looks "quiet, calm," generous for giving her extended family a place to stay. But on the inside she feels her two conflicting selves fighting for ascendance: "I always feel like I am a really mean person . . . Then I'm going like, 'Who really am I? Am I this nice person or am I this really mean person?' And then I'm like, 'Who is, you know, what is my true personality?' "

Consuelo's question "Who really am I?" relates to *culture:* From which cultural perspective do I see and judge my actions? Which cultural values do I want to embrace as my own? How can I integrate the opposing values of my two cultures? The question also relates to *personal history:* Am I the obedient good woman like my mother? Am I the person who has angry, rebellious feelings of the type punished by my father? What will happen now if I bring my feelings into relationship? It relates to *power:* Can I overthrow the internalized fear of authority and become my own authority? What will happen to me if I stand up for myself as a Mexican-American woman in this society? It relates to *morality:* What is goodness? Are anger and aggression "mean"? Do I need God's forgiveness for aggressive thoughts? And it relates to *development:* What do I want? Who do I want to become?

Because of the inner division that leaves her acting nice but feeling mean, Consuelo keeps her distance from people: "If I let the person get too close to me and then they just are like asking a lot from me, then I'm not able to say like, no, you know, this is enough." She fears that if someone "tak[es] advantage of the friendship then I'm not going to be able to, you know, see a stop to it." Like Jessie, whom we met in Chapter 3, Consuelo sees opposition as aggressive and mean. According to her schema of aggressive interactions, not being aggressive requires going along with what others want. To avoid having to choose between being mean and being taken advantage of, she keeps her distance, and this compromises her friendships and her developing strengths.

Consuelo is not a victim—of her upbringing, of the poverty she has overcome, of the cultural and gendered expectations that dictated her future as a submissive woman. With her husband, she has become assertive, saying what she thinks, creating a more egalitarian marriage. She recognizes her own strength: "I know I can make it on my own. And I know that if the marriage would not hold together, and I'd have to be on my own, I know that it would be emotionally difficult at first but I know I can make it."

In her new job at a social service agency, she will have to assert herself at work: "Otherwise I'm not going to make it out there. Because if I'm not assertive then people are going to think like, I'm really passive and I'm really dumb. They're not going to think I can handle a position, and then co-workers like take advantage of me." She refuses to be bound by devaluing images of gender and ethnicity that promote subjection of Latinas to existing power relations: she will not be seen as "passive" and "dumb." But to break free she must confront both her fear of external authority and her internal authority that tells her assertiveness is mean and wrong.

While Consuelo is able to show her positive force in going to school and being ambitious, fear surfaces whenever she thinks of opposing others: "I'm able to show all the positive that there is in me, and yet I also know that I have to cross this line where I can also show like the negative side of me in an assertive way, and then will I be completely free. And then will I not have this fear."

Consuelo describes freedom as a space free of fear, a space in which she may create herself, a space of active struggle against both inherited patterns of submissive femininity and ethnic stereotypes. To move to this space of freedom she must "cross this line" into unfamiliar territory to oppose others, to say no, to stand up for herself. While assertion is not usually seen as a negative side of self, Consuelo does not distinguish an assertion that opposes others from aggression, and this contributes to her fear and hesitation.

Inner dialogues and moral language provide a glimpse of how the relational images that mediate a woman's aggression undergo change. Consuelo's moral judgments about aggression reflect internalized cultural ideals about how to act in relationship to avoid hurt to others and herself. As she tries to live out these ideals within the challenges of daily life, she does not know what to do with her resulting anger. Her "nice" self cannot wave a magic wand to transform her negative feelings into sweetness; she wants more room to bring her feelings into relationships. At this point in her life, Consuelo is at an impasse over what to do with her anger, which contributes to the depression she feels. From either cultural perspective, she can judge herself as deficient. From one, she is unassertive and has fallen into negative stereotypes of Latinas as passive; from the other, she is selfish and has overthrown *respeto*. To move out of this impasse she must change the relational images that mediate her aggression and that provide the basis for negative self-judgment.

Depression and Destructive Aggression

Though they seem opposite in terms of outward behavior, aggression and depression share many characteristics. Both arise out of negating relationships, and both have negative interpersonal effects. Through listening to women, it becomes clear that hopelessness about the possibility of intimacy creates the despair of depression and the hostility that underlies destructive aggression. While positive aggression usually benefits relationships by removing barriers to closeness, both harmful aggression and severe depression affect relationships negatively: they cause others to back off and become hostile, compounding the distance and separation.[5]

Images of how to act in relationships play a major role in both depression and aggression. Central to women's vulnerability to depression are their images of how they "should" behave in relationship to gain and keep love (Jack, 1991). Similarly, to mediate aggression, women rely on images of how to act in relationship that focus on avoiding harm to themselves and others.

At the root of women's depression are specific images of relationship—pleasing, self-sacrifice, self-silencing, compliance—that are culturally defined as feminine attachment behaviors. They are based on the requirement that women create intimacy within unequal relationships with men. If a woman is self-effacing and compliant, she silences vital aspects of herself out of fear that voicing them would threaten her relationships. Self-silencing contributes to a fall in self-esteem and feelings of a "loss of self," inner division, and depression. Trying to keep relationships by pleasing others, the woman experiences a hidden self that is bitter, resentful, and increasingly hopeless about the possibility of intimacy. This experience of inner division, in which one part of the self turns against the other, is a key aspect of depression.

Images that mediate women's aggression are likewise grounded in assumptions about how to make relationships work that are based, in large part, on social inequality and on women's roles as nurturers. These mediating images direct women's responses to conflicts with others, guide their use of force, and shape their perceptions of the consequences of their aggressive acts. When a woman feels like hurting someone, the mediators check her actions by bringing to mind the consequences for others, for herself, and for her relationships. When the mediators fail to stop her from acting to hurt another, either her personal history has taught her that aggression is a way to connect with others, or her rage over violations overcomes her concern for consequences.

Aggression can be both creative and destructive. Women are able to use aggression positively when their schemas of aggressive interactions include images of positive ways to resolve conflict and to use their force, and images of themselves as deserving of protection. When anger or hostility arises, they use these feelings to communicate and press for change in positive ways, not to explode yet stay with the status quo, not to attack destructively to gain an illusory sense of control and connection.

When women use aggression destructively, they may turn it against others, against themselves, or against both. While women who physically attack others may appear to be "letting their anger out" and into relationship, they still feel isolated. Their actions do not connect them with others in any way that betters a situation. In fact, aggressive episodes usually make them feel more isolated as they see themselves through condemning eyes.

At the other end of the spectrum of destructive aggressiveness (unfamiliar territory), women police their thoughts to eliminate "mean," hostile images and to suppress their anger before it can slip even into their tone of voice. Suppressing anger also leads them to feel separated from others and from themselves, and frequently to become depressed through the dynamic of silencing the self. Women at both ends of the spectrum are unable to positively assert themselves to deal with relational problems. Their anger over disconnection contributes to depression as well as to destructive aggression.

As I traced the aspects of thought and behavior that characterized women's depression through their narratives of aggression, I found that the same processes were central to both: *externalized self-perception* (judging oneself by standards established by others, seeing oneself through the Over-Eye), *care as self-sacrifice* (putting others' needs first in order to maintain attachments); *silencing the self* (inhibiting self-expression in order to avoid conflict and loss of relationships); and the *divided self* (the experience of an outer self that differs from more personal, authentic thoughts and feelings). The prohibitions on voice and action that create depression also inhibit women's aggression. Perhaps, most simply, the overlap between women's inhibition of aggression and their depression exists because the relational images that affect both depression (images of how to attach) and aggression (images of how to oppose) are shaped by social realities of women's lesser social power and their vulnerability to male aggression.

Social realities not only profoundly shape the schemas that guide how women deal with relational conflicts; they also affect what choices women actually have for resolving interpersonal discord and exercising their force. Women often face higher risks of negative economic, physical, or interpersonal consequences for voicing their anger, opposition, or demands than men do (Christensen and Heavey, 1990; Jacobson and Gottman, 1998). Many depressed women are convinced that voicing opposition, anger, or "selfishness" will bring some type of negative consequence. Behind this fear of positive self-assertion lie external specifics such as violence, sexual and racial discrimination, and poverty, each of which is a known factor for women's vulnerability to depression (McGrath et al., 1990). These same factors also influence the relational images that mediate women's aggression.

Depression and aggression are interwoven, sometimes visible as separate threads, sometimes so closely entwined that they seem indistinguishable. Clearly, cultural prohibitions against women's aggression, reinforced by social structures, contribute to women's vulnerability to depression. Images of how to avoid harm to self and others mediate much more than women's destructive aggression: they inhibit women's positive force and self-confidence. Women's own wish to foster and nurture relationships joins with society's injunction against female aggression to constrain self-expression and action.

Similar feelings underlie both aggression and depression. Hostility and anger arise from anxiety over separation (Bowlby, 1973) and from perceptions of unfairness and inequality (Averill, 1982; Ross and Van Willigen, 1996). These feelings also accompany depression; depressed women are more angry and hostile than non-depressed women (Droppelman and Wilt, 1993; Weissman and Paykel, 1974). Anger and hostility often result in turning anger against the self as well as against others.

If a woman perceives her *self* as the barrier to what she yearns for—positive relationships, inclusion, success—then she may turn the powerful rage of disconnection inward against herself. She blames herself for being unworthy, or not pretty enough, smart enough, lovable enough, and so on. Culture plays a vital role in women's tendency to self-blame and self-attack, providing images of how they "should" be in relationship (caring, kind, beautiful) and holding them responsible when relationships fail.[6] Many women's narratives reveal this self-blame:

> When I was going through this [abusive relationships], because I wasn't getting any support, I felt like, "Man, I'm the trouble-maker, I'm the one that's screwing up, I'm the one that's causing these people to behave like this to me," and I totally sucked in my feelings. (Karen, age 41, white, police officer)

> I'm angry at myself for not doing anything about [my husband's beatings]. And I'm mad because I know I have to do something about it but I don't know what to do. (Angie, age 25, Native American/Latino, unemployed)

I have a boyfriend, and when I'm jealous I feel ashamed about it. So sometimes I don't tell him and that leaves me with a lot of aggression. I start blaming myself because I'm feeling like this, and he starts loving someone else because I'm like this. (Olivia, age 20, Chilean, student)

In these self-attacks, social factors contributing to women's feelings of powerlessness in relationship have been converted into hated personal deficits. The women perceive themselves as creating the interpersonal problems. Each locates *within herself* the snag that makes her relationships unworkable; she turns aggression against herself. Directing hostility inward creates depressed feeling; rarely are women taught to convert feelings of hostility into outer, positive action.

Vulnerability to depression is not due to a personal deficit, but to having internalized self-defeating images of how to relate intimately. Just as the images that give rise to depression result in self-inhibition and self-criticism, so the mediators of aggression often inhibit women's use of their positive, creative force. At times these mediators of aggression prevent social harm and promote positive actions; at other times the mediators are too broadly cast and reinforce self-silencing and depression.

5

MASKING AGGRESSION

Ways of disguising aggression are as varied as the human imagination. But the basic pattern behind the differing forms remains the same: attempts to hurt, to oppose, or to express anger go underground to reach others through hidden channels, while surface behaviors mask the intent. Women often talked about indirect aggression in their interviews.

> Men are differently aggressive than women. The women are very manipulative. Extremely manipulative. And that's how the aggression comes out . . . It's a way of survival for women, I think. It was not and still is, in a lot of cases, not acceptable for a woman to be directly verbally and physically confrontational. So she learns other ways of handling conflict. (Jodi, age 35, white, corrections officer)

> That's how I think of that kind of indirect aggression, as pretending like it's aimed at this direction and actually it's aimed at this other direction. The goal is to hurt and to get the other person to change some kind of behavior that I don't like them doing, but I'm too weasely to say it to you directly so I'll do it in a more underground kind of way. That's always been my mental image for indirect aggression—you know, it's that you tunnel somewhere and it's secret and you don't let other people know about it. It would bring people to safety. So they wouldn't get caught by the other people in power. (Wendy, age 45, white, artist)

Her husband would be violent and abusive and he'd piss her off. She'd go out and spend money, you know, and he wasn't supposed to know what she'd paid for this chair, and the kids were all party to this, they all knew about it, but he never was gonna know. But her retaliation when he pissed her off, she'd go out and spend a lot of money. I mean it's like that's what happens when you don't express your anger directly. (Anna, age 40, white, artist)

I used to hang around with white guys, yeah. I was more or less a hippie, you could say that. My family hated it and that's when I really loved it, they *hated* it. I would always bring my hippie friends in. Man, I had over about $8,000 worth of records, Jethro Tull, Black Sabbath, all that shit. I had just stacks and stacks of albums all up and down the wall. And I would turn it up real high, especially when my brother's friends would come over. "Man, what the hell's wrong with your sister, man, she's playing that white shit." And I'd turn it up higher. (Vanessa, age 37, African American, unemployed)

Using such hidden channels for the delivery of aggression allows a hasty retreat if one is confronted: "I didn't mean what you think," "I wasn't angry," "I didn't mean to hurt you." Because the aggression is elusive, not physically or verbally overt, it can leave the recipient feeling confused about intent. Without clear evidence that harm was meant, retaliation may not be so swift or so severe.

Stereotypes surround women's use of indirection: "catty," "gossipy" women destroy relationships by spreading falsehoods; wicked stepmothers send poisonous surprises; deceitful, conspiring women hide behind sweet words that cut and castrate. Such stereotypes permeate social expectations about how women behave aggressively. Women's indirect delivery of aggression is culturally prescribed, socialized at home and in schools, yet, at the same time, is culturally condemned and seen as proof that women are more devious and less principled than men. Such conflicting cultural prescriptions and judgments powerfully affect women's self-experience.

The women I interviewed had no difficulty describing indirect aggression. Each recounted purposely disguising her aggression for strategic reasons. The interviews reveal three primary factors that lead women to mask their aggression: unequal power relations, socialization, and cultural expectations about feminine nonaggression.

Why Mask Aggression?

Unequal Power

Many women say they disguise their aggression to preserve their safety (or that of their children) in situations in which they lack power. They fear physical, economic, or emotional retaliation, particularly if they openly express negative emotion or willful opposition to someone more physically or socially powerful. Fear of consequences provides a compelling reason to mask opposition, conflict, or anger. Yet going underground often reinforces women's feelings of powerlessness and arouses their anger.[1]

Power imbalances take many forms, and fear of reprisal exists within many settings. Some women fear physical violence for their overt resistance; others fear negative professional consequences if they openly challenge what they perceive as a "clear decisional boys' club." Robin (age 48, white), a partner in a large law firm, speaks about using indirect behavior to deal with situations that anger her. For years, her law firm has held a dinner for partners which includes ceremonial cigar smoking. Robin considers this ritual an "incredibly strong statement that this is a male organization."

> I finally made the point enough times that someone finally decided that was a bad idea, smoking cigars. You know how they fixed it? They invited the men's wives because none of these men would smoke cigars in front of their wives. And I thought, that's not the fix. I said screw it. Just, you know, one doesn't cooperate occasionally. I didn't go to our partners' dinner this year. Of course, it was indirect . . . But I was hostile to the thing forever and finally just decided not—you know, my way of showing hostility is not to participate.

Robin resorts to what she calls "passive-aggressive behavior" to communicate her antagonism while also preserving her safety within the firm. Leaking hostile antagonism through passivity—through "not doing"—is a way to resist existing power structures without exposing herself to retaliation.

Indirection, however, does not always provide safety from reprisal. Gloria (age 34, Latina, unemployed), who often relies on her threatening voice and manner as a wall of self-protection (see Chapter 2), also uses social manipulation to get back at others. She has found retaliation for her indirect aggression to be as harsh as that for her direct verbal aggression.

> I used to gossip a lot. I broke myself from that. *[What do you mean, "gossip a lot"?]* Start shit. Initiate stuff. But I said, "I always be the one to wind up hurt physically." So I gave that up. But, you know, everybody got to learn by their mistakes . . . *[What would happen if you started stuff?]* They would like beat me down to the cement, you know, where you have to peel your face off the cement. That kind of thing. You learn quick.

Robin and Gloria are positioned very differently in society. Gloria has no economic clout, faces racial discrimination, and has been pushed to the margins; Robin wields power as a wealthy partner in a well-established firm. The easy assumption is that women who use their voices more loudly and resort to physical aggression more freely are less likely to resort to indirect aggression. But fear of retaliation often determines the use of indirect aggression; women in all social locations experience this fear.

Socialization

Women also say they use indirect aggression because of their childhood training. Girls show less physical, overt aggression than boys, who are given much more permission to hit, kick, punch, and yell (see Cotten et al., 1994; Perry, Perry, and Weiss, 1989; Parke and

Slaby, 1983). Elementary school girls are more likely to harm others through indirect aggression than boys (Crick and Grotpeter, 1995).

By the time they reach adulthood, many women have so well rehearsed their patterns of indirect aggression that such behaviors surface almost as a habit. Anna says she uses indirect aggression "automatically, in small ways, like making a comment that's not direct but that certainly conveys that I don't like something . . . It's still difficult for me to say 'I don't like this.' I think it's almost impossible not to find yourself somehow translating that into some sort of little passive-aggressive action or comment." Such behavior, used to avoid direct confrontation, is not evidence of women's "devious, manipulative, underhanded" character. Rather, it reveals culture at work through clearly delineated and expected "feminine" ways to avoid direct conflict.

Though I describe indirect aggression from women's perspective, undoubtedly men also resort to it, though for different reasons, with different attributions of meanings, and using different masks. Men's and women's forms of resistance and accommodation to dominance and powerlessness differ. The culture hands men a "manhood" script that defines their appropriate reactions to stress, frustration, or feelings of powerlessness: act out against others. The dominant "womanhood" script calls for the opposite: turn anger and stress inward against the self to protect others (Haste, 1994). Yet women do not always turn anger and stress against the self. Often they deliver hurt to their targets from behind a pastel, pink feminine mask. As they do so, their behavior meshes with demeaning stereotypes of femininity and often lowers their self-esteem. Since negative stereotypes of men do not include indirect aggression, when they use such behaviors to hurt others, the effects on their self-concept undoubtedly differ.

Most women say they learned to avoid direct conflict by watching their mothers. In response to the question "What did you learn about aggression from your mother?" forty women explicitly described their mothers' indirect behavior. Twenty-two of these women portrayed their mothers' indirect behavior in relation to dominating or abusive men.[2] Listen to Arliss (age 27, white, student), a former air force mechanic:

> My mother is a silent manipulator. She's very, very good at that
> ... my mom married someone who was very physically abusive
> to her and emotionally abusive, which was my father ... after
> their divorce she found someone else and got remarried and that
> was my stepfather. He's a very aggressive person. He would tell
> her she couldn't do something and she would go—she would
> find some other way to do it.

Arliss's stepfather tried to prevent her mother from getting a nursing degree after having five children. "He did everything in his power to make sure that she couldn't go back to school," but she resisted his control, working and saving her money for a number of years until she was able to quietly exercise her own will. While this example portrays positive, functional aggression going underground rather than indirect hostile aggression, what Arliss learned was that her mother avoided direct conflict with those who were more powerful. She saw a strategy of compliance that allowed resistance and rebellion without overtly challenging power structures, and that did not jeopardize basic survival or security.

Women also say their mothers taught them passive-aggressive behavior as a method of control: what appears on the outside as passive inaction actually carries an active, controlling intent which affects others as surely as does a shout. Yet a shout engages and creates overt conflict; passive-aggressive behavior keeps conflict covert and refuses direct engagement around difference. Passive-aggressive control can be very effective, as Brooke (age 35, white, attorney) notes when describing her mother: "You can't get her to do anything she doesn't want to do but somehow you get the idea that something's all your fault, and she never actually actively does anything but she has control by not doing anything ... She has absolute power that way, whatever she wants she gets."

While most clinicians attribute hostile intent to passive-aggressive actions, for many women such actions may simply be safe ways of resisting others' control while attempting to exert their own. Anita (age 33, white, police officer) describes her mother as

> very submissive and very malleable. She was easily intimidated
> and, if anything, kind of like a professional victim. She was pas-

sive-aggressive, she did not get angry. Absolute refusal to get involved in a conflict. She would fade into the woodwork, go into complete denial, refuse to listen—"Oh, this is not happening"—deny my right to have feelings about certain things . . . Instead of facing up she did these things. And it drove me crazy, just an absolute refusal to deal with the problem.

Anita learned a different lesson about conflict from her brothers: "When you've got four big brothers and about twenty-five guys over at the house who are swearing and belching and drinking and carrying on, you learn how—I learned how to survive, that no matter what they said I was not going to buckle under and cry. I carried that into police work in terms of getting into a rough-and-tumble field where I could be aggressive and assertive." Anita saw that her brothers' form of aggression was more successful and empowering than that modeled by her mother. She chose a field she thought would reinforce in herself ways of relating to others that were preferable to her mother's passive-aggressive behavior.

Children do not have to follow their parents' modeling for dealing with conflict, yet the early-learned pathways of dealing with difference carry lasting effects, particularly when they are culturally condoned and learned as part of gender roles. Whether or not their mothers acted as these women portray them is less important than how the women conceptualize their own indirect behavior. Since my goal is to detail their understanding of the origins and functions of their indirect aggression, their explanations of what happened matter more than what actually took place.

Many of the women whose mothers modeled indirect aggression consciously work toward healthier ways of dealing with anger and conflict. Karen (age 41, white, police officer), holds her mother responsible for the beatings she received from her stepfather. Like most victimized daughters, she blames her mother for failing to protect her and has vowed never to get into the same position herself.[3]

My mother was a nonaggressor, but she—I can remember getting whaled on by my stepfather and begging her to help me. I can still see it, she was standing in the doorway with a smile on her face as he's beating the living tar out of me. She was getting enjoyment out of that. Then, plus I knew at one point that she was a victim of [abuse] and it had been in the family. And I told myself, "The buck stops here." And I wasn't going to have any kids because of that. I got sterilized because I was so terrified of passing it on, the sickness.

Karen felt her mother's inability to intervene was actually a refusal to do so, and considered it a form of indirect aggression against *her*.

Those women who reported habitually disguising their own aggression were critical of themselves for doing so. Wendy (age 45, white, artist) says of her indirect aggression, "I loathe it!" She learned about disguising aggression from her mother: "I saw that so much growing up—my mother didn't feel like she had the power, the position to be able to be direct with her aggression, then she was being indirect and so that looked like, to me, a horrible way of doing it." Although she tries not to repeat her mother's patterns of behavior, Wendy finds they spring forth, unbidden, in times of conflict. She consciously works, moment by moment, to state her oppositional feelings in direct, positive ways rather than to express them "sneakily" through underground channels.

Rhonda (age 32, African American, social worker) describes a mother who does not fit the stereotype of the strong, outspoken African-American woman:

I didn't see a lot of anger . . . I never seen a display of assertiveness from Mom, never. I never seen displays of aggressiveness . . . She'd always say, "You need to shut your mouth and you need to think about people's feelings," but people would take advantage of her. Mom is kind of, well, she'll be evasive, she'll hold stuff for like weeks and weeks before she'll just have the nerve to say something. I just said I wasn't going to be like that.

Even though Rhonda vowed not to follow in her mother's indirect footsteps, it has taken her most of her adult life to overcome the pattern of silencing her voice and backing down from direct conflict in relationships (see Chapter 6 for Rhonda's story).

Cultural Expectations

Women also describe masking their aggression in order to present the *appearance* of nonaggression, that is, to conform to the expectation that they will be nice and unhostile. Indirect aggression offers a way to comply with such restrictions on one level, yet to resist on another.

Many women feel they cannot overtly express their feelings, oppose others, or exercise their wills. Instead, much like the brightly painted Russian dolls that nest one inside another, they hide their intent inside a different form, and another, and another, placing feelings within charming exteriors that hold surprising contents. The recipient ends up with a doll that appears to be one form, most often that of good femininity, but that contains a complexity of hidden intentions.

Gaile (age 40, white, photojournalist), talks about this gap between what she presents and what she intends. Indirect aggression, she says, "makes me kind of squirm. It's like I'm not comfortable with this. I mean what I'd say is it's dishonesty. You're saying one thing and you're doing another. You know, you've got an ulterior motive or you're going after something but you're going to masquerade it as something else." The undermining aspect of indirection lies in its pretense of goodness. Posing as the devil when one is not so bad does not carry the same kind of moral condemnation as posing as a "good woman" when one is not.

Women often mask their aggression behind a veneer of "nice" behavior. Wendy, like Gaile, accuses herself of hypocrisy:

> In previous close relationships I have felt like all of who I am is not acceptable in that there was an underground side that couldn't—or a controlling side that wanted to shape and make the other person what I wanted them to be . . . The anger and stuff was real underground and came out in ways that are ugly. I think because I didn't feel trustworthy myself and so I would do untrustworthy things and be picky. You know, just find all the little things that I didn't like. I would loathe that in myself, the picking on him, as much I loathed the thing that I was picking on about the other person. It was destructive to me and to

the other person and to the relationship. I think it's really un- dermining. I didn't like myself very much because of being so nice, always trying to look like I was so nice and a nice person and that I wasn't that bitch, the one that was trying to mold this poor guy, and get him to do stuff and get him to be different.

The "bitch" is the woman who has a will and wants to exert control over her partner. The "nice" woman pretends to accept him and does not bring her preferences directly into relationship; her desire to control, affect, and shape her lovers subversively undermines her niceness and the relationship. Wendy is *acting nice and feeling mean,* a pattern also described by other women who see aggression as unfamiliar territory. Michelle (age 38, white, writer) elaborates on the meaning of "make nice," a way she acts when angry at some- one: "It means you would be repressing your authenticity, your genuineness. You know, your own truth, your feelings, your values, your philosophy, in order to create the perception of a peaceful interaction and 'Hey, aren't we getting along great?' . . . While the reality is I'm pissed as hell at you."

If women learn that it is hurtful to engage in direct conflict, then masking aggression can, on one level, feel "better" than caus- ing overt dissension in relationship. Denying the hostile compo- nent of hurtful words or actions conceals the "immoral" aspect of hurt and allows the woman to preserve a sense that she is morally better than one who causes overt dissension. Such obfuscation can lead to confusion over who is blameworthy: the one who engaged in indirect aggression, or the one who attempts to clarify what occurred. Masking aggression can also confuse assignment of re- sponsibility for the feelings of hurt that result from hidden acts. A person feeling hurt by disguised aggression can wonder: "Am I too sensitive? What did she really intend?" The measure of injury felt often seems unwarranted by the act, so the recipient can feel re- sponsible for the negative feelings.

Anna, who now uses anger as a "force to drive the green" (see Chapter 1), notes that her mother dealt with anger indirectly:

Honesty was being taken as the camouflage for anger. Because for my mother I can see that was probably the only aggression she was going to be able to indulge in. Anything else might kill her because of the situation she was in with my stepfather. And she could get away with a certain amount of using language to hit with, in a sense. But I don't think she wanted to acknowledge that that's what she was doing. And it's like somehow to make this repressed anger a virtue so she could feel, "I'm virtuously direct and honest." And that's quite a leap and that's quite a struggle to do it. Because there's a part that says, "It's not okay for me to be angry, I must be virtuous; but I am angry so I must make that anger a virtue." You know, it's like, "I couldn't help it, I was just being honest." I don't think so. I think it was a real twisted way to deal with something that wasn't acceptable—or safe.

Anna's mother resolves her predicament—how to hurt another yet stay safe from retaliation; how to see herself as good while acting aggressively—by donning a mask of virtue. The problem is that the disguises intended to ensure survival can also deceive the self and confuse interactions. Trying to stay good and safe, we can inflict hurt while denying it; we can get lost behind the masks, and find ourselves in psychological and ethical danger different from the danger of retaliation. When feigned honesty becomes the camouflage for anger, honesty itself becomes suspect.

Women often use stereotypes of feminine behavior to hide their aggression. For example, although Blythe (age 42, white, police officer) has changed from "working so hard to please my husband, to please other people, and failing miserably and not understanding why" to someone who is clear, direct, and stands her own ground, she can still "fall back on the other sometimes":

Sometimes I know I do this little wheedling, little-girl thing when I'm asking for something. I could just hear that little wheedly little, you know, it was *yuk!* . . . I don't like putting on that kind of face. It's talking prissy, it's talking baby talk, but it's another aspect of acting, you know. I'm acting, it's taking a different role, but again, you're trying to manipulate somebody into doing something, and I don't like the manipulation, I don't like the dishonesty.

This type of pretense—"acting" like a girl—reveals femininity to be what Judith Butler calls a "structure of impersonation." Not only are there social rules about how women should assert themselves in relationship, gender itself is a performance, "a kind of imitation for which there is no original" (Butler, 1991, 21). Lyn Brown (1998) notes that white working-class and middle-class girls, as they learn to "perform" their anger in gender-specific ways, also master how to "ventriloquate" a voice of conventional femininity. Women know what the dominant society considers the feminine style of asserting their wills from stereotypes in the media and from socialization within the home. Blythe's struggle against ventriloquating a voice of conventional femininity—one that feels "wheedling" and childish—centers on how to be direct and honest.

Women's narratives reveal that they utilize indirect aggression as a *strategy of safety*. They often exaggerate gender-stereotypic behaviors such as silence, sweetness, and an appearance of passivity in order to exert their wills, resist domination, or get back at others. Thus they outwardly comply with femininity while, at the same time, they resist femininity's central dictate—to avoid hurting others. Mandy (age 32, white, student) uses such behavior to create a safe, private space for her own thoughts:

> It's like being able to play the game of Monopoly knowing that you have to develop a strategy. You don't change the rules, but you have to develop a strategy, and so that's what I've done. For me, it's really dangerous to accept everything at face value. Really dangerous, and so my strategy is to appear that I'm accepting . . . and sort of do that pastel, you know, pink, nod my head and smile a lot and then think about just how I feel about what's happening in . . . whatever the situation might be.

Mandy doesn't change the rules of gender but uses them to her advantage. Her outer appearance of female compliance masks a willful, oppositional stance. As Gaile says, when she is "passive-aggressive" it means she is "trying to appear cool and gentle on the surface and underneath, really, have an ulterior motive or secondary plan in place."

Women both utilize and resist social conventions for female aggression. They creatively use a variety of ruses in order to avoid discovery. Sometimes these indirect means are *positive* in affording a liminal space between compliance and overt resistance, a place to practice opposition and gather strength. Or indirection can be a strategy to gain a foothold in white middle-class professional settings whose rules prohibit the kind of outspoken, confrontational honesty some women use in their home communities (Hurtado, 1996). Sometimes indirect aggression is purely *retaliatory*, intended to hurt another person, to "get back at him any way I possibly can." Sometimes its purpose is to *control*, using facades of compliance that subordinates have developed to exercise power over dominants. But in each of these instances, masking aggression carries grave dangers of self-deception about one's motives and feelings, and can preserve destructive patterns of interacting with others, primarily because it keeps conflict covert. Further, as we shall see, masking aggression creates a space of resistance that is wedged in between an appearance of "goodness" and outright rebellion that may bring swift retaliation.

Forms of Indirection

Manipulation

Manipulation carries the connotation of fraudulence: that one controls others by the "shrewd use of influence"; that one's intent is not clear, direct, and aboveboard. In large part, we consider indirect aggression to be negative because it houses the ploys and stratagems of manipulation. As a stereotype, manipulation is often ascribed to women's "character" or "personality" without inquiry into power and relational configurations. As Karen, the police officer mentioned earlier, says: "It happens in a situation of inequality, when you need to get what you want and you can't do it directly, because if you do it directly, you *know* you won't get what you want . . . I don't know, is that manipulation? It sounds like it's another survival skill . . . When women can't use their voices directly, and have to influence what they want indirectly, they manipulate." When do women use manipulation as indirect aggression? And how might they use manipulation in functional, even positive ways?

Twenty-six of the women I interviewed describe their own manipulation as a form of aggressive behavior, though they designate different meanings and actions through their examples. Mandy, who, in the process of getting sober, has learned "to be honest about who I really was and how I really felt," recalls an incident from her past:

> I remember when [my friend] and I first sobered up, then talking about the things that had happened, the violence, the incidents, and talking about how we'd . . . scuffled with our husbands. At one point when I was pregnant with my second child, my husband pushed me, and he didn't push me hard enough to make anything happen, but I backed my way out of the doorway and faked a fall down the stairs to make him feel like shit. That was my whole purpose. And to finally be able to talk with this other woman who had done nearly the same exact thing and cried victim about it, I mean, "Oh, my God, look what you did to the baby," you know. And our sole purpose in that was to make these men feel like shit, to hold them fully responsible for me and my life. I wanted them to be responsible.

When her husband pushed Mandy, she did not retaliate physically, which she knew would be likely to result in her injury. Rather, she exaggerated the harmful consequences of his acts to make him feel guilty, and to gain some control in a situation in which she felt none.

Power in relationships is determined, in part, by who defines how differences will be negotiated. Mandy's husband had set a pattern of resolving disagreements through physical and verbal assault. Wanting to stay in the relationship, and faced with the "lack of any other way to deal with the ways I felt," Mandy tried to show him the logical consequences of his pushing. Within the framework that had been set up for defining the terms of their arguments, Mandy's action was an attempt to de-escalate the physical aspects (interrupting a cycle of push-retaliate-hit-retaliate) while escalating the emotional overtones. By "crying victim," Mandy released her rage against her husband's actions but preserved her safety by employing a form of resistance that many would call manipulation.

In her honest self-appraisal, Mandy acknowledges the goal that lay behind her actions. Angry over her own drinking and her feeling of being "out of control," she attempted to make others responsible for her life. She describes this interaction as fraudulent in its indirection, and as hostile. Acts of indirect aggression must be examined on three levels: power, the actor's intent, and the means of resistance used. While *hostile manipulation* has as its goal the intent to shame or hurt another person without being detected, such actions must always be viewed in relational context, particularly with an eye to relations of power.

Other women describe their manipulation as "negative" yet without such a hostile component. Rather it appears as a conscious strategy they call on to assert their wills in relationship without being detected. For example, Karen talks about how she deals with a supervisor she detests:

> I'm one of the best manipulators that you will ever meet, and I learned it from my mom. I used that forever and ever, and to me it's negative. But I've called on it a couple of times, and I've used it for things that I needed. And it's the only way I can play the game, and I know I'm doing it, and I check in with myself before I start, and I look at everything, and then I think, "Okay, just this once," and then I'll go ahead and do it. By manipulation, I mean, I know where he's coming from, it's just that you got to play the game a little bit better, you got to be more conscious of it . . . it's like I got to make this 360-degree pass around him and figure out exactly what I'm gonna do to get what I want. What I have to say, what I have to do, what I'm willing to say, what I'm willing to do . . . it's like everything's calculated, and then when I get what I want, I walk out of his office, and I feel really good about it because I know what I've just accomplished.

This *controlling manipulation* includes a clear-eyed appraisal of what is needed to "play the game a little bit better" and accomplish what she wants. As a woman in a man's profession, Karen has encountered sexual harassment and hostility and feels she cannot be direct much of the time. With an officer who has power over her, she calculates what she needs to do to achieve a desired result. Such manipulation for control differs from manipulation that carries a specifically hostile intent.

Maggie (age 37, white, police officer) describes using this kind of controlling manipulation in intimate relationships:

> I feel like I've developed quite a few good arguing skills from arguing with my mother. And sometimes they're real manipulative and I really don't like to do that, but that just kind of comes because of those tapes that play from childhood . . . Say during an argument I might push a couple of buttons that I know really set my partner off and I'll almost time them so that I kind of have control over the argument. And then my mind's like thinking, "Okay, and then what else did I want to bring up at this time?" That is like kind of dirty manipulation. I mean it's knowing that by them getting angry, they're gonna get off track, and then I can go anywhere I want with the argument . . . That doesn't happen a whole lot anymore because I know when I'm doing that. You know, it's almost like a Jekyll and Hyde, it's like this is not really part of how, who I really am. This is a part of who I was at one time, and to me, that was my survival training, so to speak.

Maggie considers this "dirty manipulation"—but this manipulation merely seeks to control, not to harm. Her shame about using it may be rooted in a belief that anger has a functional, positive purpose and that this manipulative behavior turns what might be a useful argument into a situation she uses for her own nefarious goals.

Women also describe using manipulation for positive, functional purposes: to accomplish a greater good, or to avoid escalating a situation that might lead to harm. Sherna (age 33, white, police officer) says: "I feel smart when I manipulate . . . What I mean is that I take on the persona to make the scenario go better. It's like if I need to arrest somebody and he thinks of me as his grand-daughter and he calls me sweetie, then I'm his sweetie, you bet. 'Turn around, sir, click, click, we'll talk sweetie talk all the way home to the precinct.' I will play that role, you know."

Sherna recalls a specific example:

> It was a domestic dispute, domestics are always the worst, and it was an ex-con. He was a huge bodybuilder, he had just gotten out of prison. He was upset, we went in, we didn't have enough probable cause to arrest him, but yet he was refusing to leave. And this man was big, he was like a brick house, he was solid muscle, very intimidating, tall, muscular. Even the guys were kind of cowering away from him, and I was talking because I thought in this scenario it would be best if I tried to use my female-type persuasion to change the situation. His son came up and his son liked me and was hitting on me, "Hey baby, how's it going, ooh, ooh" . . . And I says, "Ooh, you look as strong as your dad." He says "Yeah," so I started flirting with him and I said, "You know, I bet you could do something great for me." He goes, "Oh, anything for you, babe." And I said, "Can you take your dad out of here for me?" I said, "I know your dad's really cool and things are probably pretty upsetting right now, but can you just take him for a drive and get him out of here, let things cool down?" "Oh honey, baby, anything for you." Now the officers watching this interaction think that I'm flirting with this guy and that he's somehow, you know, wowing me, but actually what I'm doing is I'm flattering him to death. He takes his dad, not only does he have him leave the house, he drives him from the scene and he thinks that he's my hero and that's great and I've just resolved the problem.

Sherna's use of her "female-type persuasion" provides a way to de-escalate conflict in a tense standoff. She manipulates the situation by assuming the guise of female flirtatious behavior, perfectly cal-culated to defuse aggression. She calls this gender performance "smart." It is brilliant. By her conscious use of *positive manipulation,* she transforms stiff-backed, edgy men into accomplices and on-lookers to her skilled handling of an explosive scene.

Silence

For centuries, silence has been a central aspect of women's roles. Physical and emotional threats by those with more power enforced this silence. Not all silence indicates compliance or inequality: both women and men employ silence as a powerful weapon of anger and control. For women, such *hostile silence* exaggerates the mandate that they not directly state their needs and feelings. It carries the flavor: "Fine, if I can't speak, I'll mock silence through my carica-ture of it, and I'll demonstrate my hostile feelings through silence." While silence maintains a facade of nonaggression, it often masks control, anger, and, at times, the intent to hurt others.

Many women recall their mothers' use of this strategy.[4] Carol (age 32, white, biologist) says of her mother: "Instead of getting angry she would just get quiet. She would just go sit in the kitchen and pretty much ignore us. Pretty much ignore—that was her anger . . . And I don't do well with being yelled at myself. I just clam up. I do the same." And Kim (age 34, social worker), whose mother was from the Philippines, says:

> My mom was really the "two-month, I won't talk to you" bit with my dad, with us. And then there was just real aggressive facial expressions, real negative body language, the sharpness of the movements—the tension was in the air. You didn't want to be in the kitchen. She wouldn't cook dinner. You fix it yourself. She's in and she's out. That, to me, is the worse aggression be-cause it's not out there. You have to guess . . . You can't approach them. They just put up the walls and there is no breaking down the walls. But if you know you can get someone to talk, then they're willing to communicate and to work this out and we'll get through. But when a person's quiet, they are saying, "Abso-lutely not. You pissed me off and I don't like you guys and so, I'm going to punish you." You feel it. You feel it hard.

Kim speaks to the confusing, controlling aspect of hostile silence: "it's not out there"; it provides nothing specific to engage with. As a tactic of control, it refuses a dialogue that could resolve disputes. In children it creates anxiety about the security of attachment, because it gives them an absent presence—a mother who is physically there but emotionally unavailable. Silence fosters disconnection, not resolution and reconnection. In partnered relationships, women's angry silence is associated with their depression (Jack, 1991, 1999a; Penza, Reiss, and Scott, 1997; Thompson, 1995).

Women are aware of the controlling aspects of hostile silence from watching their mothers. As adults, they engage in such behavior toward their own families. Nikki (39, white, teacher), who is married with two children, conveys feelings of destructiveness and anger by

> rattling the dishes around, making comments under my breath that nobody can hear—but they *can* hear. They can't hear what I'm saying, but they can hear *me*. If I say things and my family hears it, I can pretend I didn't say it. And instead of figuring out what's really bothering me and talking about that, or knowing what's really bothering me and really being afraid to talk about that because it's either going to cause a fight with him or it's about me and there's nothing to do about it—oh, I totally sabotage my family that way. It's not like I can stop it, because it's a safe outlet right now.

This poisonous rattling carries a warning as clear as the sound of a snake's tail: steer clear; I am angry but unapproachable.

Nikki struggles with depression. She often feels a deep rage that she does not understand; she watches it unfold in a "vicious circle of . . . resentment, blame, anger, and then self-blame and then guilt." When her anger explodes in screaming or name-calling, Nikki moves to the self-blame and guilt segments of this circle. She travels over and over the same ground like a tethered animal, unable to use her anger positively to break out of her well-worn paths. The alternative of muttering silence appears safer because it stays within the edict of good femininity: don't be verbally or physically aggressive. Nikki is aware of how her silence affects her family— "total sabotage"—but uses it to maintain the status quo and allow her anger to leak out. Even though angry silence leads to less guilt and self-blame than ineffective explosions, it rarely leads to dialogue and resolution. For Nikki, caught in depression, it leads nowhere.

Silence can also serve as an unhostile means of controlling others and asserting one's will. For example, Maria (age 32, Native American/Latino, attorney), whom we met in earlier chapters, does not usually bite her tongue to keep anger out of relationships, but she does purposefully withdraw through silence:

> There are times when I know, in a professional capacity and a personal one, that it's just not good that we connect or talk. We haven't resolved what the issue is, it's not going to be resolved, and sometimes time is going to be the only thing that's going to help. And one reason why I think I do that with some relationships is because I know that they're real valued and they're bigger than I can handle emotionally . . . at that time. To be honest, it's also a form of control . . . I think it isn't control like "I want to manipulate and make you feel bad" . . . it's more of "I want to be in control of what's happening here, I don't want to be at the mercy of your anger either."

This *controlling silence* is self-protective and regulates emotion in relationships without direct engagement.

Silence can also be a form of positive resistance. It can be used to pry open a small space between compliance and outright rebellion, or to create a neutral ground within a relationship filled with smoldering hostility. For women raised in cultural and familial contexts that prohibit their verbal or physical aggression, *resisting silence* becomes a strategy to preserve their agency and sense of self.

Laura (age 50, Japanese American, attorney) used silence to create a new space in her life, a space out of reach of her husband's control. Angry about the subservience her husband expected of her, she purposely disconnected from him through silence. She began by

> not saying things or not disclosing things—when I'm a really open person—but just saying less and saying less . . . And part of that, not saying things to him, was to take power over my own life in some ways. And all the time that I was in law school, I can't remember when he asked me how things were going. So

I think my not telling him anything was, this became mine. You know, I had the full power and control over this arena. And he never asked me. He was never interested. But, all the more, I wasn't going to tell him.

Laura considers this silent withdrawal a form of aggression: "Distance is aggression to me. I mean, one of the ways that I create or I give an aggressive response is to distance myself." Yet she evaluates silence and indirection as positive for the power they gave her in an unequal and deteriorating marriage.

Laura's experience as a first-generation Japanese American taught her that "my culture doesn't value aggression like the broader American culture appears to value it." When she was a girl, "a lot of emphasis was placed on being nice and proper and polite and all of the things that women are intended to do . . . As children we were supposed to be seen but not heard, that kind of upbringing." Trained into nonaggression and silence about her anger, in twelve years of marriage she developed indirect strategies to affect her husband negatively. Her aggression, she says, was "responsive in relationship": her husband's belittling comments and infatuation with another woman had inflicted "a lot of emotional damage and I didn't even recognize it."

Eventually she began to hurt him back. First she tried to express her anger directly, but "never felt acknowledged about it so that we could move from there to a resolution of whatever was causing the anger. Or even explore ways where the anger would be constructive." Then she resorted to indirection: "I have been aggressive by sarcasm. By doing, not cruel but less obvious aggressive acts. Say something that I know will . . . hurt somebody else, or throw them off balance or do something that is going to put the balance in my favor."

Like many other women, Laura felt leaving her marriage was not an option: "I come from the background of being in a marriage forever . . . I had made the commitment and had actually no thought, no real thought that I wasn't going to stay married to this man." Indirect aggression through silence and sarcasm was a way to enact her anger within the relationship without violating her moral, cultural rules. It also kept her sense of agency alive during a time when she had "lost confidence" and "felt unworthy."

Such resisting silence does not occur only within intimate relationships; resistance can also take the form of *political silence*. Aída Hurtado notes that women of color strategically suspend their voices in white communities "with a specific goal in mind and return to their own safe communities to share what they have learned and to verify the accuracy of their observations. Ultimately, the knowledge obtained by remaining silent is like a reconnaissance flight into enemy territory that allows for individual and group survival." Hurtado describes this tactical use of silence as "akin to camouflaging oneself when at war in an open field; playing possum at strategic times causes the power of the silent one to be underestimated" (1996, 382). This political silence is different from the type of self-silencing that leads to depression: women who silence themselves without a community within which to share knowledge and political purpose, who employ silence as an interpersonal strategy to keep relationship, more often end up depressed and self-alienated.

Finally, silence can be used purely for self-protection in situations in which women fear being abused but still want to convey their anger. This *safe silence* conceals as it communicates, hiding a woman's anger behind a mask whose meaning she can quickly change if necessary. Gloria (age 34, Latina, unemployed), who is now trying to find relationships with men who are not abusive, describes what she does when she gets angry: "I don't say nothing. And then the way I speak, I shorten my sentences. My boyfriend knows when I'm mad though, and he ain't even known me that long. I don't say nothing and I'll get an attitude problem, so he knows." If called on it, Gloria can quickly attribute her behavior to some other cause and deflect retaliation.

Silence, then, is a double-edged sword. When controlled, it can be wielded to protect the self, or to create a space within relationship in which to formulate new directions. Thus hostile silence, controlling silence, resisting silence, political silence, and safe silence can enhance possibilities for creating change in the self and in relational patterns.[5] But the sword can also cut the other way. Keeping anger out of relationship or leaking it into relationship through belligerent, aggressive silence brings no change in the conditions that arouse it. Silence builds no bridges to others that could lead to dialogue, reconciliation, or new relational patterns. The hostility vented through silence affects others negatively. The double nature of hostile silence is captured by the sentence "The medium *is* the message." The medium of silence communicates anger but contradicts anger's call for a response. Instead, it conveys: "There's nothing to do about it; you can't reach me or my anger on the other side of silence."

Sweetness

Women speak of masking their aggression behind "sweetness," of exaggerating "nice," feminine behavior while also defying its moral injunction not to hurt others. This tactic can confuse the recipient: Which aspect of the message is real—the sugary tone of voice, or the feeling of being hurt by what is said? Like certain forms of silence, the guise of sweet concern can allow a woman to express anger without triggering retaliation.

Kim (age 34, first-generation Filipina/Danish American, social worker) was in an abusive marriage for seven years. She and her two daughters live with her boyfriend. Her ex-husband, Ron, the father of one of the daughters, now lives at Kim's mother's house, so she sees him often. During their marriage he beat her frequently and attempted to kill her three times.

Kim's rage toward Ron is mixed with empathy. She fluctuates between wanting to hurt him and trying to understand him:

> I say, "Okay, here's this poor person, he was brought up in the projects, he's dyslexic, he's confused, he's depressed, he's this, he's that." And then I turn around and I go, "So what? I don't care." And then, so there's this battle. And I say, "Why doesn't he just get out of my life? Why doesn't he just go away, why can't I tell him, 'Go away'?" I'm constantly fighting it.

In addition to her ambivalence, Kim's fear of her ex-husband's retaliation shapes her strategies of indirect aggression. As she puts it: "I can be super sweet and be a bitch":

> I never do it in an attacking way. It's super sweet. I want to say it, but I don't want him to know that I'm really just twisting it around in his back. I'm just super nice about it. I go, "Well, gosh," you know, that really sweet—and he just looks at me. I don't go, "Hey, you animal!" I just go, "You know, well, my boyfriend, he just feels that"—just really super nice so he doesn't get really offended and he doesn't turn around and get super aggressive . . . I just think he's so stupid! . . . He looks at me just really confused because I don't think he really knows how to take it. I go, "Well, gosh, I hope I'm not offending you in any way" . . . I try to just take the rough edges off of it so it's not so apparent, so that he has to think twice about, you know, "Is she trying to be mean to me? Is she trying to—?" He tells me sometimes, "You know, I just think I'm going crazy." And I go, "Well gosh, Ron, maybe you are." Don't think that I don't! I go, "Have you ever thought about seeing a psychologist or something . . . just get it out, talk about it with someone? It really would help."

Kim acted like a female impersonator as she described these iterations, imitating sweet femininity with an exaggerated, honeyed voice. With Ron, she mimics nurturance and solicitude in order to confuse him, to disguise her attempts to control and hurt him and avoid retaliation.

Realistic fears drive Kim to mask her intent to hurt with a poisonous sweetness: "I have to watch it because I really think that he has the capability of killing me . . . He tried to run me over with a 280Z on the sidewalk . . . I know he's quite capable because he's a very dark, deep, depressed person." Labeling Kim's behavior devious and manipulative misses its context. Her indirect retaliation is a way of refusing victimization and powerlessness, a way to regain some sense of control in a situation that has damaged her for years. It allows her to resist, take control, yet outwardly comply with the norms of "good" femininity so as to *appear* unchallenging and submissive. Her sweet aggression operates as a form of safe retaliation—a way to give back some of the hurt she has received. She can see Ron as stupid: she has reversed the roles they played during their marriage and has put him in the powerless role. She sees this reversal and the hurt she can inflict as a kind of justice.

Her strategy of sweet revenge perfectly reflects both sides of her ambivalence: her concern and empathy through surface niceness, and her anger and hatred through "just twisting it around in his back." Her mean sweetness lets her preserve the ambivalent tie while, this time, she controls what happens in the relationship.

This type of intentional hurt affects Kim's self-esteem:

> I don't feel good about it. Because after I've done it, I'm always mad at myself because I think, "Kim, that is so below you. It's so petty." And I think . . . "I'm not a petty person, but why am I being petty here? It is totally unnecessary. I'm way above having to stoop so low to have to do this" . . . I don't mind hurting him and I can admit that openly and freely without a doubt and without any guilt, but what I do feel bad about is that I personally have lowered myself when I do that. It's not that I feel guilty about doing it to him but just the act of having to do that. I don't like that I would do that.

It is not the hurt she causes her ex-husband that bothers Kim, but the fact that she has "lowered herself" from her own standards to interact according to *his* standards, which allow him to purposefully cause hurt.

Kim's desire to "just cut him up any way I can, because that is what he did to me" leads her to indirect aggression. Since Ron is the father of her daughter, she cannot completely disengage from him. Trying to avoid physical costs of his retaliation, she incurs a psychological cost. This cost is revealed in her inner arguments about whether her behavior is "bad" or justified. Her aggressive self says: "I can't just tell him to go away because I think I want to torture him longer and that's something I am still battling. I'm just thinking, 'Okay, since you're making yourself within reach, any chance I get I'm just going to go . . . say something.'" But meanwhile her "good" self is saying: "I don't want to torture him. But because he's making it so easy for me to do it, I do it. I'm not a mean person; I'm more really, I'm a really good person. And I don't like to think bad about anyone and I don't like to do bad acts." At this point, such "torture" keeps Kim deeply connected to her ex-husband. It also has a negative effect on her sense of self as she judges her "bad acts." Her task is to end this destructive way of remaining connected to him.

Danielle (age 48, white, daycare worker) also tells of using sweetness to mask her aggression. Her mother taught her: "When someone is giving you shit, kill them with kindness." One Sunday after church Danielle was in line to sign up for volunteering, and an 8-year-old, developmentally delayed boy in the line was talking for a long time to the person at the desk. Danielle, who was in a hurry, interrupted to ask if she could go ahead of him. Later the boy's mother came up to her in front of other people and said she had been inconsiderate and rude: "I responded by taking the woman's arm, apologizing profusely, and it completely stopped her. My mother's phrase came to me; I did exactly what she had taught, and killed her with kindness. What I felt was anger, defensiveness, a wish to tell the woman she was out of line and rude; but what I did was to be just as nice and sweet and apologetic as I could."

Strategically turning on sweet, contrite femininity let Danielle avoid two potential traps: the shame she was bound to feel in the face of this public upbraiding, and the conflict that would be generated by her own anger in response to the mother's justified criticism. By disguising her anger behind a pink, feminine mask of profuse apology, Danielle made any genuine communication impossible and also robbed the boy's mother of her outrage by a feigned remorse. Her facade of nice, yielding, nurturing femininity disguised a host of hidden feelings and intentions.

Medusa's Stare

In the ancient world, a female face surrounded by serpent-hair was a widely recognized symbol of divine, female wisdom. Known as Neith of Egypt, Medusa represented the Destroyer component of the Triple Goddess, a symbolic acknowledgment that destruction of old forms is necessary for life. The snakes on her head were mythological symbols not only of wisdom and divinity but of power, healing, and rebirth (Walker, 1983). Freud (1959, quoted in Bowers, 1990) erroneously reduced this icon of a powerful female gaze to a "symbol of horror" representing the female genital region, an image of a "profound lack," a screen upon which others project their fears. Instead, Medusa is so terrifying because of her activity— her powerful subjectivity that has the capacity to fasten an angry, unyielding female gaze on others. If others meet her gaze, the force of her subjectivity turns them into "things," into objects of *her* perspective, and thus freezes their inner worlds.

A hostile stare can alter one's self-experience. Caught in the spotlight of another's searing gaze, self-experience shifts from perceiving to *being perceived*, from subject to object. Audre Lorde conveys the power that a hate-filled, objectifying look has to paralyze a child, freezing her in that moment as the object of someone else's contempt:

> I don't like to remember the cancellation and hatred, heavy as my wished-for death, seen in the eyes of so many white people from the time I could see . . . The AA subway train to Harlem . . . a woman in a fur hat . . . She jerks her coat closer to her . . . she has communicated her horror to me . . . When I look up the woman is still staring at me, her nose holes and eyes huge. And suddenly I realize there is nothing crawling up the seat between us; it is me she doesn't want her coat to touch . . . No word has been spoken. I'm afraid to say anything to my mother because I don't know what I've done . . . Something's going on here I do not understand, but I will never forget it. Her eyes. The flared nostrils. The hate. (1984, 147–148)

Lorde details the psychic space that lies between the hostile eyes that look at her and her "I" that looks back. To the child this space seems vast, unfathomable, full of shame. Only later does she develop the capacity to refuse to have her subjectivity turned to stone by such hatred. She becomes one who actively names, judges, and "looks back" in return.

Certain types of looks—steely-eyed hatred, cold disdain—are ways of delivering aggression indirectly. Eyes can express powerful emotions and intentions, such as a determination to hurt or destroy another. One can always deny the intent or feeling behind a malignant stare, and this makes it a relatively safe means to deliver hostility.

Verbal expressions reveal the persisting belief that the eye carries malevolent power: "If looks could kill, he would be dead." Eyes "burn holes" in others, people "look daggers," glances are sharp, penetrating, keen, deadly. The fear that the eye has the power to injure or to alter reality is captured in "Evil Eye" superstitions. Women tried as witches were often accused of looking at others in a harmful way. Cross-culturally, people share the idea that the human eye penetrates or pierces, and that it can invade personal space (Greenacre, 1926).

Patterns of looking, staring, and averting the gaze follow hierarchies of dominance and submission. Members of dominant groups have the "right" to stare, to look, to invade the personal space of others; among animals of many species, staring with an unyielding gaze communicates dominance and threat. In our culture, the "male gaze" carries power: "Men do not simply look; their gaze carries with it the power of action and of possession" (Berger, 1982, quoted in Bowers, 1990, 217). Men stare to measure and assess women's bodies, and to initiate eye contact. So as not to appear sexually inviting or aggressive, a woman averts her gaze when she wants to avoid contact. Likewise, among other animals, averting the eyes is a sign of submission. When a woman notices an unknown, ominous man, she "takes care not to meet his eyes because the mixing of looks may precipitate another form of contact. She does not dare intrude into the other's domain for fear that he will see contempt or weakness in her eyes and make her the object of his violence" (Siebers, 1983, 32). Meeting another's eyes directly and intensely—whether in anger or in affection—creates relationship; averting one's eyes creates distance.

Thus, stares carry power: they can be used to deliver hostility, assert dominance, invade another's space. Like aggression itself, they can be used for positive or destructive purposes. While not reserved for women's use alone, the powerful, paralyzing look has been emblematized in the female personage of Medusa. Her power is both destructive and creative; it becomes ambiguous as it symbolizes both. According to myth, the blood of Medusa's right side was life giving, whereas the blood from her left side caused destruction.

The women I interviewed gave striking descriptions of "the look" that paralyzes. They recall receiving this look from other women; they also speak of becoming Medusa themselves, by gathering up their forceful anger and focusing it on someone else in a laser-sharp stare. To illustrate the use of the Medusa look I will present two extended examples—those of Chrystal and Lyn—that put it in relational context.

Chrystal (age 25, African American, unemployed) recalls a look from her grandmother that paralyzed her. Of interest here is what happens to the recipient of a Medusa-like gaze. At the time of one of our interviews Chrystal lived with her grandmother, who had temporary custody of her four children. Chrystal was working out arrangements to regain custody. Also at her grandmother's house were other relatives, most of them younger than Chrystal.

The incident happened on a day that, for Chrystal, was full of critical eyes. Earlier in the day, "CPS had come by and told me 'You're not going to get your kids back 'til you do this, this, this, this, and this.' And, you know, I was really pissed off at them." The state's Children's Protective Services workers had the power to judge whether or not Chrystal was an acceptable mother. She had to open her home, her family, and her psyche to their evaluating scrutiny. On this day their treatment made her feel like "nothing." The humiliation of once more being rated unfit caused searing shame, despair, and a rage whose targets, the CPS worker and the state, were out of reach. The visit from CPS emphasized her felt lack of control over her own life.

Later that day, Chrystal's 15-year-old aunt, Lavonne,

> hit my son, and she hit him hard, she hit him so hard she knocked him down . . . I just started fighting her. I couldn't help it. I mean, it was like I was so mad it was almost like she had killed him or something. The only thing that stopped me was my grandmother came in and she was looking at me. You know,

I was looking for a knife or something—I was going to stab her.
She's only 15 and she's my blood!

Chrystal says that when her grandmother walked in, "I just
froze": "Because she has that look, when she gives you a certain
look, that means, you know, 'What the hell are you doing? Stop!'
or whatever. And when she looked at me I just froze up." In this
instance, "the look" is used to good purpose: it transfixes its recipient; it stops Chrystal from possibly injuring or killing her aunt.

Her grandmother's look paralyzes Chrystal by objectifying
her—interrupting her own subjectively determined actions with a
negative judgment from the outside. While describing this incident,
Chrystal moves from talking about her inner feelings—"I was so
mad"; "I was looking for a knife"—to evaluating herself through
"outside" eyes:

> I don't *think* that I'm normal, I don't even know what normal is.
> I see how *they* are, and I see how I am, I know they wouldn't do
> it, and since I don't know how to release that anger, and that's
> the only way I know how to do it . . . I couldn't let it out, you
> know. And it really confuses me, too, because I know that's not
> the way normal people act. It can't possibly be the way normal
> people act, but why are *they* like that and I'm not?

Chrystal searches for a perspective on herself from which to understand her actions. The "normal people," those others with
whom she compares herself and who judge her negatively, have no
specific identity. "They" are fine, she is not; she does not know
how to bridge the gap between her and them. Her poignant words
convey the depth of the alienation she feels as she sees herself
through others' eyes, prompted by her grandmother's stare that
identified her with her external acts.

For Chrystal, her grandmother's look evaluates and judges her
as her worst self. Chrystal freezes in humiliation and shame as her
grandmother's negatively evaluating eyes mirror those of the CPS
worker. After the look, she says, "I just started crying. I was thinking, 'I'm a really fucked-up person in the head.' First of all, we
shouldn't have started fighting, that was all on my part. And I'm

ten years older than she is." Her grandmother's look confirms her own negative self-evaluation. She feels exposed and shamed for actions that she herself condemns. Thus, negated from without and from within, Chrystal feels paralyzed in her familiar and dreaded position of disconnection, self-blame, and hopelessness about ever being able to connect with others.

While Chrystal vividly portrays the power of the Medusa look from the point of view of its recipient, Lyn (age 39, white, student) describes using Medusa's glare against another person. At the time of our interview, Lyn was divorced after a seventeen-year marriage. In order to understand the significance of her move from object to subject, we need to know her history.

Lyn's mother used physical force with her four children, slapping and using a paddle until they bled: "She would call us names, put us down, tell us we were idiots . . . it just crushed me." In her family, Lyn learned that conflict always involved hurt or abuse; that there was no way to assert herself without damaging consequences.

Lyn tells of many humiliating childhood incidents in which her mother shamed her in front of others and aggressively overrode any of her initiative or self-worth. Lyn married Gordon at 21, eager to leave her family and make a fresh start, including how she related to herself: "I talked to myself the same way my mom talked to me a lot of times . . . I'd always call myself, 'Oh Jonesy you're just worthless, oh Jonesy, you can't do it'—that was my last name and I would do that. Consciously when I went to get married I said, 'I'm going to be Mrs. Miller and I'm going to try and be nicer to me in this new name and try to be more myself.' "

Lyn and Gordon agreed not to have sex before marriage. On the first night of their honeymoon, Lyn attempted to initiate love-making after Gordon just "laid there," but "he rolled over to his side and went to sleep." "That's the first night! I was really devastated and I just cried myself to sleep silently."

She describes the pattern their relationship took from then on: "We played a game. The game I've been playing all my life, and that was—This is all separated from what we're doing today; today we'll be happy and we'll talk on the surface and we'll take a drive here and we'll do that and we'll have dinner and we'll push it down.

Just, it's not there." Throughout their marriage, "there was no physical relationship at all. He wouldn't touch me, he was obviously uncomfortable touching me, which made me feel like I was worthless, and I took that right in because I knew I was already. That just fed right back into that. Except when he wanted to get me pregnant and that was like a rape."

For many years Lyn stepped back from confronting her husband and continually confronted herself. She controlled her sexuality and her very life force through deadening, conventional thoughts that denied the basis of her outrage. Similar to other women who considered stating their feelings to be "aggressive," Lyn saw her options as limited: "I think because of my Christian background, you know, 'marriage is forever,' and I don't believe in divorce. On the other hand I don't believe in killing myself." She sums up her situation: "By seventeen years down the road, the girls were dying, spiritually and emotionally, and I was losing myself completely."

When she was caught in serious depression and could see no way out, something irrepressible in Lyn seemed to rise up from nowhere. She calls it her "mother bear instinct," and it came one night when

> I was standing at the stove making dinner and Gordon came in. He had just been telling one of the girls, putting them down again saying, "If you don't spend three or four hours on this homework or reading or if you don't get culturally correct"—it was one of those subjects—"then you'll just turn out to be a bum." And I turned around to him while I was stirring and I said, "Gordon stop it!" And I mean I had never done anything like that to him before.

That confrontation began unraveling the relations of power that held their marriage together. These power dynamics were held in place by social fabrications of gender and goodness, and by Lyn's fear that to confront or hurt anyone would make her like her cruel mother: "I have always had this fear because my mother is so controlling . . . that I would become like her." But Lyn's need to protect her children overrode all these considerations: "He had hurt them enough."

Lyn had not yet stood up for herself. Her first expression of her anger took the form of a Medusa look:

> I said something about "Have you got your parenthood pamphlet filled out" . . . something very neutral. And he said, "I do not know. I just do not know what you want." And I said, "I have been telling you for years what I wanted" . . . And I turned to him and said—I do not know what I said, I just had this look, I know it was a horrible look. Just a look, you know. I do not even like to look at him, and I said, whatever I was saying, in paraphrase, "It is too late, I cannot trust you anymore, you have no credibility, it is over" . . . And I said, "I think we better be real careful, because I hate you." I do not know if that is the word I used, but he got it real clearly and it really stung. I mean, I saw and he just flinched.

Lyn's "horrible look" channeled years of anger and hatred through her eyes and into expression. Her stare and her powerful words— "I hate you"—broke the game of dominance-submission that had ruled their marriage. She began to gain power when she used her "I" (eye) to aggressively stare back at her husband, under whose critical, demeaning gaze she had been pinned, and pinned herself, for so many years. Meeting her Medusa glare, he flinched from the sting of negation, the slap against his very being carried in her annihilating look. Lyn's identity shifted as she crossed a boundary to act on her own behalf: "I am going to do this or I am going to die, spiritually die."

Gazing from Medusa's eyes compels a radically new way of seeing and a different experience of self. This new, powerful subjectivity requires a woman to act in accord with its vision, and demands that she move outside the conventions of feminine "goodness."

Medusa's look is a fitting icon of female aggression. Paradoxical and ambiguous, it combines the power of destruction and of creativity; it collapses the dichotomies of divine and evil, angel and bitch, malady and cure. If women limit themselves to the maiden and mother aspects that society condones, they may be unable to discern what they need to eliminate from their lives to allow the creation of new life, new growth. If they lack the destroyer component symbolized by Medusa, they may themselves remain frozen in place.

The power of Medusa's gaze does not lie in her projection of anger or destruction. In the myth, Medusa paralyzes only those who meet her gaze. *Her gaze is interactive, relational; it holds no power unless eye ("I") contact is made.*

Medusa symbolizes the power of moving from being the object of someone else's gaze to seeing for oneself, to holding one's own perspective while interacting with others. Clear vision propels action. For Lyn, the clarity of Medusa's vision meant that she had to destroy the form of relationship that had nearly destroyed her. She had to speak truths that were hurtful to her husband and to leave her economically secure but emotionally lethal marriage. Switching from being defined to defining, she transformed her deadened existence into life.

Medusa's interactive gaze affects both giver and receiver. In Chrystal's example, we saw what happens to the recipient of a look that, as in myth, is powerful enough to paralyze and transform. While her grandmother's look froze Chrystal in shame and disconnection, it saved her from a worse fate. This event became a turning point in her determination to become one whom the stares of others no longer reduce to the status of a "thing" in the world. It prompted her to seriously engage with her rage, to relieve the "pressure in my chest" by "calling one of my advocates and talking to them." She is starting to overcome her intense feelings of alienation through words rather than through violence as self-defense against shaming.

Chrystal and Lyn, women so differently located in society, must both cross from being the devalued subject of others' looks to seeing from a position of self-respect. The gulfs they must cross differ in how they have been socially constructed and learned within their families. For Chrystal, the intersections of poverty, race, and gender increase her sense of powerlessness to bridge the gap between how she wants to live and how she lives, between how she is seen and who she wants to be. Her struggle to cross this gap is an issue of survival.

Aggressive Fantasies

Can destructive fantasy, a type of hurt delivered only in imagination, qualify as a form of aggression? Many cultures believe that fantasies of harm to others carry great power. Wishing or imagining a person dead, perhaps accompanied by symbolic rituals, is believed to lead to consequences in the physical world. Fearing harm from others' minds and spirits, people protect themselves with amulets, rituals, and prayers. Those suspected of threatening others through injurious thoughts are often punished by community shunning or death.

Angry fantasies, even when not acted upon, are forbidden by certain religious teachings, including those of Christianity. According to the Gospel of Matthew, Jesus forbids his followers even to feel or express anger, treating these offenses as comparable to murder: "You have heard that it was said to the men of old, 'You shall not kill; and whoever kills shall be liable to judgment.' But I say to you that every one who is angry with his brother shall be liable to judgment; whoever insults his brother shall be liable to the council, and whoever says, 'You fool!' shall be liable to the hell of fire" (Matt. 5:21–22; see Pagels, 1993). These verses offer a powerful moral, religious reason to suppress anger. Such teachings join cultural injunctions against *women's* anger to provide a ready source of guilt if a woman uses aggressive fantasies as outlets for her anger.

In the interviews, both abused and nonabused women report resorting to aggressive fantasy, defined here as imagining specific harm to another person within a "story" that has a beginning and an end. Twenty-one of the thirty-six abused women's narratives and eight of the twenty-four nonabused women's narratives include such fantasy. Men were the targets in 81 percent of the aggressive fantasies, women in 19 percent.[6] When women imagined aggression against other women, the motivations for their fantasies included retaliation for previous emotional hurts (six women), self-defense against women who had previously attacked them (four women), and jealousy (one woman). Physical violence was present in 80 percent of all the aggressive fantasies; 20 percent contained only verbal aggression.

Three forms of aggressive fantasies serve different purposes and carry different consequences for the self: rehearsals of resistance, substitutes for agency, and enhancements of positive self-feeling. *Rehearsals of resistance* to domination or to negative interpersonal circumstances create an imaginary space to which a woman can withdraw from her damaging outer situation. By imagining her retaliation or her triumph over those who "keep her down," a woman practices opposition and exercises her will, if only in an inner arena. This type of fantasy generally carries positive consequences for the self: it keeps a woman's sense of personal power and defiance alive when she feels unable to exercise them outwardly.

When aggressive fantasies serve as *substitutes for agency*, they reflect a woman's belief that she cannot act in her own behalf. Used as a way to cope with damaging situations, such fantasies may, in fact, foster inaction: the cognitive illusion that she is "doing something" through these fantasies, paired with the affective satisfaction of releasing hostility, may create enough sense of activity that a woman does not realize she is adapting to harmful situations. This type of fantasy usually carries negative consequences for the self if it promotes self-modification to destructive conditions.

In the third form of aggressive fantasy, *enhancement of positive self-feeling*, motives are not hostile or retaliatory. Instead, the goal is to build up a positive sense of strength and personal power, often in defiance of cultural messages that portray women as weak and yielding. These conscious forms of fantasy, often used when women know they must face dangerous situations, carry positive results for a woman's experience of self.

Rehearsals for Resistance

When a woman fears that her challenging, self-defensive actions will bring terrible consequences to her or her children, fantasy serves as a safe but unsatisfying outlet for anger and aggression.

Rehearsing what she would do if there were no restraints or consequences, she maintains an attitude of resistance that is essential for not giving up.

Fantasy seems to play such a critical role for Chrystal. She was married to a man who, after she had their first son, started beating her viciously as well as controlling her life: "One time we went to a park and you know how guys are, they see you by yourself they whistle and they hoot and all that, and when we got home he held me down by my neck and started with some clippers and cut my hair off to about an inch. It was only about an inch long. Because he said he didn't want any other man looking at me. I didn't leave the house for about two months." She was able to get through this time because "I had my baby. That's why, I think that's why I've had so many kids." Yet her attention to her first child increased the violence markedly, especially after she became pregnant again: "That's the one thing that really drove him crazy, when I was two months pregnant he socked me in the stomach for about a whole half hour, just punching me, trying to make me have a miscarriage."

In response, she turned to the safety of her imagination: "I've imagined doing things to him in his sleep, a lot." "When he was asleep was the only time I wasn't scared of him . . . And I knew if I was gonna do it that would be the only way and the only time I could do it . . . I have got to the point of boiling syrup and putting sugar and stuff like that in it and, you know, just 'When he comes back in here I'm gonna throw it at him' and stuff like that. But I could never just *do* it. I couldn't." Fantasy preserves Chrystal's image of herself as someone other than a victim. While being battered, she can also imagine herself as aggressor; she goes as far as boiling syrup to carry out her fantasy of retaliation. In fantasy she remains an agent who can act on her need to protect herself.

For most of the women who reported them, mental rehearsals of harm did not lead to action. Instead, imagination offered a place of refuge, a safe site of resistance. Imagining scenes of hurting back can be a way of coping with feelings that are considered too dangerous to enact. Most often, women's fantasies about abusive men invert the terms of the relationship by reversing who is the aggressor and who is the recipient of hurt, who is in control and who is fearful.

Chrystal's abuser carried a pager to be in contact with friends who helped him keep watch on her. When he slipped into a drunken sleep one day, she jumped from a window with her son and ran. Perhaps her aggressive fantasies had helped keep her sense of agency alive enough to take this risky action. Her sense of herself as an actor in her own life was evident both in her fantasies and in the courage it took to escape a man who had threatened her with certain death if she left him.

Fear of violence operates as a powerful means of social control by men over women, but women psychologically resist through their aggressive fantasies. While battered women are victims of abuse, they are not passive. Within their subjectivity, they actively resist, and keep their sense of angry defiance alive.

Substitutes for Agency

Aggressive fantasy is not prompted only by fear of retaliation. It can also spring from cultural and religious demands that create a feeling of entrapment as powerful as an abuser's threat. In negating relationships in which women believe that all exits lead to moral condemnation, they imagine that their husbands will die, but do not see themselves as the agents of harm. Instead, God or the impersonal hand of fate extinguishes the man's life, leaving the woman free and, she hopes, blameless. Such fantasies allow disassociation from the reality that it is "I" who wants to harm. Twelve women prayed for or imagined in detail the death of men who had harmed them. Most of these women had been abused as children and adults and felt little power to stop others from hurting them.[7]

Alice (age 46, white, secretary) found herself caught in a seventeen-year marriage with an alcoholic husband. Alice's map for how to deal with her aggression was influenced by her mother, from whom "I learned how to stuff everything. I stuffed really good. I was amazing. And I went through years of not feeling anything." Like other women who see their aggression as unfamiliar territory, Alice had no practice in bringing her anger or will into relationship.

Before her marriage, Alice worked as a secretary. When her boss gave her too much to do, she would sigh as a way to convey a complex message: "He could hear me sigh from my office to his, and I would sit there, and stop work." Through this signal,

> I was saying, "I have reached my limit, you cannot do this to me, you cannot make me type faster, you cannot make me do more, I can't work more than sixteen hours a day, so do what you want to" . . . I had no way of saying to him, "I can't do this. You're asking too much of me. You have pushed me beyond my limits." I had no way, I did not have that language at all. I never saw that happen. So I didn't know how to do it.

Having no language for the unfamiliar territory beyond her limits, Alice relies on her deep sigh as a sign of martyred resignation.

Alice took this style of dealing with difference into a marriage that quickly developed problems. Her husband drank too much, and their relationship held little intimacy or shared goals: "What was happening to him was bad enough, and I could see that, but I finally realized that what was happening to me was I was dying. I felt hopelessness, I felt despair, and I didn't think I felt anything at all, but I guess I did feel those. It took all that I had just to get through the day."

Alice had to work hard to "stuff" her anger. She could not imagine standing up to her husband and drawing limits regarding what behavior she would accept. Her self-restraint had nothing to do with fear of retaliation; he was not an abuser either physically or verbally: "He put me on a pedestal." Instead, her fears of confrontation sprang from her history and from internalized social expectations about marriage and women's goodness.

Rather than talking to her husband about his alcoholism, Alice imagined his death:

> I prayed that if he was going to have an accident coming home, because he always came home drunk, that it be a one-car accident, that he run into a telephone pole and not hurt anybody else. And that he die. And so I did actually pray for him to die, for quite a depressingly long period of time . . . I saw no other

way out, because at that point I wasn't willing to give up on the commitment I had made, which I was very serious about when I got married. That really meant something to me, and so it really was a " 'til death do us part" thing, and I couldn't see any way out of the relationship unless he died.

This prayerful fantasy offers a seemingly perfect solution to Alice's dilemma. If her husband dies, she is not guilty of breaking her marriage vows; if God engineers the death, he must approve. Thus the death-by-prayer solution offers an outlet for her hostile, angry thoughts yet preserves her moral goodness. For Alice, as in actual relationship, so in fantasy: she does not see herself as the actor or agent in her own life's drama. Fantasy serves as a substitute for agency by creating the illusion that she is doing something about her situation. Interpersonally, this aggressive fantasy allows her to endure the marriage by keeping her angry opposition active but out of relationship.

But this fantasy also affected Alice negatively, making her feel guilty: "I felt really bad about the prayer, I mean on one level. Because it was guilt, I mean, praying for anybody to die is . . . pretty serious stuff. But I literally saw no alternative. The only other alternative was divorce, which I was not at that point ready to consider."

If a woman feels all choices lead to loss, fantasy presents one possible way to find freedom. Alice perceives no exit from her relational prison, and this creates intense anxiety. The disappointments of love and her felt powerlessness also create anger. These feelings lead her to cross the line from functional fantasy, which preserves the self's felt agency, to destructive fantasy, which provides an outlet for bitter resentment but also undermines the self and relationship. Functional fantasy keeps hope for the self alive; destructive fantasy stems from despair and replaces action to change one's circumstances with inaction, waiting for something dreadful to happen. Such despairing fantasy also allows a woman to direct anger against herself, that ever present and safe target, for dwelling on such images. Finally, while images of death play in her head, such a woman outwardly silences her anger and feelings, and her silence preserves the status quo of damaging circumstances. This can lead her to feel like a victim of her situation—and to become one.

Deliverance-by-death imagery, when the woman is not the agent of harm, can be a coping mechanism which keeps anger alive while a woman either gathers her strength to move or remains stuck. In Alice's case, fantasy was a way of treading water in her relationship, converting her anger into dog-paddling to barely stay afloat. She remained where she was rather than striking off in a new direction or changing her situation. Fantasy helped her inwardly disconnect from her husband, endure a relationship that was damaging to both parties, and become severely depressed. It did not foster her sense of agency, or prepare her to act, or help her bring anger constructively into relationship. In her own estimation, it was not positive for her.[8]

Alice's use of fantasy also stands as an example of how internalization, which is a way to keep anger out of relationship, actually works. The anger and wishes to harm others, if not communicated, must be "managed" within the self in some way. Aggressive fantasy is one method by which anger is internally managed or suppressed. Keeping anger out of relationship by converting it to aggressive fantasies can bring harmful effects to the self, particularly when fantasy permits one to endure relational violations that could be changed through direct, constructive action. Observing oneself enduring such relational violations lowers one's self-esteem, and this further feeds the sense of oneself as *done to* rather than *doing*, as victim rather than agent.

The Complexities of Aggressive Fantasy

A woman's aggressive fantasy may serve as both a rehearsal for resistance and a substitute for agency. For Nancy (age 55, white, social worker), as for Alice, imagining her husband's death diverted her from facing the issues in their relationship that led to such hostility. Nancy did not see leaving her marriage as a possibility: "I didn't think I could survive on my own. I didn't think I could make enough money and work with the kids."

Nancy did not have the tools to confront her husband to demand that he change his behavior. She had been taught from childhood to defer to the men in her family and to suppress and internalize anger: "I was really a very typical Fifties middle-class white girl. My mother . . . took whatever the man in the family gave out. You accepted it. You didn't barely stand up for your own rights; whatever the man in the family wanted went. The wife cooked and cleaned and did whatever she had to do and hoped it was acceptable to the male. That's the way we lived."

Nancy took this set of expectations into her own marriage. Though her husband, Tom, was never physically abusive, he was "explosive" and "passive aggressive"; "it was constant walking on eggshells." Nancy turned to drinking to submerge her feelings of rage and unhappiness, but alcohol further stunted her ability to act positively on her own behalf. Her awareness that she drank too much made her feel "very guilty": "I could accept blame for almost everything, anything. So if I wasn't drinking and he was explosive, then yeah, he was right. Even if he wasn't right, it was probably my fault anyway."

In this unhappy marriage, afflicted by low self-esteem and lack of skills to engage in positive conflict, Nancy began to imagine killing herself:

> Not hurting myself, because what good would that have done? Suicide. A lot of suicide. I never attempted any of it because I would always get to this conclusion that I could not leave those three kids with Tom because Tom was really a terrible, terrible father to them. If I killed myself, I would have to kill all three of the kids too because otherwise I would be dooming them to living with this man who was so emotionally distant that they would just grow up in sort of a vacuum.

A powerful psychic trio lines up to threaten Nancy's survival: shame, anger/aggression, and depression. The sources of this trio are easily traced to Nancy's relational context. For example, her shame—that feeling of complete exposure of one's inadequacies to watching eyes—stems from repeated humiliations by her husband, haunting memories of her own drunken actions in public, and the sense that she is incompetent to survive on her own. Anger arises as a defense against perceived attack, including psychological attacks such as insult, humiliation, and threats that create shame (Averill, 1982; J. Gilligan, 1996; Scheff and Retzinger, 1991). Nancy's anger is continually incited by the degradation of her relationship and her alcoholism; she wants to destroy the causes of her shame. She directs her hostile rage, through fantasy, to the two people who cause her shame: her husband and herself. Suicide gets rid of one source, her self, while it punishes the other, her husband. Nancy's depression increases both her suicidal thoughts and her inability to act.

For years Nancy adapted to a relationship she hated by numbing her feelings through alcohol, and by planning, in detail, ways of killing her husband: "It was that summer that I first started doing my fantasies, doing the perfect murder in getting rid of Tom. I would lay in bed and . . . I would really have it all worked out. How you could go around the back of the apartment house and we were on the first floor and you could go in through the window, you know? *[When you had those, how would they usually end?]* Well, I'd commit the perfect murder."

I ask what stopped her from carrying out the fantasies: "I don't know. Good little girls don't do those kinds of things, I guess. It was probably a way I coped. I mean I had it all planned out even to having extra big shoes that you'd wear so the footprints . . . but I never went out and bought extra big shoes."

I ask how she felt about those aggressive fantasies:

It felt real good to plan them. Tom . . . started working on oil rigs all over the world. So he was at all times gone for periods. I used to also do a lot of praying . . . because you fly everyplace when you join a crew. With all the flying he did . . . every time there was a big airplane crash I'd say, "Why couldn't it have been the one he was on?" . . . You know, gosh, I'd be free plus I get a big insurance check.

Nancy's fantasies subdue her need to act by creating the illusion that she is doing something to address her relationship, on which she blames her entrapment in alcohol. In these fantasies, free-floating resentment coalesces into specific plans for death. This is not the kind of resentment that nibbles around the edges of awareness, but is fully conscious and feels "good" when directed at the target in fantasy. Her hostility finds some satisfaction in planning the details of death; her shame, fear of disapproval, and feelings of inferiority and powerlessness keep her from expressing the hostility directly. Nancy's fantasies allow her, like Alice, to tread water in an unsatisfactory relationship.

Nancy wandered in the labyrinth of her own anger, losing the thread of where she was going and why. Dwelling on destructive fantasies, combined with her alcoholism, led to an inability to find her way out of dead ends and kept her trapped in depression.[9]

While it could be argued that Chrystal, Alice, and Nancy all used aggressive fantasy as a rehearsal for resistance, looking closely, we see important distinctions in its uses and consequences. For Chrystal, fear was based on a realistic assessment of the dangers of her relationship and held no negative consequences for her self-experience. For Alice and Nancy, fears were derived from economic realities, from cultural demands to suppress their own will and agency, and from lifelong messages that they could not make it on their own. Their fears included disapproval from inner and outer authorities; healthy expression of aggression, as in positive confrontations or assertions of will, was inhibited by anxiety over anticipated shame. Both paths—fear of retaliation and response to social expectations—can lead to aggressive fantasy instead of to action, and both are well traveled by many women.

Aggressive fantasies of death to others hold both possibilities and dangers. As we have seen, they are positive as they create an inward, active resistance when outward expression seems too dangerous. By keeping a woman's will, agency, and anger alive, destructive fantasies serve as a place of refuge and a way of coping. They also serve as a safety valve to leak rage that, if outwardly enacted, might lead to lifelong regret.

But there are many dangers attached to murderous fantasies. When such diversions keep anger out of direct expression, anger cannot fulfill its positive function: to remove obstacles to relationship so social bonds can be restored (Bowlby, 1980; Scheff and Ret-zinger, 1991). Through hostile rumination, anger may be transformed from the anger of hope to that of despair: "Feeling ceases to be the 'hot displeasure' of anger and may become, instead, the 'malice' of hatred" (Bowlby, 1973, 248–249). Adapting to a relationship a woman hates leads her to depression, while mental fantasies of harm that promise freedom create the image that she is doing something to address her situation.

The greatest danger of violent fantasies is that they may be enacted. A critical factor that determines whether or not a fantasy becomes destructive to others lies in the link between imagination and action. Does imagination light the fires of action? Which kind of action—positive or harmful? Does the fantasy alter self-experience? These complex questions have only ambiguous answers.

Anna, whom we met in Chapter 1, presents a warning about another danger of aggressive fantasies. She prayed for the death of her abusive stepfather; he died in an accident similar to the one she had imagined. For years she was consumed with guilt. From her experience, she carries a conviction that thought may be linked to external actions in unanticipated ways. She recalls three "sleazy guys" on a bus who "were talking about how they were using women": "I had this vision, 'I'd just like to slit your throats . . . Nothing in me thinks there's any value or virtue in having you guys on this planet,' and I was just like that angry."

Anna's "vision" is an icon of retribution for male violence against women. But even though she "certainly didn't think there was any possibility" that she "was actually going to go out and do it," having this vision made her "uncomfortable": "Because that's harm. I just thought, 'Yeah, I'd just like to slit your throats,' and that's very violent imagery for me. What if every time something made me angry, my thoughts were that? My fear would be that over a period of time there just might be a point where you'd say, 'Fuck it, this seems like a real just action.'"

Anna warns us that violent fantasy might lay down ruts of thought so well worn, tracks of self-justification so deeply grooved, that action could easily follow fantasy's trail. But fantasy does not always lead to harm. For most women, fantasy serves to divert hostility into imagination so that it is *not* overtly expressed.

As Anna suggests, women's fantasies sometimes contain a rage against male domination, a sense of outrage that wants to avenge the harm done to women in general as well as to oneself. Michelle (age 38, white, writer) recognizes this element in her own vision of retaliation against a man she was dating: "I have visualized hitting him, throwing a drink in his face. Fantasized about if I were a guy, I would do more than hit him. I would probably beat him within an inch of his life. And I wonder—that kind of thought has got to be more deeply rooted. I think it speaks more to sexism in the culture. So I think there's more to the feeling than what occurred in this relationship."

Michelle ties her aggressive fantasy about this specific man to her resentment of men's privilege over women: "I get into this thing like I'm sick to death of half-grown men. And because they look good and . . . they know how to play the game, they go off and they make tons of money. They have all these opportunities to travel the globe and yet if you look at them, they are twelve-year-olds in grown-up clothes. And I'm sick to death of them. And there's—I have that rage in me too."

Responding to the question "What stops you from actually carrying out the fantasy?" Michelle says: "A feeling that it wouldn't be in keeping with who I truly am. And that it wouldn't be modeling the ethics that I hold most dear. I mean, what good does it do to hit someone?" She is not critical of herself for having such fantasies: "There are times when I've said, 'Hey, good. This is a good, healthy aggression thing.' "

Some men's actions against women deserve anger; so also do social structures that favor certain groups while they limit the access and power of other groups. Anger against such inequities can accomplish social change when constructively channeled rather than confined to hostile fantasy. But sometimes men undeservedly receive women's anger, as when a particular man serves as a symbol of the enemy.

The content of aggressive fantasies ranges from specific, detailed deaths to imagery of escape and retaliation. The amount of guilt a woman feels about aggressive fantasies does not correspond to the violence or specificity of their content. Rather, it appears related to whether or not she feels the fantasies are justified. For example, Chrystal feels no guilt for her fantasies of hurting her abusive husband because his physical brutality justifies her thoughts. Likewise, Michelle feels that her anger against men's unjust treatment of her justifies her fantasies of retaliation. Those who find no justification or explanation for their violent fantasies feel concern about them, as if the fantasies indicate they are "crazy."

Enhancements of the Self

Nine women described using fantasies of positive aggression. The theme of these fantasies is standing up to threat through powerful aggressive speech or acts. Utterly different in tone from hostile, angry fantasies, these creative imaginings use aggressive imagery to enhance positive self-feeling.

Lisa (age 43, white, self-defense instructor) names her imaginary encounters with her ex-husband "Superwoman" daydreams. They compensate for years in which "I let [my children] be hurt in certain ways when they were younger and I didn't have the power, the assertiveness, or the aggression." One of her aggressive fantasies is "my ex-husband showing up":

> He's caused a lot of pain for my kids, and it's like he's not going to cause any more because now I'm strong and powerful and I'm going to stop him. And I tell him verbally that this is the way it is, there's no negotiating . . . And I see myself in a very physical stance, you know, being ready to fight . . . It's been a situation that I've always been scared of, that always causes me pain, obviously causes my children pain, and [I imagine] it's happening again and this time I have control. And it's like in my fantasy . . . I *know* he can't hurt me. The ending of it is—well, usually I don't have to have one because he's scared. *[Do you say anything to yourself after this?]* Like "Yes! I did it! I'm strong, I'm in control, I saved my children. And I slayed the dragon, he's not going to be back."

Asked how the fantasy affects her, Lisa says: "It feels good. It's another way of not being victimized. Because, before, they could always control you, either through the law or through your passivity or through your nurturing." Lisa's fantasies restore and revise her sense of agency in relationship and offset her memories of the many encounters in which she gave way.

The police officers I talked with, who face life-threatening situations in their work, use aggressive fantasies to enlarge their confidence. Visualizations of heroic actions, portraying the self as invulnerable and admired, keep a woman feeling strong and capable in a dangerous job. They also reinforce her self-image as a protector of others instead of one who must be protected.

Anita (age 33, white), an officer with a metropolitan police force, describes such a fantasy:

> I always have this situational dream, like if I was ever confronted with a situation where I had to use deadly force, not only did I use deadly force but I was made like, to be a hero . . . The fantasy is—everything is cut and dry, no problem, and you're a hero! or heroine, whatever. It would be like a crime in progress and I was walking into the situation . . . and the person or the suspect brings out a weapon and is going to kill somebody or kill me. And I'm able to pull out my gun and use deadly force and kill the person because it was necessary. And you know, I saved people's lives or whatever, something like that. [And then how did they respond to you?] Oh, people are—tremendous accolades and I would be written up and, you know, I would be looked upon favorably.

Aggressive fantasies of assertion, confrontation, and triumph can strengthen a woman's belief in her personal force, her ability to effect positive outcomes. Fantasies of destruction can serve a purpose of survival and resistance, or can keep a woman dwelling on anger while lost in its bitterness. As with most human experiences, the deeper we look, the less easily we can say that aggressive fantasy is, in itself, positive or negative. Rather, we must consider the context, the purpose, the effect on the self and the relationship before coming to any conclusion. Fantasies of hurt to others provide a rich picture of how women manage anger and aggression behind the mask. As well, they portray what forms aggression takes when present in imagination.

Indirect aggression weaves a web of connection whose strands do not increase the possibility of intimacy but instead deliver anger and hurt, often encoded as feminine goodness. One explanation offered for women's frequent use of indirect aggression is that they calculate an "effect/danger, or cost/benefit, ratio of aggression" (Björkqvist, 1994; Björkqvist, Österman, and Kaukiainen, 1992). In this scenario, "the aggressor assesses the relation between a) the effect of the intended strategy, and b) the danger involved, physical, psychological, or social. The objective is to find a technique that will be effective, and, at the same time, incur as little danger as possible" (Björkqvist, 1994, 181).

This "effect/danger ratio" captures the larger picture of why women might use indirect aggression: calculating the costs of hurt is one of the ways women mediate their desire to hurt others, as we saw in Chapter 3. The women's examples in this chapter take us into their thoughts to reveal precisely what kinds of factors they consider to influence their use of indirection. Women's words also show how they construct the meanings and purposes of their indirect actions, and illustrate the costs to self-concept and to relationships of relying on such behavior.

But the "effect/danger ratio" explanation also leaves out some critical aspects of women's use of indirect aggression. This behavior also results from learned avoidance of direct conflict. If a woman has had no training in appropriate and direct ways to bring her anger or will into relationship, she may turn to indirect aggression more by default than from a rational calculation of costs and benefits. Well-worn, familiar paths leading underground, promising safety from detection and avoidance of consequences, pull a woman toward indirection, while rarely traveled paths to direct, constructive expression are marked with danger signs and often lead to unfamiliar territory. Norms of feminine goodness that preclude overt confrontation figure heavily in women's choices, often unconscious, to mask their aggression. The mask they choose most often is fashioned from a cloth of stereotypical feminine behavior such as sweetness, silence, and passivity. This strategic performance of femininity disguises women's intent to hurt, control, or oppose others.

Indirection often furthers separation, not connection; it rarely facilitates dialogue, change, or reconciliation, because it denies the recipient the ability to engage with the aggressor. Indirect aggression is one strategy women utilize to engage in conflict, but it is not their only choice. It is there to implement when things get too dangerous, and when a woman needs to preserve her agency and resistance.

6

CREATING NEW GROUND

Positive aggression, like all aggression, displaces another's will, but positive aggression uses force to gain equality and full participation in relationships. It takes initiative and seeks rectification. Positive aggression slays the dragon of fear that keeps one trapped in isolated, dead places. Its hallmark is constructive change. Through using their force in constructive ways, women create new ground on which to stand in relationships.

Positive aggression takes many forms—self-protection, standing up in the face of negation, leaving bad relationships, overcoming obstacles to growth, pushing for new possibilities, defending against harm. Its intent is to achieve parity and authenticity in relationship. Lynnea (age 32, white, social worker) speaks to one of its functions: "If you can't be yourself with somebody, if you can't be your true, normal, happy—or whatever yourself is that you feel comfortable with—then you're around the wrong people and get them away from you!" It leads to a clarity about how relationships affect the self, making it easier to decide how to relate to others. Positive aggression can hurt others, as for example when it ends a relationship, but the intent is self-preservative, not destructive. The goal is to change toward relationships of mutuality and equality—toward love.

Women who described a major change in their lives tied it to learning to use their force positively in relationships. As Lyn (age 39, white, student) says: "Aggression, for me, is standing up for myself. And if we define it like that, that is how I have made any changes in my life." Movement toward being able to take a stand in relationships and in the world coincides with a decrease in fear and an increase in confidence. The ability to stand one's ground and enter into conflict constructively is fundamentally related to a sense of worth and strength. Thus constructive aggression not only affects relationship; it also re-forms self-perception, allowing women to be "as big as I want to be," to perceive themselves as positive creators of their own lives and of their societies.

Needing a Backbone

Women lay the groundwork for change in themselves and in their relationships by recognizing their need for positive aggression: "I wish I had a backbone. I need a backbone to be able to stick up for myself," says Jessie (age 34, white), a single mother on welfare raising two young children. Jessie's bodily metaphor reflects her felt experience: she wants a sense of strength that will hold her up, a backbone.

Jessie presented what she called a "normal picture" of a life: a happy childhood, business school before she started work and got married. She went from this conventional path—"a good marriage, the way you're supposed to do it with the ring on the finger, buying the house, and getting the kid and the white picket fence, and everything"—to divorce, involvement with drug-using men, battering, addiction to cocaine, welfare, and now recovery. She traces this journey into destructive relationships, in large part, to her inability to oppose others: "[I've] just been walked on and let them, okay, whatever. Just let myself be the pincushion. Just through the terrible ordeals that I've lived through . . . I wish I would have been stronger."

True to her training as a "good woman," Jessie blames herself for the battering rather than holding the men responsible for their abuse. In doing so, she accepts personal responsibility for a societal problem—violence against women. Acknowledging her unrealistic shouldering of blame, let us examine how she wants to be stronger.

Jessie's body has absorbed others' blows; her physical vulnerability has been emphasized by men's abusive treatment of her: "I was beat. I was hit. I had lighter fluid drenched, sprayed all over me, and I had long hair so it was all in my hair and everything. And was told not to move or he'd throw a match on me. That was the worst." In her next relationship, "He broke my nose. I got twelve stitches in my eye and he broke my eardrum." Such brutal abuse created a sense of being beaten down bodily and psychologically, of her weakness relative to male "strength."

Leaving men who threatened to kill her if she did so, overcoming her addiction, and saving her children took incredible courage. In spite of despair and fear, Jessie has already stood her ground and taken action in the most important issues of her and her children's lives. She says her most aggressive act was "going down to the courthouse and getting a protection order . . . I felt good about myself being able to go down and do that. It was scary." Recognizing that it took strength to defy this man, Jessie acknowledges: "If I didn't have *any* backbone I know I'd be sitting in my house, doing my drugs, puffing away, not caring about a thing in the world."

Jessie is not only a woman who has been victimized; she is also someone who has used her strength to oppose others and to separate from destructive people and habits. Her drug use prompted the state to award custody of her 4-year-old daughter to her ex-husband, who, Jessie fears, harms her: "He brags that he can beat her. He can do whatever he wants with her." After losing custody Jessie used drugs even more heavily: "And then I had [my youngest child], got into Birth to Three, and got into the treatment program and worked my way up the ladder." She now sees her task as "to make my backbone stronger. To be able to stand up for myself. To be able to stand up to others and not to back away or back down. To be able to stand up for how I feel. Stand up for my rights. My kids' rights. To stand up for what I want in life." She is ready to feel and to act powerful instead of powerless.

In her understanding, such action requires self-esteem: "If you don't know when to say no, if you don't be able to have self-esteem, people start using you, and you have to have that self-esteem to stick up for yourself to know when to be able to draw those lines." Self-esteem, then, is inseparable from how she relates to others— whether she draws lines in relationships that affirm her full presence or whether she disappears in relationship by yielding to others' wishes. She says that both backbone and self-esteem require "the will to want to be able to do, whether it's to do for yourself or do for somebody else. The will. To *want* to be able." To be able to have a will and exert it in relationship means, in Jessie's words, to be able "to stand up to others and not back down and away." In relationship, these actions communicate that one is willing to advocate for oneself even if doing so leads to abandonment or retaliation. For Jessie, who has spent her life attuned to others' needs (from choice or because of brutal enforcement), this task presents a major challenge.

"Low self-esteem" is an inadequate explanation for why many women find taking a stand or opposing others so difficult. Self-esteem is an aspect of self that emerges reflexively with how we affect others and see ourselves mirrored in others' eyes. But often it is considered to be a quality of the self-contained individual, and its lack is seen as a personal deficit. Jessie's low self-esteem does not stem from within her. Rather, her conflicts about aggression and her fear of retaliation keep her from being assertive in relationships. Her lack of assertiveness, in turn, keeps her from experiencing her positive force in relationships, and this affects her self-esteem. It is not low self-esteem as such that keeps women back, but their fear and conflicts around aggression.

Jessie's desire to make her backbone stronger so she can stand up for herself is a first step toward learning how to use her force positively. She knows what she needs; she examines her past actions for evidence that she can accomplish such personal change. In a letter sent three years after her second interview, Jessie reports that she remains drug-free, has gotten new housing, and has regained custody of her daughter. Knowing what she needed, and supported in her resolve by an advocate from the Seattle Birth to Three Project, she has been able to make her backbone stronger.

Women who physically fight others *appear* to have a backbone, but their descriptions of their need for personal change are startlingly similar to Jessie's. Latisha (age 32, African American) is also a single mother on welfare raising two children. The state has custody of her older son because of her earlier drug use. Latisha has been severely abused both as a child and as an adult.

Because she is African American, the stereotypes of feminine behavior that have affected Latisha's use of interpersonal force differ from those affecting Jessie, who is white. Though each individual African-American woman experiences the convergence of race, gender, and class in a unique configuration, each must face demeaning stereotypes. Latisha undoubtedly has had to battle the "single, most frequent representation of African American adolescent women [as] the teen mother, who is generally depicted as a low-income future welfare recipient with minimal education and few transferable skills for the work place. She is assumed to be sexually irresponsible and emotionally bankrupt, and thus easily manipulated by the men in her life" (Robinson and Ward, 1991, 90–91). Given Latisha's history of abuse and abandonment, for her to avoid internalizing this racial/gender/class devaluation would be nearly impossible.

Latisha became physically aggressive to protect herself in a violent family and a world that seemed only hostile. Now in drug treatment, attending a self-help group for lesbian battered women, and out of violent relationships, she reflects:

> I'm a passive person. It's like I tend not to stand up for myself when things happen to me, I tend to wait 'til I've had enough. Then I deal with it, instead of dealing with things as they come. So I wind up being an aggressive person, because I had enough. Somebody just—it could be the next person, they don't have nothing to do with it, but they was there. I mean, that was the closest person to me, so I attack them, you know.

I ask, "What would positive aggression be for you?" Latisha replies:

> Really stand up for myself. Go for something that, certain things you might have to be aggressive in a positive way, not in a negative way, and I don't know how to do that. It's all in a negative way. Like I said, I know I keep saying it, but really standing up for myself. I'm one, I let people walk over me. You know, because I have to be liked . . . I'm starting to change, I know everybody

ain't gonna like me. Because that's life. And they don't have to like me, but I'm not gonna let them abuse me. So it's like, I'm not trying to please everybody no more.

I ask, "Does that tie in with not standing up for yourself, having to be liked?"

Yeah. You know. Because I do a lot of things that I don't want to do. I don't want to, but if I don't, they ain't gonna like me. Then they gonna walk away from me. That's something I have to deal with. It's not really the people, it's really me. It's my feeling. My own insecurities . . . I'm starting to like myself. And that's a start, because I always used to think, "Ugh." I never did like the person I be staring at, you know, but today it's like, I'm an okay person, I am who I am. This is me. I can't change the face, but I could change, you know, my behavior.

Despite the personal and social negation Latisha has experienced, she is attempting to build a life based on connection and self-affirmation. She interprets her physical aggression toward others as evidence that she is a "passive person" because she lets things happen to her until she explodes with rage. As she sees it, her developmental task is to take a self-defining stance in relationship, to be able to say, "I am who I am" and not disappear by attempting to please others.

This clear-eyed view of what she needs includes overcoming a deep rage about being humiliated and degraded. Within a relational framework, rage is a reaction to an injury, and a way to attempt to remain attached in the face of threats to basic emotional ties. In her earlier life Latisha learned two visions of relationship: others will "walk all over her" (subordination) or they will "walk away from her" (isolation). She needs to experience relationships that support her self-defining stance, such as the self-help group she has joined. She must learn that she has value in relationship and that others will listen to her. Such experiences can lead to a sense of self-recognition and self-acceptance, which lessens shame-based rage.

Latisha does not speak of the racism that also contributes to her humiliation and rage. She succumbs to the culture's suggestion that self-blame is the way to understand her problems: her suffering is unique, she, the individual woman, is the problem.[1] If her words are heard from the perspective of the deficit model of mental health, with the label "character-disordered, drug-abusing woman" filtering their impact, they can be ignored. Further, in a patriarchal culture full of socially structured racial inequality, there is a certain deafness that makes it difficult to hear this woman's meaning or to consider her point of view. Society's deafness to her words is a way to avoid any moral claim emanating from them (Levin, 1989).

Keeping in mind that women's subjectivity reflects power relations, including those influenced by poverty, gender, and race, we can trace basic beliefs that shape both physical aggression such as Latisha's and compliance/retreat such as Jessie's:

I want to be competent, powerful and positive in relation
to others.
But
my words have no power or force to affect others
in the ways I want
or
I'm not important; no one will listen to me.
Therefore
I feel powerless and under others' control.
But
I must preserve my safety and some semblance of power
and self-direction.
Therefore
(Jessie's pattern):
I will be outwardly good, passive and compliant,
but use my force indirectly or against myself.
(Leads to problems with anger/aggression: inability to be
appropriately assertive or to stand up for self, low self-esteem.)
Or
(Latisha's pattern):
I feel inwardly powerless but will outwardly attack
if pushed too far.

(Leads to violence as self-protection: inability to be appropriately assertive or to stand up for self, low self-esteem.)

In either of these patterns, a woman cannot communicate her anger or engage in conflict effectively. Both those for whom aggression is unfamiliar territory and those who use it as a wall of self-protection feel unable to channel their personal force into direct, clear communication. Both feel powerless, vulnerable, and weak, buffeted by everyone else's needs or demands.

The women's narratives reveal three kinds of turning points that change these patterns: standing their ground, connecting with a larger context, and transforming destruction into positive aggression through creativity, social action, or spirituality.

Standing One's Ground

"I see signs of me," says Jessie. "When I was able to say no to Roy, when he broke my heart and he was still bringing the drugs in . . . And I stood my ground for the first time and said, 'No, I don't want you.' "

Standing one's ground, as a metaphor, unites physical, emotional, and spiritual aspects of experience. Women use this language to describe how they affirm themselves by creating new ground in relationships and in the self. They validate a new aspect of self by opposing another person in a way that challenges devaluing patterns of interaction. This movement to "standing" in relationship, to revealing herself through opposition, is what allows a woman to experience herself as an "I" within a "we." She constructs herself differently in the very process of stepping forth to appear in relation, to disclose herself as differing from someone else. Revealing her difference is linked to a sense of self-worth, to her development as a distinct person. She achieves self-definition not by defining boundaries of a separate self but by revealing, opening up new aspects of self in relation. Thus *standing defines a new ground of being, in relation.*

For example, for Jessie to stand her ground means she will occupy space in relationship. She sees "signs of me" as she risks self-definition through opposition. To do so, she has to face her separateness, which brings to her mind fears of negation and death (retaliation) and an existential risk of aloneness. She fears that if she opposes others she will drive them away. Yet conflict, saying no, standing one's ground are ways of being connected to others; they are simply ways that hold more force and "self" than compliant disappearance. But they signal insubordination within a model of gender relations based on male dominance.

As women talk about standing their ground, they use a language of the body:

> I have a gut feeling that "This is what I need, this is what I want," and I need to dig my heels deeper in, to make my stand, to make this come across . . . Having to pull myself together and to stand up against Dan . . . I feel that I have to pull my energy together and dig my heels down and make my stand. (Martha, age 44, white, tai chi teacher)

> I am going to speak up to this or I'm going to stand up for this or I'm going to write about this or whatever. I'm definitely gonna lift my head up, and there's some choice about it all. (Patricia, age 21, white, student)

> It is kind of like a lion crouching down. Getting it all up there, you know, all ready and then, spring! And afterward it feels really good to have done that. I mean it comes back to me and says, "Wow, you really are worthwhile. You did that for *you*." (Lyn, age 39, white, student)

> I just got the guts in me and I said, "No, you're not" . . . I just stood up to her. I said, "God is with me, if God's for me, who can stand against me." (Rhonda, age 32, African American, social worker)

These women speak of an energized sense of the body made whole through focused action. Such a feeling of aliveness is tied by metaphor to the sense of standing on the earth's ground; body and nature are sources of force. As Adrienne Rich said, "In order to live a fully human life, we require not only control of our bodies (though control is a prerequisite); we must also touch the unity and resonance of our physicality, our bond with the natural order, the corporeal ground of our intelligence" (1976/1986, 21).

Gathering their forces, these women reach out to their bodies' strength, to mythic, animal archetypes, and to a broader cosmic sense than that of the narrow ego. They summon these powerful forces to offset their feelings of smallness in relation to what they stand against. They confront their conditioned fear of male strength and male prerogative. They also confront their fear that displaying their strength weakens a man, shrivels his potency, and leads to loss of relationship. The image of the castrating female comes into focus: a woman's unleashed power leads to destruction of maleness and ensures her isolation. Often women give away their aggression, both positive and negative, to men, who are permitted by culture to "be" aggressive. No wonder women must invoke powerful forces in order to stand up for themselves.

Slaying the Monster

"Standing my ground" stories occur with wide variety and hold differing degrees of risk. Yet each woman who told such a story used it to represent a time of new realizations about herself. And each described having to confront her own fears as well as possible negative consequences of her actions.

Kim (age 34, first-generation Filipina/Danish American) articulates the significance that women attach to standing their ground. I interviewed Kim twice in approximately nine months. In her first interview she described using "sweetness" as indirect aggression against her ex-husband, Ron (see Chapter 5). Although they were divorced, Kim still feared that Ron would kill her if she angered him; because they shared custody of their daughter and Ron lived at Kim's mother's house, she saw him often. Her rage against his past brutality combined with her empathic appreciation of the hurdles he faces as a black man in a racist society kept her deeply and ambivalently tied to him.

By our second interview, Kim had confronted Ron and told him how she felt.

> I thought, "Okay, Kim, this man beat you, he tried to throw you out of a car, he tried to run you over with a car. So here's all this anger. Okay, why am I hanging onto this? Why is he in your mother's house, Kim? Why, why, why? Why do you feel you have to be nice to him?" Well, one day I went over there and he was there and I go, "I need to talk to you." Here I am, Miss Aggressive, being aggressive. I go, "I need to say some things to you!"

Kim revealed both sides of her feelings to Ron:

> When I think about the past and how you used to beat me and why I even allowed myself to go through that, I hate you. But there is a part in me that I know that there is good in you. I feel it. So I think that part of you I love. I want to see that part grow. You are my child's father. I have to, in my heart, want to see you do good for the growth of my own child. I don't want my child to look at you and say "I have a bum for a dad." I said, "Because Ron, you are a bum. You don't want to work. You can't keep a job. You blame everybody for this and that. You were a rotten husband." And I said, "You are a rotten father. You are rotten." I was honest.

She says she "broke through a major barrier" by confronting him honestly. Her truthful words were helping her "need to not hate him." This powerful attachment through hate was draining her energy and "dragging her down." Ron was able to listen to her, and started "crying, crying, crying, because he knew."

This time Kim bridged the gap with her former husband through honesty rather than hostile, indirect anger. Doing so required positive aggression: speaking words that she thinks "were like a release to him." As proof of the power of positive aggression to remove obstacles to relationship, she tells of major changes that followed this confrontation: "There's a lot of equal exchange, a lot of good balance, and even though he was such a rotten person . . .

I know there is good." She and Ron now have a more supportive, understanding relationship and are able to share custody of their daughter more harmoniously.

Reflecting on this interchange, Kim says:

> I felt really good about myself, and I thought, "Kim, you did it. You came face to face with . . . it's like a demon." They're demons. When you can face head on with these five-headed dragons and beat them, you are more powerful. It's like you get the strength . . . But see, you also know their weakness so you can be strong, but you've got to pull yourself together because you are so overwhelmed with how big and powerful they look and feel and seem to you that you're unclear . . . If I can pull my strength together to attack and be direct, I've defeated. Then all the power comes to me . . . I feel powerful. It feels bigger than life. I see them shrinking. I mean I literally see them shrinking. I feel more powerful. Isn't that terrible?

Here Kim stops to question what she has just said. Such questions or comments offer glimpses into how a woman experiences herself as she speaks and how she imagines others hear her. They alert us to her awareness of a discrepancy within her self, or between what is socially expected and what she is saying. Kim comments at the precise point where she gains power and watches the man shrinking. This is culturally forbidden.

I respond to her question with a question: "Why would you say that to yourself?"

> I feel so guilty because I know that I'm sucking them dry of all their power and I'm empowering myself but I'm thinking . . . "I'm weakening these people . . . this person" even though they're big ugly monsters . . . It weakened him forever. He's not a big ugly monster anymore . . . But he listened. It hit him. It's like it was a release to him. After that I didn't see him as a monster anymore.

Kim appears to awaken from a trance as she no longer sees what she has been conditioned to see: strong man, weak woman. Culture creates this trance through repetitive, hypnotic messages of women's weakness relative to men's strength. Its power over Kim's consciousness was increased by her husband's physical abuse. As she destroys former relations of power, she destroys both a kind of connection and a way of perceiving induced by this trance. Her aggression, though only verbal, changes the terms of the relationship fundamentally. By marching through her fear to confront him, she destroys a monster.

What is it that "weakens" Ron, that changes him from "a big ugly monster"? Kim sweeps back the curtain of projection and discovers that the male figure who appeared as a larger-than-life, thundering demigod is an illusion, much like the Wizard of Oz. Once she pierces the illusion of male strength, her experience of self, particularly her sense of her personal force, changes. Having claimed the ground of her being in relation to important others, she becomes less fearful. She now speaks a clear sense of identity:

> I'm to the point in my life where I don't need anyone to confirm who I am. I am who I am. If a person doesn't like it, that's okay. The people in my life do love me and I know that. I feel that my life has a lot of value within my own family as well as my little small circle of friends. I feel very proud about that. I feel that I'm really growing a lot. I feel that I really can do anything I want. Anything I set out to do, I can do it, because I've overcome all the major barriers of my life . . . It seems like as I become stronger, I become more a part of what's natural, what's comfortable, what's relaxing, what's calm in my life. Part of the sun, the ocean, the earth, and the tree, just there . . . one with the earth . . . That's what I keep trying to get back to, and the more I make myself bigger than life, the more I become.

Kim's "I am" statements unite the psychological, existential, and spiritual aspects of her life. While the phrase "standing one's ground" usually conjures an image of the lonely hero or men on the battlefield, these women offer a new vision. Standing in relationship roots them more deeply in a broader sense of connection, to the ground of nature and of their being: "part of the sun, the ocean, the earth, the tree." Affirming themselves as one with nature, they experience their positive force as rooted in life itself.

Each woman who recounted a critical incident of standing up for herself labeled doing so an aggressive act, perhaps because it destroyed former patterns of relating based on submission and fear. Observing that her actions influenced another person in the way she intended, each woman saw herself as stronger and as more worthwhile.

Telling a story of changes remarkably similar to Kim's, Rhonda (age 32, African American) describes an act of self-defensive aggression as the turning point of her life. She now works in social services and is raising two daughters on her own. She agreed to have her story told because "I think it would help a lot of battered women."

Rhonda grew up in Seattle in an all-black neighborhood. Her mother took care of Rhonda and her four brothers and sisters, but was emotionally withdrawn and not very involved in their lives. Rhonda never saw her mother get angry or assertive, nor did her mother tell her about sex, boys, or racial prejudice. Speaking of her older brother, Rhonda says: "He be so mad at Mom to this day, because he'd get in trouble at school and it wouldn't be his fault, and . . . he wanted his mom to stand up to the teacher and this and that, and she wouldn't do it . . . She would just go down there and everything the teacher say, she agree with it. Kind of like passive. And so, I just said I wasn't gonna be like that. It used to make me so mad at her."

Rhonda got her GED, but, lacking clear goals she wanted to pursue, organized her life around the men she became involved with. The second man in her life, Derek, was "real violent." She had to "watch what you say because he'd just haul off and hit you real hard, and you won't know exactly what you said wrong, but he'll see something wrong in it." Rhonda was married to Derek, the father of her second daughter, for four years. Once his battering began, there was nothing she could do to stop it. Following a pattern common among battered women, she felt extreme anger toward his controlling, brutal behavior and tried, at times, to argue with him to create the kind of relationship she wanted, yet she also feared his violence (Jacobson and Gottman, 1998). Over time, she says,

> I was driven to a point where I didn't care, and I felt like, at that time, I didn't really have a lot of verbal skills to just know what to say, to stand up verbally to defend myself. I didn't seem to have those words because I never had to use them . . . My self-esteem was really low. And I didn't feel like I could make it, like I wasn't capable of making it because he took care of financial things . . . I was scared to leave. And I just didn't want to be alone. I just wanted to be with somebody.

Like survivors of other types of interpersonal trauma, Rhonda reacted to assault with emotional numbing, shock, denial, helplessness, and fear (Dutton, 1992; Herman, 1992; Walker, 1984). After such attacks women commonly experience depression, low self-esteem, and disturbed sleeping and eating patterns (Goodman, Koss, and Russo, 1993; Jones and Schecter, 1992). As levels of violence escalated, Rhonda's perceptions of her alternatives became increasingly restricted, as did her sense that taking action on any alternative was too dangerous to risk (see Browne, 1993).

Things got worse when her husband got involved with "this other lady that did drugs." Rhonda protested, and one time when they were arguing,

> first he was hitting me and everything and I couldn't . . . I didn't say anything but I was getting, in my mind, how I could get to that gun and get him off of me. And I did get to the gun but he started fighting me even when I had the gun. And that's how it went off in the ceiling and in the wall. And he was still fighting and then I just turned and I faced him. Because I was running. We was running through the house and that's when the bullets were going off . . . but when I turned and faced him and he got scared . . . I shot him. But it's like, I turned around and faced him because I said, "I'm not going to keep running." I turned around and faced him and I shot him.

Rhonda's bullet hit Derek in the arm. She dropped the gun; he picked it up and put it to her head. "I just closed my eyes and he didn't do it. He just says, 'See, I can't do it, I can't do it.' He says, 'You shot me, but,' he said, 'I know I've brought you to this point because I know you're not like this.'" He left the gun and went to the hospital, telling police his wound came from a drive-by shooting.

This dangerous incident, Rhonda says, "really woke me up inside." It became the catalyst for her to change her life. Before she shot him,

> I was looking at him like a monster because I was so scared of him . . . I had this concept that I was so weak and so small and he was this big beast and he was over me and I had no control and no power over him. And that I couldn't stand up and take charge of my life. That's what I felt because he controlled everything . . . But then after I did that, I realized I was just *thinking* that I was small . . . But, see, he was not the big scary thing that I thought he was.

With her new perception of her own force, Rhonda was able to take action for herself. Facing her fear that he would kill her if she left, she fled one night in a taxi with her children.

The shooting placed Rhonda on radically different ground and awakened her to the dangerous direction she had been heading: "I got to thinking, 'Boy, I could have killed him.' And see, that opened my eyes up. I said, 'I got to get out of this kind of life.'"

> It woke me up because it let me know I wasn't just a nobody . . . It woke me up to feel like I need to get away . . . and just made me know I just had something in me that I didn't know was there. Maybe it's just more, it's a strength in me or that it takes something kind of like that, the mad, to bring it out . . . I guess my self-esteem did go up. It changed. It changed in a way that I am stronger than I thought. You know? . . . Emotionally strong and just that I really do care. I care about myself more than I thought I did . . . It made me think I don't have to have this kind of man in my life. I deserve better. It woke me up to all those things.

Rhonda's psychological responses to battering had clouded her perceptions and left her feeling dazed, unable to think. The shooting "woke her up" by interrupting her conditioned terror and by reconfiguring her position in relationship to give her some sense of power.[2]

Now able to make choices rather than react out of blinding fear, Rhonda moved out, joined a church, secured a protection order against her husband, learned to drive—"I got gobs of nerve after that!"—became a daycare worker, and went to community college. Her self-defensive act, which could have had such negative consequences, instead transformed her:

> It's just that whole new different outlook I had on life. It wasn't
> dark anymore. Especially when I left him . . . I began to feel
> better about myself. My life just opened up because I had taken
> charge of my life and even though I had to put up a fight to get
> out, I did it. And I felt good about that . . . I felt more self worth
> and I didn't feel inferior. I felt just as good as anybody else. And
> I was able to stand up to people because I always felt like I didn't
> want to say much because I thought that people wouldn't listen
> or what I said wasn't really, didn't make a lot of sense. You know,
> you just kind of judge your own words . . . That was like the
> turning point where I really began to speak out and stand up for
> myself.

Rhonda also became active in church immediately after leaving her husband, and from that community drew a new sense of herself as carrying a personal force that could affect others positively. In hindsight, she feels that "it was God who helped me get to that point" of seeing that her life needed changing. In turning to the black church, Rhonda joins a long tradition of African-American women's involvement in an institution that supports community, empowers African Americans, and provides a safe space in which to learn self-respect.[3] Her activities in church clearly furthered her ability to speak out: "I started doing public speaking in my church . . . My pastor, he let me speak for the first time, you know, speak at the pulpit and give a message. I wish I had that tape of that!"

For Rhonda, the clear dualities of bad and good collapsed when she took a self-defensive action that saved her life. In her case the issue clearly was one of self-protection and survival: the act of shooting her husband, which held the capacity to destroy life, instead became life-affirming, giving her a different sense of her strength, courage, and possibilities.

Rhonda also gained a sense of positive strength from observing how the shooting affected Derek: "He said, 'I'm sorry for everything I've ever done to you.' And he says, 'Every time I'—see, he got the bullet still there—'every time I look at that, it reminds me that, you know, women had to be treated with respect. You can't just treat them any kind of way and beat on them and do this and that' . . . He said he's never hit another woman."

It is very risky to justify violent acts by their outcomes. Rhonda herself remains divided about the moral meaning of the shooting:

> It's like in a way I'm kind of proud I did that because it just really woke me up inside. I didn't know it was in me to do that, but I guess it was something in me that wanted me to survive or something that wanted to live. And I felt like I was dying inside there. That part of me is kind of glad I did it, and then there's this other side that says that's not really a positive thing to shoot somebody . . . I don't feel good about that part . . . The act itself is, I don't think it was good. But the results of what happened afterward, I think, is good. Yeah, it happened, it happened for good reasons. And good things came up out of it.

Rhonda presents an extreme example of self-defensive, positive aggression. Her narrative reveals the powerful shift that comes when a woman experiences herself as capable of standing up to others who threaten her very existence. Like all aggression, positive aggression has an intent which the person enacts by some means. Rhonda's intent was self-protection; her circumstances were such that resorting to aggressive self-defense would probably be justified in a legal test (see *State of Washington v. Wanrow*, 1977). If she had failed to protect herself, given the escalating violence and the presence of a gun in their altercation, it is very likely that she would have been killed (see Jacobson and Gottman, 1998; Jones, 1994).

According to Victoria Burbank, "Where women can take the stance of aggressor, they experience aggression differently than women who experience aggression primarily as victims" (1993, 19). Taking "the stance of aggressor" differs from initiating attack: "An aggressive stance begins as a sense of self-protection" (189) and provides a way of demanding respect and refusing to be victimized. To ensure that taking an aggressive, self-protective stance does not backfire into retaliation, women need to know that neighbors, family, and community members will protect and defend them.

The women I interviewed who stood their ground took an aggressive stance in Burbank's sense. Each stood up for herself out of a sense of self-protection, convinced that her psychological or physical survival was at stake, and most, like Rhonda, did so courageously without a protecting community at hand. Standing one's ground profoundly changes one's experience of personal force. For a woman to overcome fears of men's power over her, or to find a way out of a situation that appears hopeless, requires taking an "aggressive stance" which may be as low-key as verbal confrontation or as dramatic as physical defense of her life. The stance includes a willingness to end (destroy) relationships that threaten to destroy her.

Lynnea (age 32, white, social worker) recounts taking such a stance, which became a turning point in her life. At 20, with an infant and a toddler, she found out that her husband, who was controlling and demeaning, was cheating on her:

> That day I was probably the most aggressive I've ever been in my life. No matter what he said, he wasn't staying . . . I just laid it all out. "This is what you did and I'll never get over it." He was saying, "You know, we could just forget it." And I said, "You can forget it. I'll never forget it, my feelings have changed. I don't love you. I don't trust you. I don't respect you. So what's to hold the relationship together?" That day I really felt like I grew up.

Learning to stand up for herself constructively gives a woman a new sense of strength, maturity, and absence of fear. It is different from an act of egocentric will or from a "manly" act of bravado. It is a move to stand one's ground in the relationship through care—for one's self, for one's children, for life itself. It also affects a woman's anger and self-esteem. This is how some women describe it:

> As I feel some power to say how I'm hurt or how I'm angry, it takes away the power of telling myself I'm bad or something . . . There is a power in there that was really huge that I just kept adding to, and as I can say it, it takes power away from that inner feeling of nonworth. (Lyn, age 39, white, student)

> That sense of personal power has been so essential for me. And I just don't think anybody deserves to have every little thing screened by someone. It's just too demeaning. So I just changed and it works fine. I feel, and this is what I really learned . . . is that I'm really loving him better to not let him hurt me. (Julia, age 39, white, teacher)

> I used to be someone who was really in touch with my anger, which a lot of women actually aren't. I could get angry really quickly . . . [now] I'm calmer and I'm mellower. It's really interesting because getting somehow in touch with my strength and my power has softened everything . . . maybe the anger has to do with the fear, and you don't have to be as fearful all the time. (Lisa, age 43, white, self-defense instructor)

These women, all socialized to regard their aggression as unfamiliar territory, have felt at the mercy of everyone else's will, continually under the threat of others' possible demands. The perception of constant threat leads to fearful, hostile, and angry feelings. A woman who knows she can stand up for herself positively feels more powerful in relationship and thus less hostile and defensively angry than one who feels she cannot. Release from threat and fear brings freedom—from anger, from low self-esteem—and opens possibilities of increased love for others.

These women have faced monsters and overcome them; they have ended patterns of relating and relationships that can destroy them. When threatened, they do not shrink or ineffectively explode, assuming nothing will change. Rhonda gives an example of her new ability to deal with threats:

> Before I had this job I had a supervisor. He was controlling, like my ex-husband, totally like that . . . Oh, we clashed big time. I stood up to him. He was 6′4″, 300 pounds. Samoan. And I stood up to him and I wrote letters to his supervisor and everything. And they would get on him, you know, about the way he treated, not just me, but he would do it to Luke [a co-worker] too. Which Luke, he didn't feel like he wanted to stand up for himself. But I stood up for both of us. I could have lost my job.

After taking charge of her life, Rhonda has a different feeling of her interpersonal force. She refuses to accept demeaning treatment and meets it with positive aggression.

Standing up for oneself brings self-esteem. These narratives reveal that self-esteem is related to self-protection, to self-affirmation through one's actions. If a woman jumps from self-abnegation and feelings of powerlessness into explosive rage, there is no increase in self-esteem. She has not yet experienced herself as separate and opposed to someone else; she has not yet created a new ground of being, in relation. Learning to stand one's ground is a critical developmental step for women.

The Third Way

Once a woman learns to stand her ground, she no longer envisions a duality of subordination versus isolation—an either/or choice of silencing her anger or hurting others by saying what she thinks. She gains a new perspective that lets her transcend this duality.

Julia, whom we met in earlier chapters, tells of gaining a new perspective that led to a turning point in her marriage. After a particularly frustrating argument with her husband, Nate, Julia vowed not to let "that sinking feeling" of depression prevail:

> I left the house, and with all the energy that I felt was aggression, I just started splitting wood and I felt so strong . . . I was splitting

this mountain of firewood and I was vocalizing as I was doing it. I don't know how to describe it but almost like in childbirth, just grunting, and it was a feeling of being, of pulling together my power. And then I looked up and Nate was watching me and I felt that he felt I was really feeling like hitting him with that ax. Just kind of metaphorically.

As Julia talks she begins to cry and says, "It still moves me to remember": "It was a new—it was like a third way. I felt a confidence that I would find a way to bring to fruition what I wanted and it wasn't going to be defined by what he did. I guess I was going beyond him. And I guess also . . . what I was feeling was sort of an inner light that something was prevailing even though I was being shot down over and over again."

I ask what the third way was, and Julia replies:

I have focused many, many times on blaming him and nagging him and expressing frustrations. Then I'd give in and I'd blame and I'd feel resentful. And I didn't give in all the time but it was always one of us winning and one losing. We were driven apart by a decision. I think the difference was that sometimes in just yelling at him I was still acknowledging defeat and expecting defeat . . . So what I was experiencing was almost like coming to a dead end and then finding a way to get out that then afforded—sort of like climbing a mountain: you just can't go any farther but you find one foothold that gets you up to a plateau and then you can see the way. And that's what it felt like. And what happened that day when I was splitting the firewood, it was like . . . the firebird and the calling that brought it. That's what I was doing. I was making one of those sounds that called something to rise above what was happening.

Julia's moment of clarity sounds like the Russian fairy tale "The Maiden Czar," in which a magical firebird, called by a voice full of despair and fear, swoops down to lift the trapped hero to freedom. The tale recounts the human quest to confront one's destructive energy so as to overcome deadening limitations, to find voice and creativity. As Julia faced her familiar sense of relational disconnection and its partner, depression, this time she raged against them, chopping and "pulling together my power," physically refusing to succumb. The moment of seeing herself reflected in Nate's eyes did not hold the usual shame or defeat. Instead, she called herself to "rise above what was happening."

Before she found her new perspective, Julia had perceived only a dichotomy regarding how to deal with conflict: either win or lose, dominate or yield. Her "third way" offered the clarity of "knowing I had the power to do what I wanted to do." Her anger diminished: "I had a feeling of self-respect and calm like I didn't have to hurt him to make him see that my ideas were valid." She gained insight into their impasses: "I felt that his frustrating of me had previously limited my repertoire of what I did with my energy. That I squandered it on complaining or I squandered it on just yelling." She no longer spends her energy on power struggles: "I'm not letting him be in the way. So I don't focus on the unfulfilled desires, I don't focus on him as the reason. We just can have a lot more fun when there's not that undercurrent of 'You take something from me'— we're diminished by that."

Julia now recognizes that "my strength and my respect for my creativity and just feeling like I was a good person was the real issue." She has experienced a "transformation of wanting to prevail" over her husband into a "compassion toward him that his difficulty with me was misguided." Her third way of engaging in conflict now goes beyond him to follow an inner light that guides her toward her purpose. She now accepts responsibility for bringing to fruition things that matter to her, for fulfilling her creative desires by using her energy positively. Her new sense of personal strength and ability to transcend winner/loser thinking are keys to this third way of engaging in conflict.

Courage in Relationships

Some women have no difficulty using their positive aggression. Often these women have had models of positive conflict resolution in their families; rarely have they been in demeaning or abusive relationships. These women use their aggression creatively. They are comfortable with who they are, affirm themselves, and feel part of a nexus of community. They focus on either preventing their own fear or preventing others' wills from diminishing the enlarged space within which they live. Carla (age 38, African American, police officer) describes her stance in relationship: "I feel very well grounded in how to pursue things from my, not dictatorial standpoint, but from a fair but firm standpoint." Carla's goal is not to avoid hurt but to avoid "deceit": "If I have a problem with you, I will seek you out and talk, try to talk to you about the problem I have with you, and I would expect that from you also."

In Carla's childhood her three older brothers, her strong mother, and her father, who listened, were role models for self-assertion:

> My mom has always been very strong in fighting for us to be who we are . . . I learned that she could have anger and usually it was around us . . . And my father was a very emotional, very blustery man, and she would argue with him and she'd yell, then she'd take it down a tone, and they'd end up where he's sitting and he'd have to stop yelling so he could hear what she was saying. It was usually something that would come to a conclusion and a decision would be made. And I never saw violence between them.

Carla had to strengthen her sense of self to deal with responses she encountered as one of the first African-American women on a metropolitan police force. She also met difficulties because of her sexual orientation: "Feeling those biases and injustices, not just because I'm a black woman, but being a lesbian, makes me feel stronger in who I am. I've taken pride in who I am."

Carla uses powerful affirmations to strengthen herself to encounter the dangers she faces in her job and the discrimination she confronts as a private citizen: "They're all 'I will' and 'I am' statements. 'I will survive any threat or force used against me and come back stronger. I am a powerful woman. I am confident, capable and attentive.' " She uses these statements as

> survival techniques, so that if you do get into that situation where you're either hurt really bad by knife, gunshot, car acci-

dent, whatever, that your ingrained survival statement in your brain, in your heart, in your mind, that you will do your best to survive, and by your survival, you're ensuring that this, whoever did this to you or however this happened can be told and maybe rectified.

Carla's positive vision of herself, paired with her ability to stand up for herself, enables her to meet threats not with hostility but with positive aggression. Though surrounded by obstacles, she courageously creates a positive ground on which to live.

Facing very different threats than Carla does, Carol (age 32, white, biologist) also uses positive aggression to create an enlarged space within which to live. She has always broken stereotypes about women's behavior, particularly in terms of her physical competitiveness, her jobs, and her strength. She grew up in the wilds of Wyoming, unfettered by many of the expectations that white middle-class girls face, only loosely supervised by a mother who was occupied with raising three boys and two girls. About relationships with men, Carol learned from her mother: "Just be real submissive." Instead of expressing anger her mother would "get quiet . . . she fell in, like a depression." Carol "learned aggression when I left home and had to start dealing with life."

In her job, Carol tracks wolves, bears, and the elusive snowy owl in forests in the Pacific Northwest. She supervises a crew of four men and two women, camping out for weeks at a time. She confronts fears to overcome them, and this contributes to her sense of embodied psychological strength: "When I was working for the Forest Service, we would camp out . . . for nine days, and then off for four. And I remember putting my tent away from everybody else, just so I could quit being afraid of the woods. And sleeping in the woods alone . . . was really good for me. Because the first few nights I was just so, ooohhh, afraid, and I was camped pretty far away." Fear presents an opportunity for Carol to build her courage. As Salman Rushdie puts it in *The Moor's Last Sigh:* "With fear it's all or nothing. Either, like any bullying tyrant, it rules your life with a stupid blinding omnipotence, or else you overthrow it, and its power vanishes in a puff of smoke."

Carol's determination to vanquish her fears has led to courage in relationships. She refuses to be paralyzed by fear of losing a relationship or being rejected by others. She gives an example of having to fight to stand on equal ground when mountain climbing, the sport that is her passion:

> I was on this climb in Nepal, and this one guy just had a bad attitude about women climbing. And he happened to be our leader, the group leader . . . and he had the impression that the guy would lead up and the women stay behind, and I'm not that way. I don't want to stay behind and I want to climb at my own level and I don't want to be pushed behind because I'm a girl. And I'm not there to try and prove that I'm better than a guy. So what happens is, "Okay, so you're a girl and you think you can climb this, then you need to be as strong as I am and you need to—" And again, I stand my ground on this because I'm not as strong as men, you know. Men are stronger . . . I communicated with him and I told him how I felt and it was unfair how he was treating me.

When the other woman on the expedition got altitude sickness, the leader split the group in two, pushing Carol back to the slower group. But the other woman and her husband retreated to the lower base camp, so Carol spent the night alone, with the "wind whipping the tent," thinking of the Yeti, the Nepali counterpart of the Abominable Snowman. The next morning she decided to cross the glaciers, by herself, to join the team that was planning to attempt the summit.

I ask her what it took for her to make that decision: "Desire, I guess. I really—I had a desire, for years I wanted to climb this mountain . . . And as you get closer it's less steep and it's less intimidating and if you just take it section by section . . . You get closer and you put so much effort to getting there. So much money. So much everything. And so it's just my desire to really want to at least give it a try." Carol followed her desires, stood her ground with the unwelcoming group leader, and made it to the summit of the mountain.

What Carol calls "desire," a feeling that unites her body and psyche, guides her understanding of how to relate to others. This desire is not sexual; it is more pervasive, originating from a mysterious place that guides her path through life: "When people don't follow their desires and get kind of trapped into going a certain way in life—you know, because you always come into those intersections. And you don't follow your desires, you do what the guy wants to do. And I've done that a lot. But I think it's the situations where I took my own path and went for my own desires is when I felt really successful." Desire is part of positive aggression. It fuels the push to overcome barriers and enact goals. Emerging from some plane beyond the rational, desire requires the use of positive force to follow its intuitive feeling.

Carla and Carol illustrate the positive sense of self that comes with affirming oneself as equal in relationship. They overcome different inner and outer barriers to take such a relational stand; for both, their positive aggression creates new possibilities for self and for society.

The Aggression of Hope

Humans are social animals with innate needs for intimacy and connection. People's physical and mental health are closely related; those who are "socially isolated have at least two to five times the risk of premature death from all causes when compared to those who had a strong sense of connection and community" (Ornish, 1998, 42). From heart disease to ulcer, from cancer and strokes to arthritis, studies of illness demonstrate "a biological basis for our need to form loving human relationships. If we fail to fulfill that need, our health is in peril" (Lynch, 1977, quoted in ibid., 70).[4]

The ways we engage in conflict reflect the patterns of relating we learned as children, and lead to closeness or isolation from others. As the narratives in earlier chapters reveal, when women feel isolated and unable to connect positively, they will use destructive means. Any connection is better than isolation.

Women's narratives detail how they overcome daunting obstacles to connect with others in positive ways. Consider Anna, the artist who speaks of the "force that drives the green" (see Chapter 1). Anna prayed that her abusive stepfather would die in a car crash; when he did so, she felt "tremendous guilt." As an adult, she has overcome guilt, shame, rage, and abuse. How can anger become a force that drives the green of growth rather than a force that feeds aggressive destruction?

Connection

The theme that runs through women's stories of transforming destructive aggression—both the hurt that has been done to them and the rage they feel—into positive action is *connection*. They describe a sense of becoming part of something larger than their separate selves; their egos feel included within a greater whole. This sense of joining their emotions, their victimization, the meaning of their lives, with a larger "we" lets them transcend the devastation of isolated shame, abandonment, and suffering. They identify with something that gives meaning to suffering and offers positive pathways out of the wasteland of pain.

Sharon (age 44, Native American/white, student), gives a clear description of moving from isolated, angry disconnection to creativity and a sense of relatedness with a larger whole. Until age 8 Sharon lived with her family in Alaska and learned the traditions of her mother's tribe. Then her father took her to Oregon, where he left her with a series of people who physically abused her. She was taken into custody by the state and placed in a foster home. At this home, Sharon says:

> There was a facade going on, of some sort, you know, people were sweet but they could do the most cruel things to you underneath that. And they could do it with feelings . . . racism was like that sweet white femininity that would humiliate you . . . There's all this order being maintained, but it's a falsehood, you know, because there's a lot of violence underneath that order, that nobody was going to talk about.

Choosing to resist a situation in which people seemed to want her "to think of myself as bad, and helpless," in which "they would say mean and hurtful things and try to take my self-esteem away," Sharon protected herself by escaping. Despite the odds against her, she battled to achieve personal and racial affirmation, carrying with her the memory of the positive relationships she had early in life. She continued to run away from each foster home that demeaned her; the state interpreted this resistance to devaluation as incorrigibility. After the third or fourth foster home, Sharon realized that "what I was looking for didn't exist maybe. I was just looking for my own home." By her own home she may have meant not only her family of origin but a place that would confirm her identity in a positive way. As Dorothy Allison writes: "Resistance to hatred is not a simple act. Claiming your identity in the cauldron of hatred and resistance to hatred is infinitely complicated, and worse, almost unexplainable" (1994, 23). Sharon's running away was an attempt to resist internalizing the contempt and dismissal with which others treated her.

At 16 Sharon was placed in reform school, where she was held in maximum security because of her defiance and threats to escape. She reflects on her active resistance during that time: "Is it aggressiveness to be able to know the difference between right and wrong and be able to have a will against it? I have a will against what seems to me to be out of balance. If it's out of balance and it seems like a hurtful thing to myself or someone, people around me, then I have a will against it. I'll set myself against it."

While in detention, Sharon wrote on any scraps of paper she could find. Eight months of her writings were confiscated when discovered, because residents were not supposed to keep diaries. Aware of what had happened to Sharon, a teacher encouraged her to write about her life for a state competition. Her essay won, a victory that affirmed a creative, positive aspect of herself that had been submerged by repeated negative interactions with society.

After her eventual release Sharon married an abusive man and had a child, but she did not put up with the abuse for long. During her twenties she lived on the street, had a series of devaluing relationships, and was physically aggressive herself. Now a published poet in graduate school, she is known not only for her written words and lively intelligence but for her ability to build bridges between diverse, often hostile groups of people.

I ask, "Do you have any idea why you didn't just stay angry and full of hate?"

> When I was so isolated, I felt my relationship to humanity. Somehow or another, I sensed world pain. There is stuff that goes on in this world that is incredibly wrong, and has gone on forever. So where in hell do you put that? Inside yourself? No way—that's like ingesting evil or something. I won't do it. But people don't realize that. They think their own personal world is hell, and somebody must be responsible, so then you can just put it on them. But I've had too much experience. It's everywhere, it's in everybody, it's way more complex. It's nothing I can describe other than it's the world, it's the pain of humanity which is deep-rooted and deep-seated.

I ask how she came to this realization.

> I felt my own personal pain in the context of the world . . . I began to understand it because I started trying to figure out what, who Indians were . . . I started reading history . . . and all of a sudden it hits me. "My god, they did away with all these people. That's how come we're like we are, because they did away with us." And I started saying "us," not "me"—"they did away with *us*" . . . Well, somebody tells me another story, okay? Well, Nazis did this to Jews. Okay. And I hear another story . . . and as the picture gets larger and larger and larger, I've never lost the understanding that humankind has the ability to do incredibly ugly things to its members, to each other. So where is hate in all of that? It gets lost for me. I couldn't hate any one people, you understand what I'm saying? I couldn't hate myself.

In this powerful statement Sharon describes the transformation of a damaging life history into a creativity that nourishes both herself and the collective. At the same time that Sharon was hearing herself within a larger context, she was forming relationships that supported new ways of enacting this perception. Sharon's changes challenge the idea of an inscribed aggressive personality or the stability of aggression from childhood to adulthood; they call society to recognize the power of connection to transform lives on.

Another woman, Diana (age 51, white, Catholic lay nun), was raped by a priest when she was on a retreat. Five years later, still filled with anger and pain, she began listening to stories of Central American refugees: "I joined my experience of rape with awareness of systems of injustice in Central America, where thousands of women were raped and killed. I began to hear about the systems of injustice, and it pulled me into political action." She became deeply involved in helping refugees and transformed the rage and shame from her victimization into social action. At the same time, she formed new relationships based on healing and connection.

These women moved from the isolation of an ego-focused emotion—"I am suffering; I am angry"—to connect that pain with a wider world: "I felt my own personal pain in the context of the world." They did not stay isolated by the emotions of anger or suffering; rather, they brought their emotions into a larger dialogue. Coming into connection required *listening*, hearing the self from a broader perspective. Connecting painful experiences humanizes them. That is, it transforms them into the best qualities humans share, such as mercy, consideration, kindness, and justice-seeking. This is how the human spirit performs alchemy on the dregs of violence, hate, and fear to convert them from negativity into a force that drives positive change and growth.

Hearing the self in this enlarged way lets women come into positive relationship with the pain caused by the brutality of others. Most often, painful feelings caused by trauma lead to psychological responses called post-traumatic stress disorder, and include numbing, depression, substance abuse, and denial. These women say their ability to tolerate their painful feelings requires consciously experiencing them, staying with them, and turning them into positive action. This happens in relationship, never in isolation.

Further, these women know their capacity for destructive action and choose the positive. Sharon describes her "will," the powerful force that she uses to create change:

The essence of your humanity, your spirit, is your will, isn't it? It is to me. It's like you wake up in the morning and somehow all the things that have happened to you . . . have woven itself into whatever it is . . . It's me, it's me, and it's my will. You can't experience yourself in little pieces, you have to experience yourself as my body and my spirit and my mind, there's no separation. I'm all here. I'm a will and a force at that point. I'll reflect real deeply on things for a very long time, perhaps, but they're not for just that, they're for action. You know what I mean, they're essentially to be put into action, in my life, if not in the world.

Both Sharon and Diana transform their personal pain and resist internalizing their oppression by empathically connecting their pain with the pain of humanity. This does not mean they do not get angry; rather, their powerful anger moves them to positive action. Sharon talks about her "respectful manner," which indicates her willingness to listen to others: "You assume always that you are with them rather than against them. So I tell people, 'I hear you, I hear you totally.' And maybe I'll say something to make them understand that I do hear them, so then they're in a safe place . . . but I can't do that if I'm just in my little self." A listening compassion creates the link with others.

Creativity

Women tell of converting their isolating emotions, including their victimization, into a positive force by two additional means: creativity and spirituality. These ways of transforming pain are not the only ones available, nor are they limited to women's use. The following examples throw light on how the transformation occurs and present women's perspectives on them. In Anna's case the transformation occurs in the realm of creativity.

Anna, whose abusive stepfather died in the way she had prayed for, is now an accomplished artist. As an adolescent and a young adult she shut down her anger to avoid being like those who had hurt her. For years, keeping her anger out of awareness and out of her relationships prevented any genuine intimacy. It was not until she entered therapy to deal with her childhood abuse that she could acknowledge anger. At that time she was dissatisfied with her art:

> There was a point where I was ready to just pile all my art together and just burn it. All I was doing was pretty pictures, and I wasn't able to understand why I was so frustrated . . . There was something wrong with only doing pretty pictures for me. And I know people who say, "I'm not going to do this anger." They don't face or deal with it, and they do beautiful things. But it's like, nobody should be nice all the time. There's something wrong if everything is nice all the time . . . everything never is all wonderful, sweet, and beautiful, so there's something wrong. There's something wrong with this picture, and there was something wrong with the picture for me when all I did were pretty pictures.

Anna's integration of her anger was inextricably related to her art, and to her changing understanding of beauty:

> I didn't deliberately do any art that channeled angry energy until I actually understood that I had anger . . . For me, it was like art was to make things beautiful and that was what I did. When the world might be ugly sometimes, I took art to create beauty. And then I realized, well, I can take anger into art. I didn't create ugly pictures necessarily, but they're a whole different kind of imagery and energy and strength. I didn't feel like I was doing unbeautiful things, but I was basically understanding that anger had expanded my definition of what beauty was.

She began to find the power of anger through creativity rather than through destruction:

> Art was, in fact, the most powerful area in my life. It was creation. There's a tremendous amount of power in looking at a blank piece of paper and transforming it . . . That's the power of art for me, and then discovering that anger is not something I need to be terrified of, and that it's power. And the anger that I grew up with was abuse of power. But the problem wasn't the power, the problem was the abuse of it. And then I discovered

that I could take my anger and the energy and intensity that went with that, which certainly equaled sometimes the intense energy I have about beauty. It's like I could take anger and it could come out on a blank piece of paper and create something that was powerful and beautiful, and that conveyed anger and rage and pain and loss and suffering. But when it was all done, you stepped back and it was beautiful. And it's like, anger is part of beauty.

Now able to acknowledge pain and anger, Anna uses her art to transform such feelings into imagery that offsets the horror of violence. She recalls a violent incident in Montreal in 1989, in which a gunman killed fourteen young women:

When the women in Montreal were shot there was so much fear and anger and pain around here. And I thought, "Okay, I can do something expressive of how angry I am" . . . But I thought, "I don't want to create any more violent imagery. So what do I want to create?" And that was a very conscious thing. I want to add something loving and good . . . And if I could create a picture that expressed what I would put in its place, it would be something gentle and beautiful . . . Anger is appropriate. I mean, it's still appropriate when you think that whoever does these bad things, something terrible and awful is going to happen to them. But before I am concerned about that, it's more like how do you undo, what sort of imagery . . . That's my first thing, is taking that energy and making something that sort of neutralizes the really negative, scary stuff of anger.

The murders in Montreal, like a stone cast into a pond, sent ripples of horror and negativity through the collective. Feeling these ripples, Anna decided to create something loving and good to neutralize their impact. Profoundly connected to the pain of the women who died, to her own feelings, and to the larger "we," Anna painted a memorial that conveys the loss and rage, depicted in a beautiful form, to take the place of these women's terror-filled last moments.

This is the transformation of anger into positive aggression. To have a will and bring it to bear in the world. To influence events.

To be able to oppose things and people you think are wrong and hurtful. To be able to work for and with others for a greater cause. To do so in dialogue and in connection, not in silenced isolation.

What about women whose rage has led them to hurt others? How do they overcome the shame and guilt of knowing they have been destructively aggressive? For such women, the first step is being honest about their injurious actions. Mandy (age 32, white, student), whom we met in earlier chapters, has been violent and hurt others both physically and emotionally. She is now sober and working to build a positive life: "In terms of recovery, it's really crucial that I be completely honest with myself about who I am and where I've been. When I start trying to delude myself into thinking that all I am is a student and mother, and this great giver to people, you know, this kind of Mother Teresa thing, I think for me that's real dangerous territory. I'm capable of being hurtful to other people."

Mandy has become a writer and an artist, working to channel her destructive, unacceptable feelings into words and images. These creative outlets draw on the restless, angry energy of pain and craft it into new realizations that carry positive possibilities. Of her anger that feels aggressive, she says:

> It's the other end of the rainbow. It's the blue and the purple, and into the black, and if I shut that part of me off, then it isn't going to be very creative. It'll be sort of like that pastel in the middle area. I think that artwork can be aggressive. I mean, I don't think that the work itself is necessarily aggressive but I think that creation of the work comes from aggression. I know when I write, it's usually that part of me that's speaking. The part of me that writes isn't the part of me that was taught to be good or be nice or be polite or sit with your legs crossed and fold your hands and don't say shit if you have a mouthful, you know. The part of me that writes is the part of me that doesn't care what other people think. It's like all that stuff that I've kept inside for so many years, it comes out and people that read it tell me it's good, you know, and so I just keep going down in there and pulling more of it out.

For Mandy, this creative outlet converts the pain and shame of her former life into a desire to speak the unspoken. Her written words and painted images bring into dialogue those aspects of self which she had kept hidden.

Spirituality

Leigh (age 44, white), who teaches Buddhism, believes deeply in nonviolence. The experience of interconnection, the sense that one is part of a larger "we," is at the core of Buddhist spiritual tradition.

> We are all essentially the same, the bottom line. Life is like a field . . . whatever we do in life sows certain kinds of seeds in that field, creates that in that field. And we have a choice of creating suffering, or creating love . . . It's like when the person talked about seeing the whole universe in a grain of sand. It's like that's how incredibly powerful we are. It's like whatever we do affects the whole universe, and I see that so clearly. And so it makes it really important, you know, how I try to live my life.

Leigh's understanding of the interconnectedness of life does not preclude standing up for herself. She considers positive aggression to be "the ability to stand up for yourself and to be real clear about what your needs are and how you expect people to treat you . . . That feels grounded, and feels good." She practices a mindfulness meditation, watching thoughts and feelings go by while focusing on her breathing. She has learned to "sit with" anger and rage, to feel without having to enact. When anger comes during meditation, she attempts to "be there with it and not try to put it away or anything . . . just know it's there and touch it, let it be there." After practicing meditation for fifteen years, Leigh feels "a lot less afraid of aggression than I used to be, and I feel like I can really stand up, stand against things a lot without returning it in kind. I don't feel so caught by it."

Leigh and her husband live in a suburb of Portland with their toddler, Forrest. Leigh went through a severe test of her convictions when new neighbors moved in next door. The father in this family was a Vietnam veteran whose violent episodes, she suspected, were due to post-traumatic stress. Over time, her relationship with him deteriorated into mutual distrust. One day Leigh took a walk with her 18-month-old son perched in a backpack. She had to pass her neighbor's house. When his dogs, barking ferociously, rushed at her, she tossed a few rocks at them. He followed her, "shouting and screaming":

> And I said, "Well, what do you want me to do, walk through here with Mace?" And then I kept walking and I was really shaking because he just had been screaming at me and I didn't know what to do. I almost went up to the neighbor's to ask someone to come back with me, and Forrest was on my shoulders and I thought, "Nah, come on, . . . just let it go." So I walked back there, and he came out with a handful, a fistful of rocks and slugged me in the face. With the rocks in his hand. I mean he was just out of his mind. I was crying. Forrest was screaming and I was just backing down the road trying to get away from him—I was terrified.

After this incident Leigh was distressed, not only about the assault, but also about the seemingly unbridgeable chasm between her and her neighbor. She was painfully aware of the contradiction between her beliefs and this situation:

> Every place where you hold resentment, anger, *I* hold resentment, anger, hatred, enmity, is a place where I'm keeping separation in the world. Separating myself. And spiritually you come to a place where there's no separation at all. And you have experiences of that along the meditation path . . . It becomes very important to move always toward that everywhere you can, and where there is resentment and where there is anger, you try to heal that. And that's purifying the heart.

In this spirit of overcoming separation, she tried talking to her neighbor, without success. She tried other means, knowing that she could not and would not meet him with aggression.

I went through incredible paranoia. And fear and aggression fantasies, killing all those dogs, and dreams . . . And for a long time and working with it too, in meditation and then my practice. Where is peace here? I'm studying with this Vietnamese Zen master whose whole thing is making peace and I've got a Vietnam veteran living next door to me who wants to kill me . . . How do I live with this? I went through all sorts of things, through going up and trying to talk to him, and I mean everything, from tears to anger, the whole gamut. The whole thing of how do I work this out? And where's the compassion? Where's the understanding? This has come out of the Vietnam war. The Vietnam war's still alive right here, in my own life. And it's really an incredible lesson about war.

The massive destruction from the war's violence spreads through relationships in ever widening circles. The sufferings of those who fought the battles, as well as the pain of civilians who received the violence, create chain reactions of further aggressions that take violence farther and farther away from any "original cause." This man's suffering from the war continues to reproduce around him the pain and horror he experienced.

Leigh's relationship with her neighbor changed after a mudslide that severely damaged her house:

He was the first person down here . . . and I saw him here and it just enraged me. I didn't want this man here at all when I was dealing with this. And I was—and immediately all these thoughts, walking up to him and cussing him out, telling him to get the fuck off my property. And all that came out was this prayer. I mean this is what came out of all those years of prayer was I walked up to him . . . I put my arm around him and started to walk him up the road and said, "I hope we can use this as an opportunity to make peace between ourselves" . . . What was going on in my mind was "I hate this guy, I don't want him anywhere near my property."

Leigh's many years of crafting her consciousness to overcome separation showed its effects on this day. The practice of "being with" emotion without getting caught up in it allowed her to stop herself from expressing her wave of feeling. Her prayer for peace that "came out," seemingly unbidden, kept her tongue from forming other words. Her conscious effort to stop the violence required her to put her ego out of the way and think of the larger whole. She did not do this out of fear, but out of the conviction that where "there's not love, there's a place in us where there's still war." She did not meet fire with fire, but with empathic understanding to transform aggression into reconciliation, into connection.

Leigh's response to her neighbor was very different from self-silencing out of fear or compliance to the will of another. She actively decided not to widen the chasm of misunderstanding and anger between them. She recounts what happened after her prayer of peace: "He said, 'I've never done anything against you.' And I said, 'You hit me in the face.' And he said, 'No, I didn't.' And I said, 'There was a bruise.' And he said, 'Well, maybe I slapped you.' " Leigh felt "really good" that "at some point, he had to admit something." Mainly, she felt this interchange showed a "healthy standing up for myself" and that it was "really right for me to get to that place of not having to take it and still not having to retaliate in some way, which clearly to me was a dead end." Her actions did bring an end to the overt hostility. The two have "started waving toward each other and we've talked."

Other women also say their spiritual conviction of interconnection has helped them refuse to return destructive anger or hatred in kind. Noemi Ban,[5] age 74 at the time of our interview, survived thirteen months in concentration camps: three months in the ghetto in Debrecen, Hungary, three at Auschwitz, and seven at Buchenwald. At 20 she was taken from her native Hungary by cattle car with her mother, grandmother, sister, and brother; her father was sent to a forced labor camp. She and her father were the only survivors. Noemi knows the results of human hatred to a depth that few people experience. Noemi often speaks about the Holocaust to groups in order to "witness—to name it, to say, this exists and this is intolerable. And then it gives other people a strength to do the same about their experiences."

Until Noemi encountered the group aggression of the Nazis, she says, "With a loving family, and growing up in the upper-middle-class environment, I almost didn't know what aggression is." In the concentration camps she became acquainted with a "kind of anger that bears a close relationship with hate." At Auschwitz she saw "the result of hate":

> All of us, thousands of thousands of skeletons dying day after day ... thousands and thousands of people died daily by other human beings for one reason only. That we were Jewish. That, of itself, should have given us a lot of reason to be angry. Now during the Auschwitz days, and even in the ghetto, the over-whelming feeling was fear ... it was a fear so overwhelming that nothing else was able to sneak in there, including anger. I wish we were angry ... when you are so afraid you become almost, not a willing prisoner, but you lose all that healthy feeling of doing something about it, because anger is doing something about it, even if you don't do it. But planning, anger is a plan, is a plan for giving back or to hit or to do something that it should hurt another. And this diminished completely because we were made to fear, and it had such a tremendous power over us. There was no room for any other emotion ... I'm going to tell you about Auschwitz again—when the separation came it was so efficient—within minutes, seconds, there was nothing there. Just do what he said with his hand. Into the shower, into the room, one after the other, that whole system what was planned out, there was no time for anger ... There was no matching partner to be angry at. Because that was such a tre-mendous power over us. If you are angry at someone, you at least are on the same level or a little bit above, but not so much below.

Noemi's phenomenology of anger reveals critical truths: anger is a spur to action, an indication that one is alive with healthy fury at violations no human being should visit upon another. When fear replaces anger, it mutes anger's call to action and gives oppression an opening to invade a person's mind.

While in Buchenwald, Noemi and others were sent to work in a bomb factory:

> Then we were angry. Because we said then, that we should make a bomb or part of a bomb to hurt those that we are hoping will

liberate us? Let's do something about it! And that was an expression of anger. That was giving back. With the sabotage, we make some problem for them, some trouble for them because this bomb will not work. And we felt good about it. That meant that we were angry at them and that whatever we could, we did it.

Noemi's group successfully sabotaged bombs until they were liberated by Allied troops.

Before she could begin telling others about her experience, Noemi had to overcome an overwhelming fear of identifying herself as Jewish: "Why? Because my mother, my grandmother, my little sister, and my brother, the only reason they were killed is because they were Jewish. So that was enough reason to be afraid. And that's what I was afraid of. If I say it out loud, something will happen." Slowly she began to talk about her experiences, first in her family group, then in her own congregation, then at a Methodist church. The local newspaper interviewed her and ran a front-page article about her survival and her message:

> For days until the article appeared, I thought, "Oh boy, now what will happen, now I declared I am Jewish?" It was a very mixed feeling, anxiety, and I was a little proud of myself too. And then finally when it was in the newspaper, and people called me or sent me articles, slowly I did notice that they are not coming after me anymore. And that it is all right to be Jewish and nothing happened. Now I always use this as an example for any group I'm talking to . . . to show that you can overcome your fear. That it is all right to have fear. But you could overcome it and then it's a victory. It feels good that you finally share it. And that's healing. I got more encouraged and started to go to schools. I was amazed that I was standing there in front of the kids and I had no fear, I was sharing with them. From then on, when I went to schools and talked to the children, the adults and civic groups, it eased up in me that fear, and I find the benefit of it. That sharing is healing.

In her talks Noemi emphasizes how critical *dialogue* is to overcome the hatreds and rifts resulting from human cruelty. Both sides of dialogue, the speaking and the listening, are essential: "I think listening is so important for many reasons, but one coming from my own pain—I know that by people listening to me, it was healing."

Others often ask Noemi how she can be so warm and loving after all she has been through:

> I don't know why. I don't know if it is something in my personality, my genes, or upbringing or what. But I did see the results of what happened if you are hated. I saw, in the thousands, what happened in people if they are hated, and if they hate . . . And there is no end to the tragedy. It is so tremendous that even though I was there, it is still too much to measure. Now, it is not my plan that on a day, on that hour, from ten to eleven o'clock, I will be kind because I suffered in Auschwitz. It's not that. My whole being—I've been through this terrible trauma, focused only on one little—one thing. One day at a time. Just one little smile or warmth or love, can do more than hate. And that's as rich as—that is the driving force. That's my purpose.

She describes the transformation that occurred within her as she continued to tell her story:

> My heart and my whole being opened up, because at the beginning, not selfishly, but naturally, I was busy with my own hurts. Not that I lived in them on some island alone, but . . . more and more I was able to see that there are other people and hurts. And this also gives me a strength not to hate, that we have to live without hate, and what I learned about hate in Auschwitz and how this relates to others' pain. So it is a combination of a lot of growth, learning, opening my eyes, and of course the best teacher is . . . that I survived Auschwitz . . . In a very strange way, I use the survival of that terrible trauma to almost change it into a strength. That's what's happening to me. Because instead of losing my head if something happens, I go back here: "Oh! You survived that one. You can survive anything."

In Noemi's life, the hatred that was the Holocaust is stopped, transformed into love and social action. This alchemy, performed by her psyche within community, in dialogue with others, overcomes destructive hatred. Her pain no longer isolates her, nor does she allow the hatred that caused her pain to pass through her and on into more lives. Noemi's courage and love as she reaches out to teach others about this human tragedy cannot be measured in words.

Humans differ from animals in their capacity to organize mass destruction and to gain some sort of enjoyment from cruelty. The possibility of brutal aggression in the world will never be eradicated; it comes with human freedom and imagination. Yet, as these women demonstrate, a person can transform brutal aggression— whether undergone through victimization at another's hands, through organized genocide, or even through one's own actions— into a positive force. Each of these women does so by connecting her personal experience to a greater whole. Each achieves such connection by hearing herself in a larger context and by entering into the world to exert her positive force.

When one has been victimized, or when one has hurt others, it is easiest to explain the pain by assigning blame: it's my fault; it's his or her fault. Instead, these women, hearkening to wider rings of sound, hear a more complex story, one that transcends any specific culture. It connects them to humanity and to history. One person's experience of violence and hatred is linked to what happened to a people, to a group, years ago, centuries ago. One's pain or rage is joined with the ordeals of others in one's group—other Jews, other Native Americans—and then with those of humanity itself. These women's awareness no longer focuses on personal experience alone. Yet awareness of others' pain does not create a deeper despair but creates a meaning that transcends their own egos. This expanded meaning allows them to move out of woundedness and into dialogue and empowerment. Pain no longer feels isolating; anger activates a determination to right the imbalance that has caused the injury or violence. The destruction that affected them does not have to be carried forward in more reverberations of hatred but can be stopped, integrated, and transformed into empathy and social action.

Further, this new way of hearing their anger and pain resists and reframes prevailing cultural explanations, which so often lapse into we/them, right/wrong, victim/victimizer dualism. These women take a more complex, empathic stance, recognizing that hatred and violence affect both perpetrator and victim. They also change their images of personal force, seeing themselves as agents of positive force and realizing that in the particular lies the universal: daily acts of love can transform pain and violence in ways that affect larger contexts. As Noemi Ban says, "Just one little smile or warmth or love, can do more than hate . . . that is the driving force." As Anna says, it is "the force that drives the green." Guided by a belief that their suffering carries a meaning beyond themselves, these women create new ground in self and society by working to prevent the kind of pain that affected their own lives.

These women have moved from ego-focused ways of listening to their own pain and anger into spacious, dialogic ways of listening that enable them to transcend tit-for-tat responses to injustice. Dialogic ways of listening are never permanent in any sense. When the ground suddenly gives way to leave them at a seemingly unbridgeable gap in relationship or feeling unbearable pain, these women again create new ground in relationship and in the self by acts of self-affirmation that do not destroy others. Their narratives reveal that they refuse to be pulled into culturally expected yielding, or into dominating. They do not forget how to interact in ways that preserve the greater fabric of which they feel they are but a small part.

Women's experience of their own aggression has gone uncharted. The foundation for understanding their aggression lies in their everyday lives. Listening to women, we learn that forms of relationship critically shape their aggression. Their narratives provide a powerful account of the damage caused by inequality, oppression, isolation, and violence. Each person's individual experience is inextricably related to social standing, including ethnicity and class. Unequal and abusive forms of relationship and gaps in community provide the contexts in which harmful aggression becomes a person's chosen way of relating.

The sixty women whose voices fill this book repeatedly came to junctions at which they had to decide how to use their force: positively, destructively, to push for change, to survive. At such junctions, an act of aggression is not an isolated event. It is part of a long series of interactions from which a woman has learned how to use her force. In the moment, her decision is influenced by her calculation of the risk of hurt, her beliefs about what is worth fighting for, and her sense of vulnerability in relationships.

Some women draw from a wide range of possible aggressive responses. As children, they learned self-confidence within supportive relationships; as adults, they are confident they will be heard; they have the freedom to respond constructively to threat and inequality. Their communities support their use of creative aggression to overcome violations, to push against restricting limitations. Still, they may elect a more hurtful course. They have the power to choose.

Other women's choices about the use of aggression are more constrained, limited by lessons taught by relationships. For some, histories of abuse, lack of self-esteem, and marginalization have taught them to react to threatening situations with destructive acts against others or themselves. These women long for positive ways to make connections; they often lack the skills and support to make them.

Women who have not learned a full range of aggressive possibilities enter adulthood believing that they must use their force against themselves. They seek to keep themselves under tight control in order to be good so as not to destroy others or be destroyed. The compliant pleasing of others becomes their protective shield. They feel fearful and unable to exercise their agency, leaving them with little choice regarding the use of their own force.

Using positive aggression to stand up for oneself is a crucial developmental step for women. Without standing her ground, a woman cannot exercise her force positively in the world. Healthy relationships require mutuality (being with), but they also require positive aggression (being opposed). For a woman to grasp her potential for positive aggression, she must both exercise her own will and also find the support of a community that accords her safety, equality, and respect.

NOTES
REFERENCES
ACKNOWLEDGMENTS
INDEX

Notes

Hearkening to Women's Voices

1. Fink and Heidegger (1979), 128, quoted in Levin (1989), 229.

2. Most violence against women is committed by their partners: 76 percent of women raped and/or physically assaulted at age 18 or older were assaulted by an intimate, a former intimate, or a date (Tjaden and Thoennes, 1998). Differences among ethnic/racial groups are statistically significant, in decreasing order of incidence: American Indian/Alaska Native; mixed race; African American, white, and Asian/Pacific Islander (ibid.). In America, women in families with annual incomes below $10,000 are more likely than other women to be violently attacked by an intimate (Bachman and Saltzman, 1995). Men with low incomes sanction slapping wives more than do middle-class men (18.5 vs. 14.4 percent) and are more likely to admit hitting their wives (Kantor and Straus, 1990). Linda Gordon (1989), who examined social work records documenting family violence in Boston between 1880 and 1960, concluded that chronic, intergenerational poverty was a chief risk factor. In low-income families, asymmetry in income favoring women, rather than total family income, predicts men's frequency and severity of abuse toward their wives (McCloskey, 1996).

3. I sent all reachable women their typed interview transcripts and sent most women drafts of chapters that contain their stories. Elsewhere I have described my methods of listening and analysis (Jack, 1999b).

4. The Seattle Birth to Three Project began in 1991 at the University of Washington under the direction of Therese Grant and Ann Streissguth. It is an advocacy program that employs paraprofessionals with histories and cultural experiences similar to those of the women for whom they advocate (Grant, Ernst, and Streissguth, 1999).

5. The women of color included two Asian-American, three Latina, four dual-heritage, two Native-American, and eight African-American women. I have chosen to designate cultural communities by these terms primarily because women used them in describing themselves. The terms are not meant to suggest biological, unscientific notions of race but to indicate a woman's social identity.

6. Ethnograph software makes it possible to code interview data and select coded segments across all interviews for comparison and contrast. It also allows "nesting"—coding data with multiple indicators—and selection of cases for analysis by key variables such as abuse, social location, or age. For example, when I selected segments of text coded "hurt" and printed them out by the abuse variable (abused as child, as adult, as both child and adult, and not abused), I was able to listen to hurt across all the women in order to discern patterns not visible through reading each interview separately. The Ethnograph is available from Qualis Research Associates, P.O. Box 2070, Amherst, MA, 01004; email: Qualis@MCIMail.com.

7. While I interviewed only women, the more I learned about the relational nature of aggression the more skeptical I became that this work describes women exclusively. Many of my observations about women's aggression may be true for men as well, particularly regarding the relational definition of aggression, the usefulness of listening to metaphors of force and space, and the importance of moral themes in people's talk about their aggression.

1. The Puzzle of Aggression

1. Dylan Thomas, "The Force That through the Green Fuse Drives the Flower" in *Collected Poems* (New York: New Directions, 1957), 10.

2. See, e.g., Geen, 1990; Gladue, 1991; Maccoby and Jacklin, 1974; McCabe and Lipscomb, 1988; Segall, 1989; Simon and Landis, 1991; White, 1983.

3. Federal Bureau of Investigation, 1994. Arrest statistics have well-known limitations in measuring the true incidence of violent crimes because many crimes are unreported or unsolved.

4. In 1995 scientists reported that a deficiency of testosterone, rather than its excess, could lead to the negative behaviors usually associated with this hormone of male violence and aggression: "The relationship between aggression and androgen levels . . . in humans is much less clear than that shown in data from animal studies. The evidence available from humans, which suggests that T[estosterone] may have an effect on human aggressive behavior, is usually obtained from correlation studies, observer reports, or self-ratings in response to specific situations. These studies were often performed in selected groups of men and may not reflect the response of normal or hypogonadal men" (Wang et al., 1996, 3582). Further, it appears that the increase in male aggression in adolescence may have more to do with estrogen levels than with testosterone (Finkelstein et al., 1997). Endocrinologists remind us how little we know about the links between hormones and aggressive behav-

ior, but the cultural belief remains that testosterone is responsible for male dominance.

5. See esp. Bandura, 1973; Baron and Richardson, 1994; Berkowitz, 1990; Eagly and Steffen, 1986; Lightdale and Prentice, 1994; Maccoby and Jacklin, 1974; White and Kowalski, 1994. For the argument for the social determinants of aggression see Gilligan, 1996; see also Ray and Smith, 1991; Sommers and Baskin, 1992.

6. While much of this violence can be explained by mental illness, substance abuse, battering experienced by the woman, and the fact that women spend more time alone with children than men do (see, e.g., Belsky, 1993; Egami et al., 1996; McCloskey, 1996), it must also be considered against the backdrop of economic jeopardy and insufficient social support for large numbers of mothers and their children.

7. *Price Waterhouse v. Hopkins,* 490 U.S. 228 (1989), 278, 288.

8. Letter from Acting Executive Director, X Hospital, March 10, 1995, supplied by Dr. Jones.

9. Letter dated February 17, 1994, provided by Dr. Jones.

10. The Bem Sex Role Inventory (Bem, 1974) codes the following adjectives as masculine: ambitious, analytical, assertive, athletic, competitive, dominant, forceful, independent, individualistic, self-reliant, self-sufficient, and strong. Feminine qualities assume nonaggressiveness: affectionate, cheerful, childlike, compassionate, flatterable, gentle, gullible, loyal, sensitive, shy, soft-spoken, sympathetic, tender, understanding, warm, and yielding. See also Lenney, 1991.

11. Many researchers would disagree with this statement; see Macaulay, 1985; White and Kowalski, 1994.

12. Society assumes that men are less capable of nurturing because they are more easily aroused to aggression and less able to internally pacify their aggressive tendencies toward infants. Men's absence from caretaking, as well as socialization for aggressiveness, has affected their nurturing behavior more than any inherent factors.

13. Haste (1994) argues that gender roles are usually sustained by the central concept of "otherness" or difference, which defines male as not-female. Positive female qualities come in two versions: the carer and the neutralizer. Certain characteristics, such as types of aggression and irresponsibility, are perceived as essentially male and are negatively judged. Society may deplore them, but they do not detract from masculinity, in fact, they may affirm it.

14. Harrison et al. (1995); Jordan et al. (1991); Jordan (1997).

15. Crick and Grotpeter (1995) use the term *relational aggression* to characterize girls' indirect practice of "harming others through purposeful ma-

nipulation and damage of their peer relationships," such as through "angrily retaliating against a child by excluding her from one's play group; purposefully withdrawing friendship or acceptance in order to hurt or control the child; spreading rumors about the child so that peers will reject her" (711). They found that girls more often employ relational aggression and boys, overt aggression (physical, verbal, or intimidation). I use the term more broadly, to indicate that women wish to *affect the relational space between people.*

16. In married couples, men "use whatever means possible (which are usually withdrawal, avoidance and rationality) to manage the level of negative affect so it does not escalate. In dissatisfied marriages, this rational, avoiding style of males, combined with the emotional, engaging style of females leads to the escalation of the intensity of negative affect by females and to withdrawal by males" (Gottman and Levenson, 1988, 196).

17. "The typical instigation to anger is a value judgment. More than anything else, anger is an attribution of blame. The attribution may not always be correct or free from self-serving biases, and it may be influenced by a host of factors (e.g., frustration, arousal, stimulus-response associations, anonymity) that are in themselves value neutral" (Averill, 1983, 1150).

18. In a national probability sample of 2,031 adults, women had higher levels of anger than men. Economic hardship and inequitable distribution of parental responsibilities were found to explain this difference. Findings support a hypothesis that anger results from perceptions of social inequality in the family (Ross and Van Willigen, 1996).

19. The topic of assaults on men by women is highly controversial. Straus (1980) and Straus and Gelles (1986, 1990) found that while women direct nearly as much aggression against men as men direct against women, much of women's aggression against men is self-defensive, and men's actions result in far greater injury than women's actions. Dobash et al. (1992) argued that the claim of symmetry in marital violence is greatly exaggerated. Courts, police, and women's shelters find that wives are much more likely than husbands to be victims. Finally, while men and women kill their partners in a 1.3:1 ratio, "unlike men, women kill male partners after years of suffering physical violence, after they have exhausted all available sources of assistance, when they feel trapped, and because they fear for their own lives" (Dobash et al., 1992, 81).

2. Ways of Occupying Space

1. In a very different way than I do here, Freud and object relations theorists use spatial metaphors in relation to aggression. They rely on a model

of an "inner" world—filled with psychic entities and structures described in spatial terms like intrapsychic "distances," "ego-splitting," "boundaries," and "borderlines"—which relates to an "outer" world. In their model, aggression, broadly speaking, results from internal tensions or strains related to object-seeking.

2. Johnson discusses seven common metaphor structures related to force: (1) compulsion, the sense of a force moving a person on a path that the person is unable to resist; (2) blockage, the experience of an obstacle that blocks or resists our force; (3) counterforce, the "head-on meetings of forces"; (4) diversion, when forces collide and cause a change in the direction of one of them; (5) removal of restraint, when a barrier is removed, or when a potential restraint is absent; (6) enablement, a felt sense of power or lack of power to perform some action; (7) attraction, a force pulling one toward an object.

3. Bringing the body into discussions of mind does not imply essential differences between genders: preverbal, preconceptual learnings about force are patterned through bodily experience in similar ways in male and female infants (Johnson, 1987). Also, the embodied schema of force differs from Freud's (1923) idea of the "body ego." The physiological distinctions between male and female were a core determinant in the formation of the body ego and the self. This led to the "anatomy is destiny" argument, whereby personality organization is organ-based. Erikson (1950, 1968) elaborated a variety of modes available in relating to objects, which he thinks are initially created out of the various erogenous body zones such as mouth, anus, and genitals. These modes become generalized to pervasive mental attitudes and conflicts. Erikson described the female's mode of the genital zone as incorporative, leading her to elaborate inner space. The embodied schema of force that Johnson describes is not anatomically based as are these psychoanalytical notions. Force is experienced throughout the body; social norms affect the patterning of interactions through which the growing child experiences force.

4. I am indebted to Johnson (1987) for some of these ideas.

5. Men fill up space in a way that researchers call "relaxed aggressiveness," leaning back in chairs, resting limbs on furniture, loosening restrictive clothing, sitting with ankles apart and legs angled open, while women keep arms and legs close to the body and take up less space. Klein (1984, 128) speculates that the male position reflects dominance by "increasing the contour of masculine stature" and "prevents the close approach of another individual."

6. Women of color and white women often face different issues related to their bodily presence in dominant society. A woman of color in a white profession, for example, can experience herself as "a body in a system that

has not become accustomed to [her] presence or to [her] physicality" (hooks, 1994, 135).

7. The line that women draw around their own self-assertion into public and private spaces copies the line that society draws to mark off and evaluate women's voices, activities, and contributions as less valuable than men's. Belenky, Bond, and Weinstock (1997) detail the devastation caused by society's discounting women, particularly their form of community leadership, which draws out the voices of the silenced and makes communities more nurturing places to live. Because this form of women's leadership runs counter to the conventional images of leadership, these powerful women remain largely invisible, and society fails to reap the full benefit of their contribution.

8. The Christopher Commission called into question not whether women are aggressive enough but whether aggressiveness is a useful quality in a police officer (Case, 1995, 88). It concluded that women's particular characteristics in policing—their skills in communication, their ability to defuse potentially violent confrontations, and their more sensitive responses to violence against women (which make up as much as half of the calls to police departments)—should be more highly valued on police forces.

9. "Back me" refers to serving as backup protection for an officer on a dangerous call.

10. The media report that women are arming themselves with handguns, primarily for protection from male violence. Smith and Smith (1995) estimate that 11 to 12 percent of women own guns and that "male ownership of handguns surpasses that of women by almost four to one."

3. Why Not Hurt Others?

1. Philosophers such as Hume (1975) argue that feelings like empathy (sympathy and benevolence) are primary motives that underlie moral thought and action. Precursors of empathy can be seen in the capacity for co-feeling manifested by primates and human infants (de Waal, 1996).

2. Numerous researchers have found that empathy inhibits aggression, though the cognitive mechanisms through which inhibition occurs are unclear (Mehrabian, 1997; Miller and Eisenberg, 1988; Richardson et al., 1994). Interventions designed to reduce violent aggression often rely on empathy training as a key element of their programs (Wiehe, 1997). Though some studies find that girls score higher than boys on measures of empathy (Cohen and Strayer, 1996), psychologists have not been able to consistently correlate the suppression of aggression through empathy with gender (Miller and Eisenberg, 1988). Some of the inconsistency in findings is related to problems of definition (of

both empathy and aggression) and the usual variations in research design and measurement.

3. Other researchers have found that women deal with anger by adopting a "nonhostile" strategy: they prevent their aggressive acts by concentrating on unaggressive thoughts (Frodi, 1976). Women have been found to report (by questionnaire) more guilt and anxiety about their own aggressive acts than men do, more vigilance about the harm aggression causes its victims, and more concern about the danger their aggression might bring to themselves (Eagly and Steffen, 1986). But listening to women talk about their lived experiences reveals more complex mediators that restrain their urges to hurt others.

4. I began the interviews certain that women's most common reason for inhibiting aggression would be either fear of losing relationships or empathy with the hurt they would cause others. Not until I had coded all the interviews and used Ethnograph to analyze frequencies did I realize how often the women mentioned fear of retaliation. I think my inability to register what I was hearing came from being deadened to the impact of violence in our culture, particularly the impact of violence against women. It also points to the way language masks an uncomfortable reality.

5. Researchers have defined empathy in a number of ways ranging from cognitive to emotional (see Duan and Hill, 1996). Cognitive definitions equate empathy with imagining how the other person is affected by his or her situation (Batson, 1987; Hoffman, 1976). Definitions of emotional empathy suggest that empathy is an emotional reaction in which one matches one's affect to that of another (Eisenberg and Strayer, 1987; Wispe, 1991). In women's descriptions, empathy that offsets aggression appears to be both cognitive and emotional, but most often identifies with the pain of the prospective victim.

6. Compare a boy's feelings in a similar situation. He is torn between empathy for his mother and identification with his father; the culture tells him that aggression is manly, that his mother is weak for "taking it" and being a victim. While a girl may be appalled by her mother's "weakness," the culture pairs that weakness with goodness, making it more difficult for her to learn to stand up for herself without feeling like an aggressor.

7. In real-life situations, the inhibition of aggressive and antisocial reactions often is mediated by factors other than empathic responding (see Miller and Eisenberg, 1988; Cohen and Strayer, 1996; Lisak and Ivan, 1995; Tantam, 1995).

8. To put Deborah's remarks in context, consider the following: in 1998 women represented about 14 percent of law enforcement positions in the nation, up half a percentage point from 1997. Since 1990 their numbers have

increased by 3.2 percent. In a survey of 176 police departments, more than one-third had no women in top command ranks and nearly three-quarters had no high-ranking women of color. Of the 10 big-city police departments with the most female officers, eight were forced to hire more women by federal court orders (National Center for Women and Policing, 1998).

9. The ways in which people talk about controlling their emotions have been called "powerful devices by which domination proceeds" (Lutz, 1990, 74). The language of avoiding hurt operates more subtly than these "discourses of emotional control."

10. Teenage prostitution is linked to childhood victimization and neglect (see Widom and Kuhns, 1996).

4. The Rage of Disconnection

1. Self-defense is not an aspect of destructive aggression because it does not seek to hurt the other but only to defend the self. Drug and alcohol abuse, which is strongly correlated with physical and sexual abuse, makes it easier for a woman to engage in destructive aggression.

2. In earlier work (Durbin and Bowlby, 1939) Bowlby had named functional anger, or the anger of hope, "simple aggression" (Bacciagaluppi, 1989). He named dysfunctional anger, or the anger of despair, "transformed aggression": that is, when anger protesting the disruption of a bond cannot be expressed to the attachment figure(s), it appears in other forms (Bowlby, 1939, cited in Bacciagaluppi, 1989).

3. In a column headlined "This is one strong woman who's not afraid to whine," Donna Britt (1998), an African-American columnist for the *Washington Post*, addressed the "undying stereotype—and often, undeniable truth—about women of African descent: Whatever comes, we will be *strong*." Britt discussed the downside of this stereotype: that it denies black women their vulnerability, which Britt defines as "desperately needing someone else's strength." The stereotype of the strong woman can make needing others into a weakness when in fact it is a necessity for all of us.

4. Depression is associated with self-silencing in both women and men (see Jack, 1999a; Gratch and Jack, 1999).

5. See Joiner and Coyne (1999) on interpersonal causes and effects of depression.

6. Self-blame and self-attack also affect one's physiology. Droppelman, Thomas, and Wilt (1995) list physiological and emotional conditions that relate to suppression of anger, including hypertension, coronary heart disease, breast cancer, depression, migraine headaches, and obesity. Women often take

full responsibility for relationship problems by becoming sick instead of angry.

5. Masking Aggression

1. The metaphor of sending thoughts and feelings underground to avoid detection was also used by Brown and Gilligan (1992) to describe adolescent girls' sudden loss of voice as they encounter the ideal of "the perfect girl," that precursor of good femininity. Their sample was primarily white and middle class, but the small subsample of girls of color and white working-class girls suggests a different, more openly assertive and political pathway into womanhood. Other research reveals that adolescents of color use their voices more directly to oppose others. Niobi Way (1995), in a longitudinal qualitative study of twelve urban, poor, and working-class girls (ten of whom were girls of color), found they spoke out, including their anger and disagreement, in all relationships except those with boyfriends. Hurtado (1996) describes resisting the racism and devaluation she encountered as a Latina adolescent through outspoken, challenging anger rather than dissimulating, compliant silence. See also Walker (1995). As women describe the labyrinth of tunnels used to affect others negatively yet preserve relationships, they appear much more aware of what they are doing and why than adolescent girls who were beginning to practice the technique.

2. Only five women said their mothers directly expressed their anger through aggressive behavior—spanking, occasional slaps, yelling—in ways that did not feel destructive or cruel. These women felt their mothers' aggressive behavior was motivated by love. These five women also described their mothers as having power within the family. Eight women reported that their mothers physically abused them, and one reported abuse by stepmothers. Five women reported their mothers were dominant and controlling, using verbal aggression and withholding to deal with conflict.

3. See Jacobs (1994) on mother-blaming by daughters sexually abused by their fathers or stepfathers. Jacobs ties mother-blaming to the wider culture and to mothers' powerlessness to stop men's actions.

4. Twenty-three women described their mothers as using silence as a tactic to convey anger. For example: "My mom will stay angry for weeks, days, weeks, like if we had an argument or if there was some problem in the evening I would wake up the next morning and be over it, I would have forgotten it, but my mom would slam the cupboards and slam the dishes down and then there would be silence" (Sherna, age 33, white, police officer). "My mom didn't get angry, she would be cold and distant . . . it was such a quiet, subtle

sort of thing" (Leigh, age 44, white, teacher). "She registered disapproval in silence. If you did something wrong, she just didn't say anything. And in what she didn't say, you knew as much as what she would say" (Gaile, age 40, white, photojournalist).

5. These patterns of silence all exist in relation to power and to culture. Some cultures, such as Laura's Japanese-American tradition or Julia's white middle-class norms, require indirect strategies. Cultural norms become indistinguishable from moral imperatives; a woman violates her own moral guidelines if she steps outside cultural norms. On the relation of silence to cultures see Goldberger (1996).

6. While Burbank (1987) finds women, worldwide, more often physically aggressive against other women (most probably because of fear of injury from men's retaliation), in fantasy the reverse may be true. Because fantasy does not necessarily lead to consequences or action, it is a safe place to enact revenge and retaliation against men whom women fear.

7. Twelve women imagined in detail the death of men who had harmed them. Four of these had not been abused; one had been abused only as a child; two had been abused only as adults; the remaining five had been abused as both children and adults.

8. Alice and her husband did divorce, at her instigation, after three years of prayerful fantasy.

9. Nancy was able to take positive steps to leave the marriage after she went into recovery for alcoholism. Her anger then served as an activator to help her move, find a job, and create a new life. While alcoholism appeared to be the major problem, Nancy's inability to express her anger directly and constructively or to engage in positive conflict was probably a major contributing factor to her alcoholism.

6. Creating New Ground

1. "The scapegoat is different from the martyr; she cannot teach resistance or revolt. She presents a terrible temptation: to suffer uniquely, to assume that I, the individual woman, am the 'problem' " (Rich, 1976, 278).

2. The psychological responses of women who are battered by their husbands can be diagnosed as post-traumatic stress disorder, and include the symptomatology and sequelae attached to that disorder (see Browne, 1993; Herman, 1992). My discussion of Rhonda's example does not do justice to the extensive knowledge of the dynamics and effects of battering; I focus on her self-change that surrounded her self-protective act.

3. Belenky (1996), documenting black women's involvement in "public homeplaces" that support the development of the community's most vulnerable members, underscores the importance of the church as a place for personal and community empowerment (see also Goldberger et al., 1996; Collins, 1990; hooks, 1990; Greene, 1988).

4. See also Amick and Ockene, 1994; Kennell et al., 1991; Medalie et al., 1992; Reynolds et al., 1994; Schwartz and Russek, 1998; Spiegel, 1993.

5. Noemi Ban asked that her real name be used as part of her effort to overcome the fear of being identified. Her oral history is available on videotape in "Survivors of the Shoah: So Generations Never Forget What So Few Lived to Tell," Shoah Visual History Foundation.

References

Allison, D. 1994. *Skin: Talking about sex, class and literature.* Ithaca: Firebrand Books.

Amick, T. L., and J. K. Ockene. 1994. The role of social support in the modification of risk factors for cardiovascular disease. In S. A. Shumaker and S. M. Czajkowski, eds., *Social support and cardiovascular disease.* New York: Plenum.

Ardrey, R. 1966. *The territorial imperative.* New York: Atheneum.

Averill, J. R. 1982. *Anger and aggression: An essay on emotion.* New York: Springer-Verlag.

———. 1983. Studies on anger and aggression: Implications for theories of emotion. *American Psychologist 38,* 1145–60.

Babcock, J. C., J. Waltz, N. S. Jacobson, and J. M. Gottman. 1993. Power and violence: The relation between communication patterns, power discrepancies, and domestic violence. *Journal of Consulting and Clinical Psychology 61,* 40–50.

Bacciagaluppi, M. 1989. The role of aggressiveness in the work of John Bowlby. *Free Associations 16,* 123–134.

Bachman, R., and L. E. Saltzman. 1995. *Violence against women: Estimates from the redesigned survey.* Special report. Washington: U.S. Department of Justice, Bureau of Justice Statistics, NCJ 154348.

Bandura, A. 1973. *Aggression: A social learning analysis.* Englewood Cliffs, N.J.: Prentice Hall.

Baron, R. A., and D. R. Richardson. 1994. *Human aggression.* 2nd ed. New York: Plenum.

Batson, C. D. 1987. Prosocial motivation: Is it ever truly altruistic? In L. Berkowitz, ed., *Advances in experimental social psychology,* vol. 20. New York: Academic Press.

Bederman, G. 1995. *Manliness and civilization: A cultural history of gender and race in the U.S., 1880–1917.* Chicago: University of Chicago Press.

Belenky, M. F. 1996. Public homeplaces: Nurturing the development of people, families, and communities. In N. R. Goldberger, J. M. Tarule, B. M. Clinchy, and M. F. Belenky, eds., *Knowledge, difference, and power.* New York: Basic Books.

Belenky, M. F., L. A. Bond, and J. S. Weinstock. 1997. *A tradition that has no name.* New York: Basic Books.

Belenky, M. F., B. M. Clinchy, N. R. Goldberger, and J. M. Tarule. 1986/1997. *Women's ways of knowing: The development of self, voice, and mind.* 10th anniversary ed. New York: Basic Books.

Belsky, J. 1993. Etiology of child maltreatment: A developmental-ecological analysis. *Psychological Bulletin 114,* 413–434.

Bem, S. L. 1974. The measurement of psychological androgyny. *Journal of Consulting and Clinical Psychology 42,* 155–162.

Benjamin, J. 1988. *The bonds of love: Psychoanalysis, feminism, and the problem of domination.* New York: Pantheon.

Berger, J. 1982. *Ways of seeing.* Harmondsworth: Penguin.

Berkowitz, L. 1990. On the formation and regulation of anger and aggression: A cognitive-neoassociationistic analysis. *American Psychologist 45,* 494–503.

Bing, V. M., and P. T. Reid. 1996. Unknown women and unknowing research: Consequences of color and class in feminist psychology. In N. R. Goldberger, J. M. Tarule, B. M. Clinchy, and M. F. Belenky, eds., *Knowledge, difference, and power.* New York: Basic Books.

Björkqvist, K. 1994. Sex differences in physical, verbal, and indirect aggression: A review of recent research. *Sex Roles 30,* 177–188.

Björkqvist, K., K. M. Lagerspetz, and A. Kaukiainen. 1992. Do girls manipulate and boys fight? Developmental trends in regard to direct and indirect aggression. *Aggressive Behavior 18,* 117–127.

Björkqvist, K., and P. Niemelä. 1992. New trends in the study of female aggression. In Björkqvist and Niemelä, eds., *Of mice and women: Aspects of female aggression.* San Diego: Academic Press.

Björkqvist, K., K. Österman, and A. Kaukiainen. 1992. The development of direct and indirect aggressive strategies in males and females. In K. Björkqvist and P. Niemelä, eds., *Of mice and women: Aspects of female aggression.* San Diego: Academic Press.

Block, J. H. 1983. Differential premises arising from differential socialization of the sexes: Some conjectures. *Child Development 54,* 1335–54.

Bordo, S. 1993. *Unbearable weight: Feminism, Western culture, and the body.* Berkeley: University of California Press.

Bowers, S. R. 1990. Medusa and the female gaze. *NWSA Journal 2,* 217–235.

Bowlby, J. 1969. *Attachment and loss,* vol. 1: *Attachment.* New York: Basic Books.

———. 1973. *Attachment and loss,* vol. 2: *Separation: Anxiety and anger.* New York: Basic Books.

———. 1980. *Attachment and loss,* vol. 3: *Loss, sadness and depression.* New York: Basic Books.

Briere, J., and E. Gil. 1998. Self-mutilation in clinical and general population samples: Prevalence, correlates, and functions. *American Journal of Orthopsychiatry 68,* 609–620.

Britt, D. 1998. The burden of always being strong. *Washington Post,* April 24.

Brown, L. M. 1998. *Raising their voices: The politics of girls' anger.* Cambridge, Mass.: Harvard University Press.

Brown, L. M., and C. Gilligan. 1992. *Meeting at the crossroads: Women's psychology and girls' development.* Cambridge, Mass.: Harvard University Press.

Browne, A. 1993. Violence against women by male partners: Prevalence, outcomes, and policy implications. *American Psychologist 48,* 1077–87.

Brownley, K. A., K. C. Light, and N. B. Anderson. 1996. Social support and hostility interact to influence clinic, work, and home blood pressure in black and white men and women. *Psychophysiology 33,* 434–445.

Burbank, V. K. 1987. Female aggression in cross-cultural perspective. *Behavior Science Research 21,* 70–100.

———. 1993. *Fighting women: Anger and aggression in aboriginal Australia.* Berkeley: University of California Press.

Butler, J. 1991. Imitation and gender insubordination. In D. Fuss, ed., *Inside/out: Lesbian theories, gay theories.* New York: Routledge.

Campbell, A. 1993. *Men, women, and aggression.* New York: Basic Books.

Case, M. A. C. 1995. Disaggregating gender from sex and sexual orientation: The effeminate man in the law and feminist jurisprudence. *Yale Law Journal 105,* 1–105.

Chase-Lansdale, P. L., L. S. Wakschlag, and J. Brooks-Gunn. 1995. A psychological perspective on the development of caring in children and youth: The role of the family. *Journal of Adolescence 18,* 515–556.

Christensen, A., and C. L. Heavey. 1990. Gender and social structure in the demand/withdraw pattern of marital conflict. *Journal of Personality and Social Psychology 59,* 73–81.

Cicchetti, D., and V. Carlson, eds. 1989. *Child maltreatment: Research and theory on the causes and consequences of child abuse and neglect.* New York: Cambridge University Press.

Coghlan, A. 1996. Why women don't start wars. *New Scientist 151,* no. 2048, 13.

Cohen, D., and J. Strayer. 1996. Empathy in conduct-disordered and comparison youth. *Developmental Psychology 32,* 988–998.

Collins, P. H. 1990. *Black feminist thought: Knowledge, consciousness, and the politics of empowerment.* Boston: Unwin Hyman.

Cotten, N. U., J. Resnick, D. C. Browne, S. L. Martin, D. R. McCarraher, and J. Woods. 1994. Aggression and fighting behavior among African-American adolescents: Individual and family factors. *American Journal of Public Health 84,* 618–622.

Crick, N. R., and J. K. Grotpeter. 1995. Relational aggression, gender, and social-psychological adjustment. *Child Development 66,* 710–722.

Davis, M. A., P. A. LaRosa, and D. P. Foshee. 1992. Emotion work in supervisor-subordinate relations: Gender differences in the perception of angry displays. *Sex Roles 26,* 513–531.

de Waal, F. 1996. *Good natured: The origins of right and wrong in humans and other animals.* Cambridge, Mass.: Harvard University Press.

Dijkstra, B. 1996. *Evil sisters: The threat of female sexuality in twentieth-century culture.* New York: Henry Holt.

Dobash, R. P., R. E. Dobash, M. Wilson, and M. Daly. 1992. The myth of sexual symmetry in marital violence. *Social Problems 39,* 71–91.

Dodge, K. A., and J. D. Coie. 1987. Social-information-processing factors in reactive and proactive aggression in children's peer groups. *Journal of Personal and Social Psychology 53,* 1146–58.

Dollard, J., L. Doob, N. Miller, O. Mowrer, and R. Sears. 1939. *Frustration and aggression.* New Haven: Yale University Press.

Droppelman, P. G., S. P. Thomas, and D. Wilt. 1995. Anger in women as an emerging issue in MCH. *MCN: American Journal of Maternal Child Nursing 20,* 85–94.

Droppleman, P. G., and D. Wilt. 1993. Women, depression, and anger. In S. P. Thomas, ed., *Women and anger.* New York: Springer.

Duan, C., and C. E. Hill. 1996. The current state of empathy research. *Journal of Counseling Psychology 43,* 261–274.

Dunn, K. 1994. Just as fierce. *Mother Jones 19,* 36–39.

Durbin, E. F. M., and J. Bowlby. 1939. *Personal aggressiveness and war.* London: Routledge and Kegan Paul.

Dutton, M. A. 1992. *Empowering and healing the battered woman: A model for assessment and intervention.* New York: Springer.

Eagly, A. H., and V. J. Steffen. 1986. Gender and aggressive behavior: A meta-analytic review of the social psychological literature. *Psychological Bulletin 100,* 309–330.

Egami, Y., D. E. Ford, S. F. Greenfield, and R. M. Crum. 1996. Psychiatric profile and sociodemographic characteristics of adults who report physically abusing or neglecting children. *American Journal of Psychiatry 153,* 921–928.

Eisenberg, N., and J. Strayer. 1987. Critical issues in the study of empathy. In Eisenberg and Strayer, eds., *Empathy and its development*. New York: Cambridge University Press.

Erikson, E. 1950. *Childhood and society*. New York: Norton.

———. 1968. Womanhood and the inner space. In *Identity, youth, and crisis*. New York: Norton.

Eron, L. D., and L. R. Huesmann. 1989. The genesis of gender differences in aggression. In M. A. Luszcz and T. Nettelbeck, eds., *Psychological development: Perspectives across the life-span*. Amsterdam: North-Holland.

Felson, R. B., and J. T. Tedeschi. 1993. *Aggression and violence: Social interactionist perspectives*. Washington: American Psychological Association.

Fine, M. 1992. *Disruptive voices: The possibilities of feminist research*. Ann Arbor: University of Michigan Press.

Fink, E., and M. Heidegger. 1979. *Heraclitus seminar, 1966–1967*. Tuscaloosa: University of Alabama Press.

Finkelstein, J. W., E. J. Susman, V. M. Chinchilli, S. J. Kunselman, M. R. D'Arcangelo, J. Schwab, L. M. Demers, L. S. Liben, G. Lookingbill, and H. E. Kulin. 1997. Estrogen or testosterone increases self-reported aggressive behaviors in hypogonadal adolescents. *Journal of Clinical Endocrinological Metabolism 82*, 2433–38.

Fordham, S. 1993. "Those loud black girls": (Black) women, silence, and gender "passing" in the academy. *Anthropology and Education Quarterly 24*, 3–32.

———. 1996. *Blacked out: Dilemmas of race, identity, and success at Capital High*. Chicago: University of Chicago Press.

Foucault, M. 1977. *Power/knowledge*, ed. and trans. C. Gordo. New York: Pantheon.

———. 1983. The subject and power. In Hubert Dreyfus and Paul Rabinow, eds., *Michel Foucault: Beyond structuralism and hermeneutics*. Chicago: University of Chicago Press.

Freud, S. 1923/1961. The ego and the id. In *The standard edition of the complete psychological works of Sigmund Freud*, vol. 19, ed. and trans. J. Strachey. London: Hogarth Press.

———. 1923/1959. Medusa's head. In *Collected papers*, ed. J. Strachey, vol. 5. New York: Basic Books.

Frodi, A. 1976. Experiential and physiological processes mediating sex differences in behavioral aggression. *Psychological Reports 6*, 113–114.

Fromm, E. 1973. *The anatomy of human destructiveness*. New York: Holt, Rinehart and Winston.

Geen, R. G. 1990. *Human aggression*. Pacific Grove, Calif.: Brooks/Cole.

Gilligan, C. 1982. *In a different voice.* 2nd ed. Cambridge, Mass.: Harvard University Press.

Gilligan, J. 1996. *Violence: Our deadly epidemic and its causes.* New York: Putnam.

Ginorio, A. B., L. Gutierrez, A. M. Cauce, and M. Acosta. 1995. Psychological issues for Latinas. In H. Landrine, ed., *Bringing cultural diversity to feminist psychology.* Washington: American Psychological Association.

Gladue, B. A. 1991. Aggressive behavioral characteristics, hormones, and sexual orientation in men and women. *Aggressive Behavior 17,* 313–326.

Goldberger, N. 1996. Cultural imperatives and diversity in ways of knowing. In N. Goldberger, J. Tarule, B. Clinchy, and M. Belenky, eds., *Knowledge, difference, and power.* New York: Basic Books.

Goldberger, N., J. Tarule, B. Clinchy, and M. Belenky, eds., 1996. *Knowledge, difference, and power.* New York: Basic Books.

Goleman, D. 1995. *Emotional intelligence.* New York: Bantam.

Goodman, L. A., M. P. Koss, and N. F. Russo. 1993. Violence against women: Physical and mental health effects. *Applied and Preventive Psychology 2,* 79–89.

Gordon, L. 1989. *Heroes of their own lives: The politics and history of family violence.* New York: Viking.

Gottman, J. M., and L. J. Krokoff. 1989. Marital interaction and satisfaction: A longitudinal view. *Journal of Consulting and Clinical Psychology 57,* 47–52.

Gottman, J. M., and R. W. Levenson. 1988. The social psychophysiology of marriage. In P. Noller and M. A. Fitzpatrick, eds., *Perspectives on marital interaction.* Clevedon, U.K.: Multilingual Matters.

Grant, T. M., C. C. Ernst, and A. P. Streissguth. 1999. Intervention with high-risk alcohol and drug-abusing mothers: I, Administrative strategies of the Seattle model of paraprofessional advocacy. *Journal of Community Psychology 27,* 1–18.

Gratch, L. V., and D. C. Jack. 1999. Gender issues and factor structure on the Silencing the Self Scale. Manuscript.

Greenacre, P. 1926. The eye motif in delusion and fantasy. *American Journal of Psychiatry 5,* 555–580.

Greene, M. 1988. *The dialectic of freedom.* New York: Teachers College Press.

Hall, N. 1980. *The moon and the virgin.* New York: Harper and Row.

Harrison, A. O., M. N. Wilson, C. J. Pine, S. Q. Chan, and R. Buriel. 1995. Family ecologies of ethnic minority children. In N. R. Goldberger and J. B. Veroff, eds., *The culture and psychology reader.* New York: New York University Press.

Haste, H. 1994. *The sexual metaphor*. Cambridge, Mass.: Harvard University Press.

Hawkins, W. E., M. J. Hawkins, C. Sabatino, and S. Ley. 1998. Relationship of perceived future opportunity to depressive symptomatology of inner-city African-American adolescents. *Children and Youth Services Review 20*, 757–764.

Hayles, N. K. 1986. Anger in different voices: Carol Gilligan and *The Mill on the Floss*. *Signs 12*, 23–39.

Herman, J. 1992. *Trauma and recovery: The aftermath of violence*. New York: Basic Books.

Higginbotham, E. B. 1992. African-American women's history and the meta-language of race. *Signs 17*, 251–274.

Hillman, J. 1975. Betrayal. In *Loose ends: Primary papers in archetypal psychology*. Zurich: Spring Publications.

Hoffman, M. L. 1976. Empathy, role-taking, guilt, and the development of altruistic motives. In T. Lickona, ed., *Moral development and behavior: Theory, research, and social issues*. New York: Holt, Rinehart and Winston.

hooks, bell. 1989. *Talking back: Thinking feminist/thinking black*. Boston: South End Press.

———. 1990. *Yearning: Race, gender and cultural politics*. Boston: South End Press.

———. 1994. *Teaching to transgress: Education as the practice of freedom*. New York: Routledge.

———. 1996. *Killing rage: Ending racism*. New York: Henry Holt.

Horney, K. 1937. *The neurotic personality of our time*. New York: Norton.

Huesmann, L. R., N. G. Guerra, A. Zelli, and L. Miller. 1992. Differing normative beliefs about aggression for boys and girls. In K. Björkqvist and P. Niemelä, eds., *Of mice and women: Aspects of female aggression*. San Diego: Academic Press.

Hume, D. 1975. *Enquiries concerning human understanding and concerning the principles of morals*. 3rd ed. New York: Oxford University Press.

Hurtado, A. 1996. Strategic suspensions: Women of color theorize the production of knowledge. In N. Goldberger, J. M. Tarule, B. M. Clinchy, and M. F. Belenky, *Knowledge, difference and power*. New York: Basic Books.

Jack, D. C. 1991. *Silencing the self: Women and depression*. Cambridge, Mass.: Harvard University Press.

———. 1999a. Silencing the self: Inner dialogues and outer realities. In T. E. Joiner and J. C. Coyne, eds., *The interactional nature of depression: Advances in interpersonal approaches*. Washington: American Psychological Association.

————. 1999b. Ways of listening to depressed women in qualitative research: Interview techniques and analysis. *Canadian Psychology 40*, 91–101.

Jack, D. C., and D. Dill. 1992. The Silencing the Self Scale: Schemas of intimacy associated with depression in women. *Psychology of Women Quarterly 16*, 97–106.

Jacobs, J. L. 1994. *Victimized daughters: Incest and the development of the female self.* New York: Routledge.

Jacobson, N. S., and J. M. Gottman. 1998. *When men batter women.* New York: Simon and Schuster.

Jacobson, N. S., J. M. Gottman, J. Waltz, R. Rushe, J. Babcock, and A. Holtzworth-Munroe. 1994. Affect, verbal content, and psychophysiology in the arguments of couples with a violent husband. *Journal of Consulting and Clinical Psychology 62*, 982–988.

Jaudes, P. K., E. Ekwo, and J. Van Voorhis. 1995. Association of drug abuse and child abuse. *Child Abuse and Neglect 19*, 1065–75.

Johnson, M. 1987. *The body in the mind: The bodily basis of meaning, imagination, and reason.* Chicago: University of Chicago Press.

Joiner, T. E., and J. C. Coyne, eds. 1999. *The interactional nature of depression: Advances in interpersonal approaches.* Washington: American Psychological Association.

Jones, A. 1994. *Next time she'll be dead.* Boston: Beacon.

Jones, A., and S. Schechter. 1992. *When love goes wrong: What to do when you can't do anything right.* New York: HarperCollins.

Jones, J. 1985. *Labor of love: Labor of sorrow.* New York: Basic Books.

Jordan, J. V., A. G. Kaplan, J. B. Miller, I. P. Stiver, and J. L. Surrey, eds. 1991. *Women's growth in connection: Writings from the Stone Center.* New York: Guilford.

Jordan, J. V., ed. 1997. *Women's growth in diversity: More writings from the Stone Center.* New York: Guilford.

Jung, C. G. 1970. Four archetypes. Trans. R. F. C. Hull. In *The Collected Works of C. G. Jung*, Bollingen Series, vol. 20. Princeton: Princeton University Press.

Kantor, G. K., and M. A. Straus. 1990. Response of victims and the police to assaults on wives. In M. A. Straus and R. J. Gelles, eds., *Physical violence in American families: Risk factors and adaptations to violence in 8,145 families.* New Brunswick: Transaction Publishers.

Kennell, J., M. Klaus, S. McGrath, S. Robertson, and C. Hinkley. 1991. Continuous emotional support during labor in a U.S. hospital: A randomized controlled trial. *Journal of the American Medical Association 265*, 2197–2201.

Kirsta, A. 1994. *Deadlier than the male: Violence and aggression in women.* New York: HarperCollins.

Klein, Z. 1984. Sitting postures in males and females. *Semiotica 48*, 119–131.

LaFromboise, T. D., S. B. Choney, A. James, and P. R. Running Wolf. 1995. American Indian women and psychology. In H. Landrine, ed., *Bringing cultural diversity to feminist psychology: Theory, research, and practice.* Washington: American Psychological Association.

Lahr, J. 1997. Speaking across the divide. *New Yorker*, Jan. 27, 35–42.

Leavitt, K. S., S. A. Gardner, M. M. Gallagher, and G. Schamess. 1998. Severely traumatized siblings: A treatment strategy. *Clinical Social Work Journal 26*, 55–71.

Lenney, E. 1991. Sex roles: The measurement of masculinity, femininity, and androgyny. In J. P. Robinson, P. R. Shaver, and L. S. Wrightsman, eds., *Measures of personality and social psychological attitudes.* San Diego: Academic Press.

Levin, D. M. 1989. *The listening self: Personal growth, social change and the closure of metaphysics.* New York: Routledge.

Lightdale, J. R., and D. A. Prentice. 1994. Rethinking sex differences in aggression: Aggressive behavior in the absence of social roles. *Personality and Social Psychology Bulletin 20*, 34–44.

Lisak, D., and C. Ivan. 1995. Deficits in intimacy and empathy in sexually aggressive men. *Journal of Interpersonal Violence 10*, 296–308.

Lorenz, K. 1966. *On aggression.* New York: Harcourt, Brace and World.

Lorde, A. 1984. *Sister outsider.* Trumansburg, N.Y.: Crossing Press.

Lutz, C. A. 1990. Engendered emotion: Gender, power, and the rhetoric of emotional control in American discourse. In C. Lutz and L. Abu-Lughod, eds., *Language and the politics of emotion.* New York: Cambridge University Press.

Lynch, J. J. 1977. *The broken heart: The medical consequences of loneliness.* New York: Basic Books.

Macaulay, J. 1985. Adding gender to aggression research: Incremental or revolutionary change? In V. E. O'Leary, R. K. Unger, and B. S. Wallston, eds., *Women, gender, and social psychology.* Hillsdale, N.J.: Erlbaum.

Maccoby, E. E., and C. N. Jacklin. 1974. *The psychology of sex differences.* Stanford: Stanford University Press.

MacDonald, E. 1991. *Shoot the women first.* New York: Random House.

Massey, D. 1994. *Space, place and gender.* Minneapolis: University of Minnesota Press.

McCabe, A., and T. J. Lipscomb. 1988. Sex differences in children's verbal aggression. *Merrill-Palmer Quarterly 34*, 389–401.

McCloskey, L. A. 1996. Socioeconomic and coercive power within the family. *Gender and Society 10*, 449–463.

McCloskey, L. A., A. J. Figueredo, and M. P. Koss. 1995. The effects of systemic family violence on children's mental health. *Child Development 66*, 1239–61.

McGrath, E., G. P. Keita, B. R. Strickland, and N. F. Russo. 1990. *Women and depression: Risk factors and treatment issues.* Washington: American Psychological Association.

Medalie, J. H., K. C. Stange, S. J. Zyzanski, and U. Goldbourt. 1992. The importance of biopsychosocial factors in the development of duodenal ulcer in a cohort of middle-aged men. *American Journal of Epidemiology 136*, 1280–87.

Mehabrian, A. 1997. Relations among personality scales of aggression, violence, and empathy: Validational evidence bearing on the Risk of Eruptive Violence Scale. *Aggressive Behavior 23*, 433–445.

Merleau-Ponty, M. 1962. *Phenomenology of perception.* London: Routledge and Kegan Paul.

Miller, A. 1981. *The drama of the gifted child.* New York: Basic Books.

Miller, D. 1996. Challenging self-harm through transformation of the trauma story. *Sexual Addiction and Compulsivity 3*, 213–227.

Miller, J. B. 1976/1986. *Toward a new psychology of women.* Boston: Beacon Press.

———. 1991. The construction of anger in women and men. In J. V. Jordan, A. G. Kaplan, J. B. Miller, I. P. Stiver, and J. L. Surrey, eds., *Women's growth in connection: Writings from the Stone Center.* New York: Guilford.

Miller, P. A., and N. Eisenberg. 1988. The relation of empathy to aggressive and externalizing/antisocial behavior. *Psychological Bulletin 103*, 324–344.

Milner, J. S., and C. Chilamkurti. 1991. Physical child abuse perpetrator characteristics: A review of the literature. *Journal of Interpersonal Violence 6*, 345–366.

Mitchell, S. A. 1988. *Relational concepts in psychoanalysis: An integration.* Cambridge, Mass.: Harvard University Press.

Mullings, L. 1994. Images, ideology, and women of color. In M. B. Zinn and B. T. Dill, eds., *Women of color in U.S. society.* Philadelphia: Temple University Press.

Napholz, L. 1994. Dysphoria among Hispanic working women: A research note. *Hispanic Journal of Behavioral Sciences 16*, 500–509.

National Center for Women and Policing. 1999. Equality denied: The status of women in policing, 1998. April 13. www.feminist.org/police/status1998.html

Noddings, N. 1989. *Women and evil.* Berkeley: University of California Press.

Obejas, A. 1994. Women who batter women. *Ms. Magazine 5*, (Sept./Oct.), 53.

Ornish, D. 1998. *Love and survival: The scientific basis for the healing power of intimacy.* New York: HarperCollins.

Pagels, E. 1993. The rage of angels. In R. A. Glick and S. P. Roose, eds., *Rage, power, and aggression: The role of affect in motivation, development, and adaptation.* New Haven: Yale University Press.

Painter, N. I. 1995. Soul murder and slavery: Toward a fully loaded cost accounting. In L. K. Kerber, A. Kessler-Harris, and K. K. Sklar, eds., *U.S. history as women's history: New feminist essays.* Chapel Hill: University of North Carolina Press.

Palmer, P. M. 1983. White women/black women: The dualism of female identity and experience in the United States. *Feminist Studies 9*, 151–170.

Parke, R. D., and R. G. Slaby. 1983. The development of aggression. In P. Mussen, ed., *Handbook of Child Psychology*, 4th ed. New York: Wiley.

Penza, K., A. Reiss, and H. Scott. 1997. Sexual orientation and communication in relationships: Self-silencing, mutuality and power in heterosexual and lesbian relationships. Paper presented at the Annual Meeting of the American Psychological Society, Washington.

Perry, D. G., L. C. Perry, and R. J. Weiss. 1989. Sex differences in the consequences that children anticipate for aggression. *Developmental Psychology 25*, 312–319.

Phelps, R. E., N. M. Meara, K. L. Davis, and M. J. Patton. 1991. Blacks' and whites' perceptions of verbal aggression. *Journal of Counseling and Development 69*, 345–350.

Piaget, J., and B. Inhelder. 1971/1997. *Mental imagery in the child.* New York: Routledge.

Price Waterhouse v. Hopkins. 490 U.S. 228 (1989).

Puka, B., ed. 1994. *Reaching out: Caring, altruism, and prosocial behavior.* New York: Garland.

Putallaz, M., P. R. Costanzo, C. L. Grimes, and D. M. Sherman. 1998. Intergenerational continuities and their influences on children's social development. *Social Development 7*, 389–427.

Ray, M. C., and E. Smith. 1991. Black women and homicide: An analysis of the subculture of violence thesis. *Western Journal of Black Studies 15*, 144–153.

Reid, P. T. 1993. Poor women in psychological research: Shut up and shut out. *Psychology of Women Quarterly 17*, 133–150.

Renzetti, C. M. 1992. *Violent betrayal: Partner abuse in lesbian relationships.* Newbury Park, Calif.: Sage.

Report of the Independent Commission on the Los Angeles Police Department. 1991. Warren Christopher, Chair. July 9.

Reynolds, P., P. T. Boyd, R. S. Blacklow, J. S. Jackson, R. S. Greenberg, D. F. Austin, V. W. Chen, and B. K. Edwards. 1994. The relationship between social ties and survival among black and white breast cancer patients: National Cancer Institute Black/White Cancer Survival Study Group. *Cancer Epidemiology, Biomarkers and Prevention 3*, 253–259.

Rich, A. 1976/1986. *Of woman born.* New York: Norton.

Richardson, D. R., G. S. Hammock, S. M. Smith, W. Gardner, and M. Signo. 1994. Empathy as a cognitive inhibitor of interpersonal aggression. *Aggressive Behavior 29*, 275–289.

Robinson, R., and J. V. Ward. 1991. "A belief in self far greater than anyone's disbelief": Cultivating resistance among African-American female adolescents. In C. Gilligan, A. G. Rogers, and D. L. Tolman, eds., *Women, girls and psychotherapy: Reframing resistance.* New York: Haworth.

Rodriguez, C. M., and A. J. Green. 1997. Parenting stress and anger expression as predictors of child abuse potential. *Child Abuse and Neglect 21*, 367–377.

Ross, C. E., and M. Van Willigen. 1996. Gender, parenthood, and anger. *Journal of Marriage and the Family 58*, 572–584.

Schapiro, B. A. 1994. *Literature and the relational self.* New York: New York University Press.

Scheff, T. J., and S. M. Retzinger. 1991. *Emotions and violence: Shame and rage in destructive conflicts.* Lexington, Mass.: Lexington Books.

Schwartz, G. E., and L. G. Russek. 1998. Family love and lifelong health? A challenge for clinical psychology. In D. K. Routh and R. J. DeRubeis, eds., *The science of clinical psychology: Accomplishments and future directions.* Washington: American Psychological Association.

Segall, M. H. 1989. Cultural factors, biology, and human aggression. In J. Groebel and R. A. Hinde, eds., *Aggression and war: Their biological and social bases.* Cambridge: Cambridge University Press.

Shipley, J. T. 1967. *Dictionary of word origins.* Totowa, N.J.: Littlefield, Adams.

Shorris, E. 1992. *Latinos: A biography of the people.* New York: Norton.

Siebers, T. 1983. *The mirror of Medusa.* Berkeley: University of California Press.

Simon, R. J., and J. Landis. 1991. *The crimes women commit, the punishments they receive.* Lexington, Mass.: D. C. Heath.

Smith, T. W., and R. J. Smith. 1995. Changes in firearms ownership among women, 1980–1994. *Journal of Criminal Law and Criminology 86*, 133–149.

Sommers, I., and D. Baskin. 1992. Sex, race, age, and violent offending. *Violence and Victims 7*, 191–201.

Spain, D. 1992. *Gendered spaces.* Chapel Hill: University of North Carolina Press.

Spelman, E. 1989. Anger and insubordination. In A. Garry and M. Pearsall, eds., *Women, knowledge, and reality: Explorations in feminist philosophy.* Boston: Unwin Hyman.

Spiegel, D. 1993. *Living beyond limits: New hope and help for facing life-threatening illness.* New York: Times Books.

Spillar, Katherine. 1991. Testimony before the Independent Commission on the Los Angeles Police Department. May 13.

State of Washington v. Wanrow. 559 P.2d 548 (1977).

Stern, D. 1985. *The interpersonal world of the infant.* New York: Basic Books.

Storr, A. 1991. *Human destructiveness.* New York: Routledge.

Straus, M. A. 1980. The marriage license as a hitting license: Evidence from popular culture, law, and social science. In M. A. Straus and G. T. Hotaling, eds., *The social causes of husband-wife violence.* Minneapolis: University of Minnesota Press.

Straus, M. A., and R. J. Gelles. 1986. Social change and change in family violence from 1975 to 1985 as revealed by two national surveys. *Journal of Marriage and the Family 48*, 465–479.

———, eds. 1990. *Physical violence in American families: Risk factors and adaptations to violence in 8,145 families.* New Brunswick, N.J.: Transaction Publishers.

Suyemoto, K. L. 1998. The functions of self-mutilation. *Clinical Psychology Review 18*, 531–554.

Tannen, D. 1991. *You just don't understand: Women and men in conversation.* New York: Random House.

Tantam, D. 1995. Empathy, persistent aggression and antisocial personality disorder. *Journal of Forensic Psychiatry 6*, 10–18.

Taylor, J. M., C. Gilligan, and A. M. Sullivan. 1995. *Between voice and silence: Women and girls, race and relationship.* Cambridge, Mass.: Harvard University Press.

Thomas, D. 1957. The force that through the green fuse drives the flower. In *Collected Poems.* New York: New Directions.

Thompson, J. M. 1995. Silencing the self: Depressive symptomatology and close relationships. *Psychology of Women Quarterly 19*, 337–353.

Tjaden, P., and N. Thoennes. 1998. Prevalence, incidence, and consequences of violence against women: Findings from the National Violence against Women Survey. Washington: U.S. Department of Justice, Bureau of Justice Statistics, NCJ 172837.

Vasquez, M. J. T. 1994. Latinas. In L. Comas-Días and B. Greene, *Women of color: Integrating ethnic and gender identities in psychotherapy.* New York: Guilford.

Walker, B. G. 1983. *The woman's encyclopedia of myths and secrets.* New York: Harper and Row.

Walker, L. E. 1984. *The battered woman syndrome.* New York: Springer.

Walker, R. 1995. *To be real: Telling the truth and changing the face of feminism.* New York: Anchor.

Wang, C., G. Alexander, N. Berman, B. Salehian, T. Davidson, V. McDonald, B. Steiner, L. Hull, C. Callegari, and R. S. Swerdloff. 1996. Testosterone replacement therapy improves mood in hypogonadal men: A clinical research center study. *Journal of Clinical Endocrinology and Metabolism 81,* 3578–83.

Way, N. 1995. "Can't you see the courage, the strength that I have?" *Psychology of Women Quarterly 19,* 107–128.

Weisman, L. K. 1992. *Discrimination by design: A feminist critique of the man-made environment.* Chicago: University of Chicago Press.

Weissman, M. M., and E. S. Paykel. 1974. *The depressed woman.* Chicago: University of Chicago Press.

White, J. W. 1983. Sex and gender issues in aggression research. In R. G. Geen and E. Donnerstein, eds., *Aggression: Theoretical and empirical reviews,* vol. 2: *Issues in research.* New York: Academic Press.

White, J. W., and R. M. Kowalski. 1994. Deconstructing the myth of the non-aggressive woman. *Psychology of Women Quarterly 18,* 487–508.

Widom, C. S., and J. B. Kuhns. 1996. Childhood victimization and subsequent risk for promiscuity, prostitution, and teenage pregnancy: A prospective study. *American Journal of Public Health 86,* 1607–12.

Wiehe, V. R. 1997. Approaching child abuse treatment from the perspective of empathy. *Child Abuse and Neglect 21,* 1191–1204.

Wispe, L. G. 1991. *The psychology of sympathy.* New York: Plenum.

Wood, J. T. 1994. *Gendered lives: Communication, gender and culture.* Belmont, Calif.: Wadsworth.

Wrangham, R. W., and D. Peterson. 1996. *Demonic males: Apes and the origins of human violence.* Boston: Houghton Mifflin.

Wray, M., and A. Newitz. 1997. *White trash: Race and class in America.* New York: Routledge.

Wright, P. 1993. Variations in male-female dominance and offspring care in non-human primates. In B. D. Miller, ed., *Sex and gender hierarchies.* New York: Cambridge University Press.

ACKNOWLEDGMENTS

This book was made possible by the openness and trust of the women whose voices fill its pages. I thank them for their time and their help, and for sharing aspects of their lives usually kept hidden. Discussions with participants after they received transcripts of their interviews, as well as after they read a draft of their words for this book, deepened our dialogue. Many participated out of a wish to help others; I share their desire that the book clarify some of the pain and confusion, as well as the positive possibilities, surrounding women's aggression.

Fairhaven College and the Bureau for Faculty Research of Western Washington University provided institutional support, for which I am grateful. Students in my courses on the psychology of women and on aggression offered lively and challenging questions about early drafts of Chapter 5. Kristen Penza commuted from the University of Washington to code interviews, and Fairhaven students also helped with analysis: Sarah Pearson managed Ethnograph software and frequencies, while Samya Clumpner and Athena Stephens coded the anger segments of the narratives. I am grateful to my friend Therese Grant, director of the Seattle Birth to Three Project, and to Ann Streissguth, co-investigator, for their generous help. Women enrolled in the Birth to Three Project who agreed to interviews were valued teachers. Norman Marr helped locate police officers who wanted to be interviewed, and Advocates for Abused and Battered Lesbians contacted women who were interested in interviews. I deeply appreciate their assistance.

Lois Holub, Lynne Masland, Candy Wiggum, Linda Vaden-Goad, Linda Krebs, Summer Graef, Kathryn Anderson, and Pat Fabiano read early drafts of chapters and offered encouragement and suggestions. My colleague Kathryn Anderson also offered unfailing support and discussions of concepts. I profited immensely from Janet Miller's nuanced comments on many drafts, and from our discussions of methodology. At later stages, Lyn Brown's careful reading of four chapters helped sharpen and focus my ideas, as did a writing group with Jennifer Hahn and Ara Taylor. Thanks, also, to Tony Bernay and Nancy Goldberger for reading the manuscript and offering helpful suggestions. I also benefited from sharing aspects of this work at the Mayo Clinic Conference on Women and Health in 1997, the Marshfield Clinic in 1995, and the Chicago Illinois Psychological Association Preconvention Conference in 1995.

Angela von der Lippe was instrumental in the beginnings of this project. Her enthusiasm helped focus my interest. Elizabeth Knoll guided the work through its final stages, and Camille Smith's careful editing, done with humor, patience, and a steady hand, significantly improved the book.

My love and appreciation go to my family—Rand, Darby, Kelsey, and my mother, Dorothy Beach. Fourteen years of studying depression and aggression have not been an entirely cheerful endeavor. My loving, supportive, and often hilarious family have made it possible through their caring interest and help. Rand's willingness to read, discuss, and edit difficult sections was essential, and I am deeply grateful. A special thanks to Kelsey, from whom I have learned so much about backbone in the last two years.

I have written this book with the deep hope that it might influence our understandings of aggression in women and focus attention on preventing the rage that comes from disconnection. I join many others who warn of the dangers of isolation and emphasize the importance of positive relationships for all aspects of human functioning, including aggression.

INDEX